# ETHICS
## in the Workplace

**3<sup>e</sup>**

## Dean Bredeson, J.D.

Senior Lecturer
University of Texas at Austin

## Keith Goree

Former Director
Applied Ethics Institute
Saint Petersburg College

The third edition of *Ethics in the Workplace* is dedicated to the memory of William Keith Goree, who passed away on 16 July 2009. Keith taught Applied Ethics at St. Petersburg College for over twenty years and wrote books and numerous articles on the subject. In 2005, he became the Director of the Applied Ethics Institute and was key to establishing its first Advisory Board. His work and teaching touched thousands of students' lives and influenced faculty and professionals in the field of ethics.

SOUTH-WESTERN
CENGAGE Learning

Australia • Brazil • Japan • Korea • Mexico • Singapore • Spain • United Kingdom • United States

SOUTH-WESTERN
CENGAGE Learning™

**Ethics in the Workplace, Third Edition**
Dean Bredeson
Keith Goree

Editorial Director: Jack W. Calhoun

Vice President/Editor-in-Chief: Karen Schmohe

Associate Acquisitions Editor: Michael Guendelsberger

Senior Developmental Editor: Penny Shank

Editorial Assistant: Anne Kelly

Marketing Communications Manager: Tom Guenette

Associate Marketing Manager: Shanna Shelton

Content Project Management: PreMediaGlobal

Media Editor: Lysa Kosins

Senior Manufacturing Coordinator: Kevin Kluck

Production Service: PreMediaGlobal

Senior Art Director: Tippy McIntosh

Internal Design: PreMediaGlobal

Cover Design: Lisa M. Langhoff

Cover Image: © Maciej Noskowski, Getty Images

Rights Acquisition Director: Audrey Pettengill

Rights Acquisition Specialist: John Hill

For product information and technology assistance, contact us at
**Cengage Learning Customer & Sales Support, 1-800-354-9706**

For permission to use material from this text or product, submit all requests online at **www.cengage.com/permissions.** Further permissions questions can be e-mailed to **permissionrequest@cengage.com.**

Apple, iPhone, and iPad are trademarks of Apple Inc., registered in the U.S. and other countries.

Intel is a trademark of Intel Corporation in the U.S. and/or other countries.

Microsoft and xBox 360 are either registered trademarks or trademarks of Microsoft Corporation in the United States and/or other countries.

"Hard Choices" and "Ethics & Work" excerpts are © Cengage Learning.

Library of Congress Control Number: 2011925164

ISBN-13: 978-0-538-49777-0

ISBN-10: 0-538-49777-7

**South-Western**
5191 Natorp Boulevard
Mason, OH 45040
USA

Cengage Learning products are represented in Canada by Nelson Education, Ltd.

For your course and learning solutions, visit **www.cengage.com.**
Visit our company website at **www.cengage.com.**

Printed in the United States of America
1 2 3 4 5 6 7 15 14 13 12 11

# Brief Contents

Preface   vii

CHAPTER **1**   **Welcome to Ethics**   1

CHAPTER **2**   **Ethical Principles**   15

CHAPTER **3**   **Personal Ethical Development**   31

CHAPTER **4**   **Shareholder Theory and Stakeholder Theory**   51

CHAPTER **5**   **Ethical Selling, Marketing, and Advertising**   67

CHAPTER **6**   **Technology, Testing, and Workplace Privacy**   87

CHAPTER **7**   **Ethics and Discrimination**   101

CHAPTER **8**   **Ethics for Employees**   115

CHAPTER **9**   **Ethical Lending and the "Great Recession"**   131

CHAPTER **10**   **Two Global Issues: The Environment and Sweatshops**   151

CHAPTER **11**   **Critical Thinking in Ethics**   165

Glossary   183

Index   189

# Contents

Preface | vii

CHAPTER **1** **Welcome to Ethics** | **1**

What Is Ethics All About? | 3

Standards of Behavior | 6

*Ethics @ Work* Intentional Deception:
When (If Ever) Is It Ethically Justified? | 9

Chapter 1 Assessments | 12

CHAPTER **2** **Ethical Principles** | **15**

Basing Morality on Consequences | 17

Basing Morality on Rights, Duties, and Virtues | 19

*Ethics @ Work* Cooper Fan Company | 24

Chapter 2 Assessments | 27

CHAPTER **3** **Personal Ethical Development** | **31**

Kohlberg's Justice Model of Moral Development | 33

Rest's Four Components of Moral Behavior | 39

*Ethics @ Work* Microinsurance | 44

Chapter 3 Assessments | 47

CHAPTER **4** **Shareholder Theory and
Stakeholder Theory** | **51**

Shareholder Ethics | 53

Stakeholder Ethics | 55

*Ethics @ Work* The Winds of Change | 60

Chapter 4 Assessments | 64

CHAPTER **5** **Ethical Selling, Marketing, and Advertising** **67**

    Ethics in Advertising      69

    Ethics in Selling      75

    *Ethics @ Work* Five Commercials      79

    Chapter 5 Assessments      82

CHAPTER **6** **Technology, Testing, and Workplace Privacy** **87**

    Privacy Law      90

    Drug Tests and Polygraph Exams      92

    *Ethics @ Work* Trouble at Greentown Bank      96

    Chapter 6 Assessments      99

CHAPTER **7** **Ethics and Discrimination** **101**

    Discrimination      103

    Sexual Harassment      106

    *Ethics @ Work* Workplace Blues      108

    Chapter 7 Assessments      111

CHAPTER **8** **Ethics for Employees** **115**

    Ethical Violations by Employees      117

    Character Traits of Excellent Employees      120

    *Ethics @ Work* Don't Be a Hero      125

    Chapter 8 Assessments      128

CHAPTER **9** **Ethical Lending and the "Great Recession"** **131**

    Ethical Issues in Lending      133

    Special Issue: Mortgages and Foreclosures      136

    Applying Ethical Principles to Financial Issues      140

    *Ethics @ Work* Strategic Defaults      144

    Chapter 9 Assessments      147

CHAPTER **10**   **Two Global Issues: The Environment and Sweatshops**   **151**

Environmental Ethics   154
International Ethics: Sweatshop Labor   156
*Ethics @ Work* Sweatshop Labor   159
Chapter 10 Assessments   162

CHAPTER **11**   **Critical Thinking in Ethics**   **165**

Logical Fallacies and Ethical Reasoning   168
Ethical Dilemmas and Reasoning   172
*Ethics @ Work* Unusual Needs and Layoffs   175
Chapter 11 Assessments   178

**Glossary**   **183**
**Index**   **189**

# Introduction to Students

A woman finds a wallet with $500 inside, and she returns it to its owner. One student is caught cheating on an exam, while another student in the same class volunteers for several hours every week tutoring elementary school children. An employee in a department store establishes a new recycling program for his firm, while a coworker steals merchandise from the store. Ethical choices confront us at every turn.

In this textbook, you will explore what makes actions right or wrong, why people choose to do what is right, and how to apply those ideas to the workplace. Before you begin your study of ethics, however, there are a few important things about this book that you need to know.

## *Ethics in the Workplace* will . . .

- Help you become more sensitive to ethical issues in everyday life and at work. Once you learn to recognize ethical issues, you will be amazed at all the places you see them—at home, at school, in your community, and around the world.

- Encourage you to learn to think more clearly, critically, and logically about difficult ethical issues and questions. Carefully thinking through an ethical problem is the first step in finding the best answer.

- Offer tools necessary to make more mature and responsible ethical decisions—decisions on which you can look back later with pride, rather than regret.

- Help you understand the vastly different consequences of ethical and unethical behavior at work.

- Give you an opportunity to raise your own personal ethical standards to new, higher levels. You must choose to raise these standards for yourself. This higher road is not an easy one, or more people would take it. However, as you grow in moral maturity, you will find that people treat you more as an adult and less as a child. They will respect and trust you more.

- Assist you as you set sail on what is hoped will be a lifelong search for the best answers to life's problems, the best ethical principles to live by, and a good life.

## *Ethics in the Workplace* will not . . .

- Provide you with a list of rules and regulations to obey in life. The goal of studying ethics is to learn to make responsible and mature moral decisions on your own.

- Give you a list of opinions with which you are expected to agree. This book is about the process of making decisions about right and wrong.

- Try to manipulate or control your moral beliefs or opinions. An important part of ethical maturity is developing your own beliefs and opinions for your own reasons.

## Organization of *Ethics in the Workplace*

The first three chapters represent the foundations of ethics. In them, you will investigate the nature of ethics, as well as principles that can be used in making ethical decisions. You will learn about the process of moral development. You will also acquire critical thinking skills that can be useful in finding answers to ethical questions.

Chapters 4 through 11 focus on specific ethical issues in the workplace. The issues are quite timely and relevant. You may be surprised to find how frequently you see the topics discussed in class on the front page of the newspaper and on the evening news.

Each chapter offers a thorough discussion of specific ideas relevant to business ethics. In addition, each chapter includes reinforcement activities (sometimes with a creative twist!), critical thinking exercises, and a variety of opportunities for personal reflection and growth.

## What's New in This Edition?

- *New and updated coverage* This edition features new and expanded discussions of stakeholder ethics, employee privacy, the appropriate use of technology in the workplace, diversity policies, sustainable practices, international "sweatshop" labor, and ethical lapses that contributed to the economic meltdown and the "Great Recession."

- *Hard Choices* This feature seeks to immediately engage you by presenting ethical dilemmas as they actually come up in companies. They are often dramatic and should provoke interesting class discussions.

- *Ethics @ Work* Each chapter ends with an expanded presentation of how ethics arises in real workplaces. Most are written as screenplays, and like the Hard Choices features, they should generate debate in class.

- *Review* Objective questions on key points in the chapter will help you to review the chapter concepts.

- *Applications* These activities will require you to go beyond repeating information and to apply critical thinking skills.

- *The Bottom Line* This activity asks you to give a final assessment of the main ideas in the chapter.

## CourseMate

The more you study, the better the results. Cengage Learning's CourseMate for *Ethics in the Workplace* helps you make the most of your study time by accessing everything you need to succeed in one place. CourseMate features include:

- An interactive eBook with highlighting, note taking, and an interactive glossary.

- Interactive learning tools—read your textbook, take notes, review flash-cards, watch videos, and take practice quizzes online.

- Affordability—about half the cost of a traditional printed textbook.

If you received a printed access card with the purchase of your text, you can redeem this at www.cengagebrain.com.

To access additional course materials including CourseMate, please visit www.cengagebrain.com. At the CengageBrain.com home page, enter the ISBN of the book (from the back cover) using the search box at the top of the page. This will take you to the product page where these resources can be found.

## Tips for Getting the Most from This Course

- Focus on understanding new concepts and learning to apply them to ethical questions. Simply memorizing definitions won't do you much good. Keep asking yourself these questions: What does this mean? How can I use it?

- Stay open-minded to new ideas and different points of view. Someone said a mind is like a parachute—it only functions properly when it is open. You cannot learn anything as long as you think you already have all the answers.

- Keep holding yourself up to the ethical mirror. Evaluate your own ethical strengths and weaknesses as honestly as you can. If you think of this course simply as new words to be learned and blanks to be filled in, you'll miss the most important lessons.

## Challenge to Students

As the author of this textbook, I issue you this challenge: keep this book and the comments you will write in it and refer back to it as your career unfolds.

The goal of this course is to provide you with tools that will be useful in thinking through the countless ethical dilemmas you will face in a typical business. Tremendous care has been given to presenting realistic scenarios that get at the real and difficult decisions that come up in real companies. Whatever you do for a living, you will have to face many of these scenarios in your career.

That being the case, this book can be a valuable reference to have on your office bookshelf. It can serve as a reminder of what you once thought and can thereby give you added confidence in navigating the dilemmas you will face. It can also help you to recall what your professor and peers had to say about business problems and can give you insight into how others perceive ethical dilemmas.

I have a 20-year-old course packet from a class I took as an undergraduate called "leadership issues." Its binding is weak and worn out, and its pages are yellowing, but I still look at parts of it every semester.

In the same way, I believe this book could be a useful thing for you to have in the future.

**Dean Bredeson**
Austin, Texas

# ■ Acknowledgments

We are grateful for the feedback of the following reviewers, who offered excellent suggestions and encouragement.

**Michael A. Carey**
Business Education and Computer Technology
    Teacher
Central Heights Schools
Richmond, Kansas

**James A. Cheslek**
Dean of Academic Affairs
Brown Mackie College
Albuquerque, New Mexico

**Julia M. Clark**
Dept. Chair of General Studies
Brown Mackie College
Ft. Wayne, Indiana

**Yvonne Drake**
Business Dept. Adjunct
Pensacola Junior College
Pensacola, Florida

**Kristina Halloran**
Business Information Technology Instructor
Career Technology Center of Lakawanna County
Scranton, Pennsylvania

**Scott R. Higgins**
General Education Program Director
Kaplan College
Columbus, Ohio

**Martin Hyatt**
Associate Professor and Writing Center Coordinator
ASA Institute
Brooklyn, New York

**Lisa R. Jeter**
Business and Computer Science Dept. Chair
Bainbridge High School
Bainbridge, Georgia

**Valerie A. Jones**
Business Teacher
Somerset Area School District
Somerset, Pennsylvania

**Ronny Perez**
Business Teacher
Mater Academy Charter High School
Miami, Florida

**Michelle K. Roe**
Business Dept. Teacher
Beaverton High School
Beaverton, Michigan

**Kimberly A. Rose**
Business Education Teacher
McKeesport Area School District
McKeesport, Pennsylvania

**Margaret Stafford**
Curriculum Coordinator
Valley College
Martinsburg, West Virginia

**Anne-Marie Zenni**
Office Technology Dept. Head
Diman Regional Vocational Technical High School
Fall River, Massachusetts

# ■ About the Authors

Dean Bredeson has been on the faculty of the University of Texas for over 15 years specializing in business ethics, business law, and discrimination law. He has received several rare teaching awards including the Lockheed Martin Excellence Award for three years running. He is also among the youngest recipients of the Board of Regents Teaching Award and was UT's nominee for the Carnegie Foundation's United States Professor of the Year Award in 2010. Professor Bredeson recently published the *Student Guide to the Sarbanes-Oxley Act* with Robert Prentice and is coauthor of *Business Law and The Legal Environment* with Jeffrey Beatty and Susan Samuelson. He earned his undergraduate degree from the McCombs School of Business and his J.D. from the School of Law at the University of Texas.

Keith Goree taught Applied Ethics at St. Petersburg College in St. Petersburg, Florida. He was also the Director of the Applied Ethics Institute from 2005 to 2009 and helped to develop programs for students, including the Ethics Bowl and the High School Leadership Academy. He received the 1997 Professor of the Year and the National Teacher of the Year awards in 2005. In 1999 he received the Carol Burnett Prize for Ethics in Journalism; in 2005, he was awarded the William H. Meardy Faculty Member Award. Professor Goree wrote several articles and books on the field of ethics.

# Welcome to Ethics

The fundamental question in ethics is, How should people behave? In many situations, people act (or choose not to act) to avoid negative consequences. But what about decisions in which no choice is illegal, and no choice will lead to any particular problems for the decision maker? If a person has a genuine free choice, what principles should guide his or her actions?

## Objectives
- Identify common ethical principles and sources of ethical beliefs.
- Distinguish among etiquette, law, and ethics.

## Key Terms and Concepts

ethical principles, p. 3
relativism, p. 3
legalism, p. 3
authority, p. 4
culture, p. 4
morality, p. 4

intuition, p. 4
reason, p. 4
standard of etiquette, p. 6
standard of law, p. 7
standard of ethics, p. 7

**HARD CHOICES**

Ed the Entrepreneur buys a cheap piece of California land in the middle of the Mojave Desert. It is located a mile back from a major highway, and it is exactly between the two closest gas stations, which are 85 miles distant in either direction. In the summertime, average high temperatures are often above 110 degrees.

Ed then builds a shack and paints it bright orange so that it is easily visible from the highway. He installs a phone, a large refrigerator, and the strongest air conditioner available. He adds a giant HDTV, a couch, and a PlayStation®3. Usually, weeks or months pass without anyone dropping in. From time to time, however, desperate people knock on his door. When they do, Ed offers to let them have a gallon of cold water, the use of his phone, and a chance to wait for their ride inside. His price is $50,000.

If his customers don't have the money handy, Ed makes them sign a contract promising to pay him later, out of future wages if necessary. If they refuse to pay or sign, Ed throws them out, locks the door, and goes back to playing PlayStation®3 after telling his surprised visitors to "say hello to the vultures." In the end, everyone signs the contract. Ed makes a profit of about $300,000 per year.

No one has ever walked away and met with harm in the heat. In his heart, Ed knows he would not allow someone to remain outside, even if he or she refused to sign the contract.

Ignore the fact that a court would probably invalidate the contracts. Assume the contracts would stand up in court, and answer the following question strictly from an ethical perspective.

## {**WHAT** Do You Think?}

Is Ed's operation ethically justifiable as it is currently run?

# What Is Ethics All About?

**Ethical principles** are general statements of how people should or should not act. These principles are often the reasons behind a person's actions, thoughts, and beliefs. Some ethical principles are frequently described as universal, meaning that rational people thinking logically would have to agree that everyone should follow them. A popular universal ethical principle is known as the golden rule—you should treat others as you would want to be treated. Other common ethical principles include the following:

- People should respect the rights of others.
- They should keep their promises.
- They should be honest.
- People should take responsibility for their actions.
- They should act in the best interests of others.
- They should help others in need when possible.
- People should be fair.

## Do Right and Wrong Exist?

Do moral right and wrong really exist? Some people argue that they are mere social inventions created to control people's behavior. Others assert that they are little more than emotional reactions or social agreements. Such skepticism is often based on two arguments.

The first is **relativism**, the belief that because ethical values vary so widely, there can be no universal ethical principles that apply to everyone. After all, no two individuals, societies, or religions agree completely on what is right or wrong. If a set of moral guidelines did exist for all people, wouldn't it seem logical that everyone could agree on what those guidelines are? Since everyone does not agree, the argument continues that moral right and wrong cannot be anything more than personal opinion.

The problem with that criticism of ethics is that people *do* agree, at least most of the time. That may not seem to be the case, since people tend to focus more on their differences than their similarities. How many people believe that helping others or standing up for the truth in a difficult situation is wrong? Most people agree about the vast majority of life's ethical questions.

The second criticism of ethics is legalism. **Legalism** is the belief that because there are laws and policies to cover issues of right and wrong, ethics is irrelevant. It's not necessary to discuss whether people should be allowed to smoke marijuana because doing so is illegal. If an action is illegal, it must be wrong. If someone isn't sure whether an action is right or wrong, all he or she has to do is find out what the law says.

You may already understand that this problem is based on a fundamental misunderstanding about law and ethics. Yes, societies write laws to back

> Ours is a world of nuclear giants and ethical infants.
>
> —Jef I. Richards

up and formalize their ethical values, but the laws don't take the place of those values. They only reinforce them. At times, the laws don't even do that. Sometimes societies discover that their laws are actually in conflict with their ethical values. That's what happened when Americans decided that laws allowing slavery, the second-class status of women, harmful child labor practices, and discrimination of all kinds had to be changed. "Legal" is not the same as "ethical." In fact, the ethical standard is usually higher, as you will see later in this chapter.

## Sources of Ethical Beliefs

Since it seems reasonable to assume that moral right and wrong do exist in some form, where do people get their ethical principles and values? Some are the result of lessons taught at home, in school, or in religious training. Others are the result of individual life experiences. Some people acquire their principles and values from messages that society sends through television, music, magazines, and books. In other words, people's ethical beliefs come from a variety of sources. However, writer and philosopher Richard Doss has pointed out that some sources are more influential than others. When asked where they acquired their beliefs about an ethical issue, most people tend to identify one or more of the following sources.

One source of ethical beliefs is **authority**. According to this approach, an action is right or wrong because someone important said so. This way of thinking is often seen in religious ethics, but other moral authorities in history have included political leaders (for example, monarchs).

Another source of ethical beliefs is **culture**, the idea that the morality of an action depends on the beliefs of one's culture or nation. **Morality** refers to that part of human behavior that can be evaluated in terms of right and wrong. This approach says that cultures and nations, like individuals, have different values and principles based on their different experiences and histories. A belief that works well for one culture may be harmful for another.

A third source of ethical beliefs is **intuition**, which is the idea that principles of right and wrong have been built into a person's conscience and that he or she will know what is right by listening to that "little voice" within. This reliance on intuition is very common. People often seem to know instinctively whether actions are right or wrong.

A fourth source of ethical beliefs is **reason**, the idea that consistent, logical thinking should be the primary tool used in making ethical decisions. If stealing is judged to be wrong, for example, then there should be solid arguments and logical principles that back up that judgment. In other words, the arguments against stealing are stronger than the arguments for stealing. With the appeal to reason, an action is not wrong *just* because an authority says so, *just* because it is unpopular within a culture, or *just* because someone's inner voice warns against it. Instead, this approach suggests that a person look open-mindedly at the arguments on both sides of an issue and then use reason to carefully choose the stronger arguments.

Some companies set a "tone at the top" by placing their values in a mission statement, statement of core values, or credo. These statements can offer guidance to employees as they face dilemmas. They can also serve as a useful tool for prospective investors, who may be attracted by a mission statement that reflects strong values. Companies are well served by stating guiding principles up front, and Johnson & Johnson certainly does this.

## The Johnson & Johnson *Credo*

We believe our first responsibility is to the doctors, nurses and patients, to mothers and fathers and all others who use our products and services. In meeting their needs everything we do must be of high quality. We must constantly strive to reduce our costs in order to maintain reasonable prices. Customers' orders must be serviced promptly and accurately. Our suppliers and distributors must have an opportunity to make a fair profit.

We are responsible to our employees, the men and women who work with us throughout the world. Everyone must be considered as an individual. We must respect their dignity and recognize their merit. They must have a sense of security in their jobs. Compensation must be fair and adequate, and working conditions clean, orderly and safe. We must be mindful of ways to help our employees fulfill their family responsibilities. Employees must feel free to make suggestions and complaints. There must be equal opportunity for employment, development and advancement for those qualified. We must provide competent management, and their actions must be just and ethical.

We are responsible to the communities in which we live and work and to the world community as well. We must be good citizens—support good works and charities and bear our fair share of taxes. We must encourage civic improvements and better health and education. We must maintain in good order the property we are privileged to use, protecting the environment and natural resources.

Our final responsibility is to our stockholders. Business must make a sound profit. We must experiment with new ideas. Research must be carried on, innovative programs developed and mistakes paid for. New equipment must be purchased, new facilities provided and new products launched. Reserves must be created to provide for adverse times. When we operate according to these principles, the stockholders should realize a fair return.

Reprinted courtesy of Johnson & Johnson.

Are companies better off adopting a statement like Johnson & Johnson's, or do you imagine most people would pay no attention?

1. Look back at the seven ethical principles listed at the beginning of this section. Which three do you think are most important?

2. Return to the opening passage on Ed the Entrepreneur and reexamine his operation. Support your critique of it with the three ethical principles you listed in your answer to the last question.

3. Everyone would presumably be in favor of a convenience store at Ed's location that charged $5 for water and let customers use a phone and rest inside for free. Let's change the price points for Ed's services. Circle the amount that is the *most* you think Ed can ethically charge.

   $50      $500      $5,000      $50,000      $500,000      $5,000,000

4. Are your opinions about Ed's business shaped most by authority, culture, intuition, reason, or some other source? What makes you say so?

## ■ Standards of Behavior

Honor is better than honors.

—Abraham Lincoln

A standard, or norm, is an accepted level of behavior to which people are expected to conform. The level may be set low (a minimum standard), in the middle (an average standard), or very high (a standard of excellence). Whatever the level, all standards involve some kind of expectation. To say that stealing is wrong does not mean that it is wrong for just one person or even for a few people. If stealing is forbidden by a social standard, then the assumption is that stealing is wrong for everyone. Certainly, there are ethical issues that are individual and personal, too, but ethics often deals with principles that apply to everyone. People's actions can be evaluated according to many standards, but three of the most common standards are those of etiquette, law, and ethics.

### Etiquette

The **standard of etiquette** refers to expectations concerning manners or social graces. Societies and cultures have their own rules of etiquette that their members are expected to meet. Most people understand their social etiquette standards and try to live up to them. Thus, a person knows to knock before entering someone's office and tries to remember to say "please" and "thank you." It is assumed that everyone understands these rules, even though many of them are not written down. People who violate the standards of etiquette run the risk of being embarrassed or of having others look down on them. Some large corporations actually send their employees to etiquette classes—proper manners can be that important to the company's image.

In a crowded, busy, and stressed society, etiquette also reduces social friction and makes it easier for people to live together as a community. There is an important difference, however, between the standards of etiquette and ethics. That difference is *seriousness*. The issues covered by the standard of etiquette are not as serious as those that pertain to ethics. People rarely die due to poor manners, but the ethical standard applies to many life-and-death issues such as abortion, euthanasia, war, and capital punishment. Even ethical issues that are not associated with death, such as censorship, honesty in government, and sexual ethics, still have serious implications.

## Law

The **standard of law** has to do with rules of behavior imposed on people by governments. Like ethics, this legal standard can be serious, too. After all, many laws deal with life-and-death issues, including rules forbidding murder, drunken driving, drug use, and child abuse. Yet while legal and ethical standards are serious, there is an important difference—people *must* follow legal standards, or they will face specific negative consequences.

## Ethics

The primary factor in determining the validity of a law is whether the creator of the law had the legitimate authority. With the ethical standard, however, authority is not what matters. The **standard of ethics** refers to social expectations of people's moral behavior. The ethical principles and rules making up this standard are made valid by *the reasons and arguments supporting them*. If you say, "The death penalty is morally wrong," what you're really saying is that the reasons and arguments supporting that statement make more logical sense than the reasons and arguments on the other side of the debate. For ethical statements to be valid, they must make logical sense.

Because of that crucial difference, legal standards and moral standards do not always agree. Some laws may be morally wrong. Many people in history have gone to prison—and even to their deaths—rather than violate their ethical beliefs.

Another difference between legal and ethical standards is in when and how they change. Legal standards (based on authority) may change as authorities change. Ethical standards (based on reason) change only when new information causes people's thinking about the standards to change.

1. How is the standard of ethics different from the standard of etiquette?

2. What is the difference between the standard of ethics and the standard of law?

3. Provide an example of a time when you had to make a difficult ethical decision. How did the concept of the ethical standard apply to your situation?

# ETHICS @ WORK

This chapter has provided a framework for thinking through ethical dilemmas. The following scenarios are your chance to apply the ideas to a new situation. Answer the questions that follow each scenario, and be prepared to respectfully argue for your point of view in class. The two most valuable things about an ethics course are these:

- The chance to learn new ways of thinking through problems
- The exchange of ideas with other people—learning from and influencing your classmates

## Main Issue and Options

**Issue:** The question presented in these scenarios is simple: When, if ever, is lying *good*?

**Options:** In both scenarios, the actors may be truthful or deceptive.

## Intentional Deception: When (If Ever) Is It Ethically Justified?

### Background

We are taught from an early age that we must tell the truth to our parents, teachers, and others. Usually, honesty is clearly the best policy. The consequences of lying can be severe: children are grounded, students are suspended, employees are fired, and witnesses are convicted of perjury. Sometimes the problems are more subtle but still significant: a loss of trust or a loss of opportunities.

In some specific circumstances, however, intentional deception is tolerated and even admired. In sports, for example, athletes spend countless hours perfecting techniques designed to trick opponents. If Peyton Manning looks one way and throws the other, no one is upset even though his intention is to deceive the defensive backs.

The first scenario focuses on D-Day, the turning point of World War II. Until the 1944 invasion of Normandy by the Allies, the Nazis had spent the last several years imposing their will on much of Europe. Eleven months after D-Day, the Nazis surrendered, and the war in Europe was effectively over.

The invasion's success was due largely to the fact that the Nazis were fooled about where it would take place. Adolf Hitler expected a massive invasion at the Pas-de-Calais, and he kept 19 of his Panzer divisions there. An enormous number of tanks were far from Normandy and were useless to the Nazis. Hitler didn't simply blunder on his own, however. He was led to believe that the invasion would be at the Pas-de-Calais by an elaborate deception called Operation Fortitude.

### Dover, England: February 1944

The corporal opened the tent's flap. "The new man is here, Major."

Major Cole looked up from a stack of papers. "Excellent. Send him in, Corporal."

"Yes, sir." The corporal was soon replaced by an officer, who offered Cole a crisp salute. "Lieutenant Thatcher, 55th Infantry, Lancashire, reporting, sir."

"At ease, Lieutenant," Cole said, returning the salute. "Have a seat," he added.

"Thank you, sir."

Cole smiled. "I imagine you are full of questions."

"Yes, sir. I, ah, was not briefed on the, ah . . ."

"Nature of this operation?" Cole's grin widened.

"Correct. Sir. I was told only to bring my men here to rendezvous with the 58th Infantry and await further instructions."

Cole laughed. "Hmm, yes (snort)—the 58th."

"Sir?"

Cole got his chuckling under control, but a gleam remained in his eye. "There's no such thing as the 58th, Lieutenant," he said.

"I, ah . . . I'm not surprised, sir. After what I've seen around the camp so far."

"Yes. I apologize for laughing—not very sporting of me. Everyone who comes here reacts the same way in the beginning. Shall I fill you in on Operation Fortitude?"

"Yes, sir. Please."

"You've probably seen the tanks."

"Yes, sir. Are they . . . inflatable? Like . . . giant toys?"

"Indeed they are. We have about 500 blown up now, but some of your boys will be helping us inflate another 10,000 over the next few months."

"Ten thousand rubber tanks?"

"Just so. You'll also be building thousands of artillery pieces from plywood."

"Plywood?"

"Yes. Life-sized and painted to look like the real thing. The people we need most, though, are your communication specialists. We're going to set up several radio tents around the perimeter of this base, and we're going to broadcast false orders around the clock. We'll encrypt them, but we'll be using an easy-to-break code. So, Lieutenant . . . can you guess what we're up to here?"

"We're . . ." Lieutenant Thatcher trailed off. Then his eyes sharpened and he said tentatively, "We're, ah, we're creating a fake invasion force . . . to . . . mask a real invasion force somewhere else?"

"Excellent, Lieutenant! Spot on!" Lieutenant Thatcher smiled at the praise. Major Cole continued. "Our orders are to make it look as if 150,000 men are massing for an invasion. When German spy planes fly high overhead, we want them to see and report back on a growing number of barracks, tanks, artillery, landing vessels, and the like. And when they listen to the airwaves, we want them to get the amount of radio traffic you'd expect with a force of that size."

"Outstanding."

"Indeed. And word is that next month General Patton will be joining us on a regular basis for photo ops. He's been deemed the most widely recognized Allied commander. We'll be staging a lot of photos in front of a few of the real tanks and so forth that we'll have scattered around so the newspapers can run stories like, 'General Patton Inspects Troops at Dover,' that kind of thing. Meanwhile, General Eisenhower will be gearing up for the real thing 'somewhere else,' as you say."

"That's brilliant."

"Just so. While the Nazis are cooling their heels and waiting for us at the Pas-de-Calais, we'll land somewhere else. And once we have secure supply lines open, we can beat Adolf back to Berlin and bloody well go home. Be nice to get back to my wife."

"Yes, sir."

"And to get the football league going again. I bloody miss football. I'd give a week's pay to listen to an Arsenal match on the wireless. And a month's pay to see a game at Highbury. Who are you for, Lieutenant?"

"Blackburn, sir."

"Ah, the Rovers. Well, one day soon if we all do our jobs, then, what?"

"Yes. sir. One day soon."

## What Do You Think?

1. How, specifically, can Operation Fortitude be justified as a "good lie"? Use ideas from the chapter to support your answer.

2. Speaking generally now, when is making a misrepresentation acceptable? (Check all that apply.)

_____ To protect life or the physical safety of people

_____ To protect a job

_____ To protect another person's feelings

_____ To gain an advantage

_____ To get out of trouble

_____ When others expect it and may do the same (war, poker, football)

# Greentown, Illinois: Present Day

Harold finished his explanation to his brother. "There's just no other way to do it," he said.

"You can't be serious," replied Harold's brother Tom. "You're just going to walk in there."

"Yes."

"And hand off a file of fake documents? And walk out with a $100,000 loan you can't get without lying?"

"I am."

"You're nuts."

"As I said, it's the only way."

"Harold," Tom paused and rubbed his eyes. "Man, you've done some dumb things in your life, but this is just . . . what if you get caught?"

"I won't get caught. I'm only exaggerating the numbers a little, and I've never fudged a single thing in 15 years of banking with them. They won't look too closely."

"You're nuts."

"I won't miss payroll, Tom. I have 20 employees with families to support who are counting on me to make it work. I'm going to make it work."

"Harold . . ."

"It's not as if the bank is going to lose its money. Orders are already picking up, and they'll return to normal, just as they did in the last two recessions. I'll pay the bank every penny back—with interest—this time next year. Who gets hurt?"

"You get hurt if you're wrong about anything you just told me."

"I'm a big boy, Tom. It might go badly, but I don't think so. Besides, I'm willing to chance it."

"I wish you wouldn't."

"I know you do. But you've always worked for somebody else, Tom. You don't know what it's like to be on the other side, to have good people depending on you. It'll be fine. You'll see."

## What Do You Think?

3. Rate Harold's plan to lie to his bank to secure the $100,000 loan to pay his employees.

COMPLETELY WRONGFUL ——————————— COMPLETELY JUSTIFIED

1    2    3    4    5    6    7

4. Assume a year passes and business picks up for Harold's company. He repays the loan. No one is laid off or misses a paycheck, and Harold's lie is never caught. Is your rating the same with the benefit of hindsight? Do the ends at least partially justify the means?

COMPLETELY WRONGFUL ——————————— COMPLETELY JUSTIFIED

1    2    3    4    5    6    7

5. Describe the reasons for your ratings in Questions 3 and 4. Use ideas from the chapter to support your response.

# Summary

Ethical principles are general guidelines for how people should live. They often lie behind a person's actions, thoughts, and beliefs. Some of these principles are widely shared.

Two arguments critical of the existence of moral right and wrong are relativism and legalism. Both are controversial. Legalism is the idea that laws dictate what is right and wrong, and relativism argues against the existence of universal principles.

While people's ethical beliefs come from a variety of sources, they tend to be based on one or more of the following sources: authority, culture, intuition, and reason. The standard of law is based on authority. In contrast, the standard of ethics is based on reason and logical thinking.

# Key Terms and Concepts

**Match each definition with a key term or concept.**

a. authority

b. culture

c. ethical principles

d. intuition

e. legalism

f. morality

g. reason

h. relativism

i. standard of ethics

j. standard of etiquette

k. standard of law

_____ 1. A source of ethical beliefs holding that principles of right and wrong have been built into a person's conscience

_____ 2. A source of ethical beliefs holding that an action is right or wrong because someone important said so

_____ 3. The belief that because there are laws and policies to cover issues of right and wrong, ethics is irrelevant

_____ 4. The belief that because ethical values vary widely, there can be no universal ethical principles that apply to everyone

_____ 5. A source of ethical beliefs holding that consistent, logical thinking should be the primary tool used in making ethical decisions

_____ 6. A source of ethical beliefs holding that the morality of an action depends on the beliefs of one's culture or nation

_____ 7. Refers to rules of behavior imposed on people by governments

_____ 8. Refers to social expectations concerning manners or social graces

_____ 9. Refers to social expectations of people's moral behavior

_____ 10. Ideas that act as guides for behaving ethically

_____ 11. The part of human conduct that can be evaluated in terms of right and wrong

# Review

1. Name three common ethical principles.

2. True or false: Legalism is the idea that because ethical concepts vary so widely, there can be no universal ethical principles that apply to everyone.

3. Describe the four sources of ethical principles discussed in the chapter in your own words.

4. If a behavior is evaluated as right or wrong by asking "According to whom?" the standard of _____ is being applied.
   a. etiquette
   b. law
   c. ethics

# Critical Thinking

5. Sometimes ethical principles conflict. For example, keeping an old promise might not be the best way to be fair, or being honest might not be the best way to help others. Consider the ethical principles described at the start of this chapter. When you find yourself in situations in which satisfying some principles will mean violating others, how should you proceed?

# Applications

6. Ziba works part-time helping to take care of an elderly neighbor, Miss Chura, who suffers from early-stage Alzheimer's disease. She buys Miss Chura's groceries, drives her to appointments, and sometimes cooks and cleans. Ziba knows that Miss Chura has a drawer full of cash in her dresser. She is considering borrowing $100 from the drawer without asking permission. She intends to repay the $100 as soon as she receives her next paycheck.

   a. How is the standard of law relevant to Ziba's plan?

b. How does the standard of ethics apply?

c. List three ethical principles Ziba might consider when she is reasoning about what she should do.

7. Terri is applying for a job. The employment application asks for her college grade point average. Terri's overall GPA was 2.91, but in her major, her GPA was 3.35. She decides to enter the major GPA, and while she is at it, she rounds it up to 3.4.

a. How is the standard of law relevant to Terri's plan?

b. How does the standard of ethics apply?

c. List three ethical principles Terri might consider when she is reasoning about what she should do.

## Digging Deeper

8. Seven universal ethical principles are listed early in this chapter. Go online and enter "universal ethical principles" in a search engine. Find at least two ideas that are not outlined at the beginning of this chapter. Do you find either of your new ideas more useful or compelling than the seven included here? Why or why not?

## The Bottom Line

9. The one ethical principle that I find most important is . . .

10. The one source of ethical principles that influences me most is . . .

# Ethical Principles

How can we assess whether a decision is right or wrong? Is a moral decision one that tends to lead to favorable outcomes, or is it one that was made for good reasons in the first place? Do we have a duty to "do good" and to respect the rights of others?

## Objectives
- Evaluate the role of consequences in ethical decision making.
- Explain the concepts of human rights, moral duties, and moral virtues.

## Key Terms and Concepts

value system, p. 17
consequences, p. 17
egoism principle, p. 17
utility principle, p. 18
right, p. 19
principle of rights, p. 20
duty, p. 20

principle of duties, p. 21
universality, p. 21
respect for persons, p. 21
virtue, p. 21
principle of virtues, p. 22
golden mean, p. 22

Bridget Allen, chief executive officer of a major car company, sits at a meeting and listens as her division chiefs made proposals.

"Ms. Allen, the Kaflor Belt is a breakthrough technology. We estimate it could prevent 3 percent of total annual fatalities in car accidents. It's that much better. Drivers and passengers can take a much harder hit and survive because of the way the Kaflor Belt is designed. We're in the prototype stage now, and the belt should be ready for the production line in 12 to 18 months."

"That's terrific," Allen responds. "Have we patented it yet?"

"Not yet. The team wanted me to ask if you . . . thought we should consider making this design available to everyone."

"As in, not seek a conventional patent?"

"Yes. Volvo patented the first three-point seat belt in a way that made it freely available to other car manufacturers. Some of the designers want us to think about doing the same thing. They feel this technology is too important for us to lock up for ourselves for the next 20 years. If we really can reduce fatality accidents by 3 percent, that's about 1,200 lives a year that could be saved, if everybody uses the technology. If the Kaflor Belt is only on our vehicles, then maybe only 200 people a year can be saved."

"Yes, but we could patent the Kaflor Belt and let others use the technology if they pay us licensing fees."

"That's true. Some of our competitors wouldn't pay, though. Nevertheless, I'm just presenting the idea. Some of the designers disagree with it. We invented the Kaflor Belt, after all. Maybe we *should* own it. It would certainly be a selling point."

## {**WHAT** Do You Think?}

**Should Allen keep the Kaflor Belt technology exclusively for her company?**

# ■ Basing Morality on Consequences

Not all people look at ethical issues and questions the same way. This is especially obvious in the cultural melting pot of America. People living in the United States come from many different backgrounds, and each can have its own unique **value system**, meaning its own way of viewing ethical right and wrong. In addition, a person's ethical beliefs are affected by his or her experiences in life, peer groups, and other factors, some of which are not yet understood. It's almost a wonder that people agree on anything at all! There are some ethical answers, however, on which most people agree because humans share many common ethical principles. In this chapter, you will investigate some of those principles.

A typical way of considering morality is to think of actions as having good or bad consequences. **Consequences** are the effects or results of what people do (Figure 2-1). According to this way of looking at ethics, a moral action is one that brings about good consequences, and an immoral action is one that causes bad consequences. Thus, killing another person is usually considered wrong because it leads to bad consequences. Families and friends are left devastated and grieving. However, people who see ethics from the consequential perspective might argue that if the killing of another person had good results, it would be the right thing to do. Consider, for example, a scenario in which a police officer has to kill one armed criminal to save the lives of many hostages. Do the officer's ends (intentions) justify his or her means (the shooting)? Most people would probably think so. Two main ethical principles, discussed next, are part of consequential ethics.

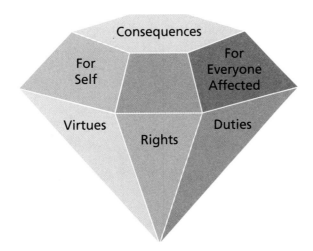

**FIGURE 2-1**
Consequences

## The Egoism Principle

This principle states that you should consider only the effects an action will have on yourself and your interests. The **egoism principle** is the idea that the right thing for a person to do in any situation is the action that best serves that person's own long-term interests (Figure 2-2). No one else's interests need be taken into account. If you are trying to decide whether to steal money from the cash register where you work, the egoism principle would lead you to think about the effects the act would have on you. Would it be better for you in the long run to steal the money or to leave it in the register? The answer probably depends on how badly you need the money and what you think your chances are of getting caught. According to the egoism principle, you do not need to consider the consequences for the store owner, your coworkers, or customers. The egoism principle maintains your only moral obligations are to yourself.

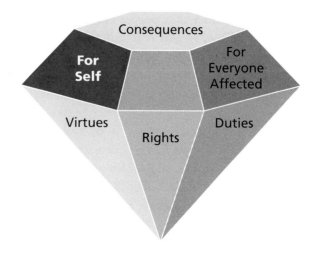

**FIGURE 2-2**
Egoism

## The Utility Principle

The **utility principle** is the idea that the morally right action is the action that produces the best consequences for everyone involved, not just for one individual (Figure 2-3). Think back to your decision about stealing the money. Using the utility principle requires that you consider the effects your action would have on everyone: you, the store owner, your coworkers, and the store's customers. In this situation, if stealing produces more *total* good or happiness for everyone than not stealing, taking the money would be the right thing to do. If not, you should leave it in the drawer.

> The greatest happiness of the greatest number is the foundation of morals and legislation.
>
> —JEREMY BENTHAM

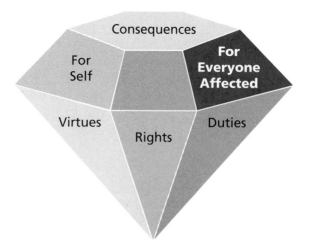

**FIGURE 2-3**
Utility

## Strengths and Weaknesses of Consequential Ethics

These consequential approaches to ethics have several strengths. For instance, they are fairly easy to use, and they seem very natural to people. In addition, it is certainly wise to consider the consequences of an action before deciding whether or not to take it.

However, the two principles have some serious weaknesses, too. First, both require you to accurately predict the consequences of your actions. Can you really do that consistently? The consequences of your actions often surprise you. Second, neither approach considers any action to be always right or always wrong. Killing an innocent person can be justified by the egoism principle when it is in a person's long-term best interests. Killing an innocent person can be permitted by the utility principle when it produces enough total happiness for everyone. Third, both approaches allow people to exploit or harm individuals for their own benefit (egoism) or for the benefit of the larger group (utility). Although considering the consequences of your actions is clearly a good idea, making sound moral decisions often requires more.

## CHECKPOINT **2–1**

 **1.** Return to the opening passage. If Allen bases her decision on the principle of egoism, what will she decide to do?

 **2.** If Allen bases her decision on the principle of utility, what will she decide to do?

 **3.** If you were in Allen's shoes, would you patent the Kaflor Belt technology? Why or why not?

**4.** In your own life, do you more often follow the principle of egoism or the principle of utility? Give a few examples.

## ■ Basing Morality on Rights, Duties, and Virtues

Another way of thinking about ethics is in terms of rights, duties, and virtues. These three principles very often lead to the same conclusion, or "right answer" to an ethical dilemma.

### The Principle of Rights

This principle calls for basing moral decisions on individual rights. A **right** refers to a way in which an individual is entitled to be treated by others (Figure 2-4). For example, your *right to life* implies that others should not take away your life because they owe you the opportunity to live. Your *right to property* implies that others should not steal your material possessions. The Declaration of Independence and the Constitution of the United States specifically refer to many such rights, including life, liberty, the pursuit of happiness, free speech, and a fair trial. In more recent years, society has debated whether individuals have the right to die with dignity, the right to have access to health care, and the right to smoke cigarettes in public places.

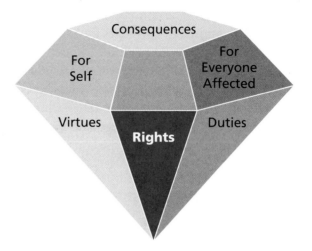

**FIGURE 2-4**
Individual rights

According to the **principle of rights**, an action is considered moral when it respects the rights of others and immoral when it violates another's rights. Therefore, stealing from the cash register would be considered wrong because, in taking other people's money, you are violating their property rights. Good or bad consequences are not what make an action right or wrong. Stealing from someone would nearly always violate that person's rights, even if the consequences of the theft were good for you or for a larger group.

A strength of the principle of rights is that it gives people a great deal of moral freedom. As long as you don't violate the rights of others, you can do whatever you want. This emphasis on independence and personal freedom is probably why the founders of the United States made rights such an important part of the government and the legal system. However, the rights approach has drawbacks, too. One is that people do not always agree on what their rights are. A 15-year-old may think he has the right to stay out all night, but his parents probably disagree. If it were easy to sort out what rights people have, debates over issues such as abortion, the death penalty, and euthanasia would have been settled long ago.

## The Principle of Duties

Another approach to considering ethics focuses on moral duties. A moral **duty** is an ethical obligation that one individual has to others (Figure 2-5). Notice that this definition is the opposite of the one given for a right. In fact, rights and duties can be thought of as opposite sides of the same coin. Your right to life implies that others have a moral duty not to kill you. Your neighbor's right to privacy implies that you have a duty not to read her mail without her permission. Other universal moral duties include obligations to help those in need, to tell the truth, and to provide for your children or aging parents.

> Everyone is really responsible to all men for all men and for everything.
>
> —Fyodor Dostoyevsky

The **principle of duties** maintains that you should do what is ethically right purely because you have a moral obligation to do so. A classic explanation of ethical duties came from the German philosopher Immanuel Kant (1724–1804). He wrote that fulfilling moral duties is the very heart of ethics. A person's primary moral duty is to base his or her actions on good reasoning. Kant believed sound reasoning will lead all people to accept two main ethical principles: universality and respect for persons. The concept of **universality** is the idea that you should act as you would want others to act in the same situation. According to the concept of **respect for persons**, it is always wrong to use other people in ways that harm them for your own benefit. In other words, it is wrong to take unfair advantage of others for personal gain.

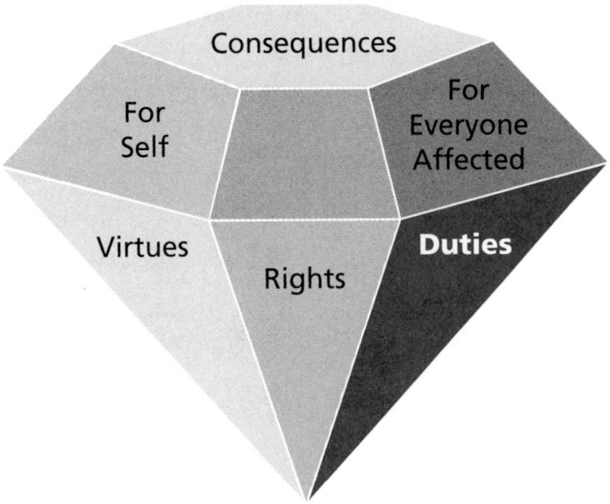


**FIGURE 2-5**
Moral duties

A strength of basing ethics on duties is that this principle motivates people to the highest levels of ethical behavior. Concepts like universality and respect for persons are extremely challenging to live up to. On the other hand, people do not seem to agree with one another about what their moral duties are. How could a society agree on what people's moral duties should be?

## The Principle of Virtues

A final ethical principle focuses on the role of moral virtues. A **virtue** is an ideal character trait that people should try to incorporate into their lives. These traits are considered good in themselves, not good because of their consequences. Examples of ethical virtues include ideals such as honesty, loyalty, respect, responsibility, self-discipline, compassion, and courage. An action that is consistent with virtues like those is considered to be good, or moral. An action that conflicts with such virtues is considered bad, or immoral.

The **principle of virtues** states that ethics is based on being a good person, that is, on incorporating ideal character traits into your life. How do you do that? How do you become honest with, responsible to, or generous toward others? More than 2,000 years ago, the Greek philosopher Aristotle wrote that the key is simply to make the virtues habits. In other words, if you don't think of yourself as an especially kind person, make up your mind to do one act of kindness today. Then do another kind act tomorrow, and so on. Eventually kindness will become a habit to you; at that point, kindness will have become ingrained into your character. You will be a kind person.

## Do the RIGHT THING

America's biggest shopping day of the year is the Friday following Thanksgiving Day. However, you might be surprised to learn that one of the biggest *online* shopping days of the year is the following Monday. Evidently, many people wait until they are back to work to go online and order gifts for the holidays. Remember, many of these people just had several days at home when they could have completed their online shopping. Meanwhile, many employers have policies that forbid employees from using their work computers for personal matters.

1. Is it ethically wrong for employees to use company computers for Internet shopping?

2. Are employers justified in forbidding it? Explain.

Thus, this principle would judge stealing money from the cash register at work to be wrong because doing so conflicts with the ethical virtues of honesty, integrity, and fairness (Figure 2-6). Whether this particular act of stealing would have good or bad consequences does not matter. One's moral duties and the rights of others are not especially relevant. The principle of virtues would judge stealing to be inherently bad because it is inconsistent with the kind of person you should want to be.

Precisely what does it mean to be courageous or generous? How do you know when you have achieved kindness or truthfulness? Aristotle addressed such questions with a unique concept called the **golden mean**, defining virtues as perfect balances between opposite and undesirable extremes.

If you want to know exactly what it means to be courageous, you have to determine the undesirable extremes. Not having enough courage is cowardice. That is one extreme. Can a person have too much courage, however? Aristotle said yes. There is an opposite extreme of courage to the point that the behavior doesn't make sense. It might be referred to as foolhardiness, that is, taking irrational, unnecessary risks. Real courage, the virtue that you should try to incorporate into your life, is perfectly balanced between the two extremes.

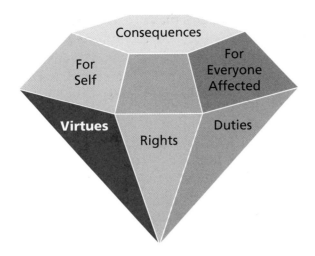

**FIGURE 2-6**
Virtues

A strength of using virtues as a basis for making decisions is that the virtues encourage people to achieve high levels of moral behavior. Like Aristotle, some philosophers of ethics, including Plato, have maintained that the key to becoming a morally mature person is acting on virtues until they become habits. However, the principle also has its weaknesses. One problem is that some actions might promote one virtue while violating another. In addition, when such a conflict exists, people do not always agree on which virtues are most important. For example, if a coworker asked you to tell a lie to cover up something that he or she had done, you would be forced to choose between the competing virtues of loyalty and honesty. When virtues alone are used to find answers to ethical questions, the conflicts may be irresolvable.

## CHECKPOINT 2–2

1. Which rights are most important to you (free speech, for example)? List five.

2. Do you feel duties toward family members? friends? your employer? your nation? any other groups?

3. Do you act in accordance with the principle of universality in your own life? Do you think other people do?

4. List five virtues you try to exhibit in your own life.

 5. Return to the Hard Choices scenario at the start of this chapter. If the CEO follows the principle of rights, what will she decide to do with the seatbelt technology?

# ETHICS @ WORK

This chapter has presented several ideas that can be used when addressing ethical dilemmas. The following scenario is your chance to apply the concepts to a business situation. Which idea makes the most sense to you? Why? Answer the questions that follow the scenario, and be prepared to respectfully argue for your point of view in class.

## Main Issue and Options

**Issue:** Does Mark owe an ethical obligation to his customers? If so, how can he meet it?

**Options:** Mark can order an immediate safety recall, delay a recall until after his company secures a large contract, or not order a recall.

## Cooper Fan Company

### Assembly Line

"OK, this all looks good," Mark talked loudly over the substantial noise inside Manufacturing Building 2. "If we get that big account as hoped, we should be able to add a third shift sometime this summer."

"If we add 75 jobs, we can double our tax credit with the city," Ernie said.

"That should be doable—if we get that contract."

"I'll keep my fingers crossed," Ernie said as a heavy machine "gronked" loudly and spit out several dozen newly cut ceiling fan blades.

"What?"

"I say I'll keep my fingers crossed!"

"Yeah. We should know something in the next month. Now, what was that other thing you wanted to talk about?"

Ernie paused. "One of our testers says there's a problem with the CPRF-300 model."

"What kind of a problem?"

"Let's go ask her."

"Lead on."

Ernie took the plant manager to a side door with a sign reading "Quality and Design" above it. He hung his hard hat on a peg beside the door before he went through it, and Mark did the same.

### Quality and Design Lab

"This," Ann said, "is the standard remote control for the CPRF-300." She handed Mark a small remote control device with buttons marked "Low," "High," "Off," and "Reverse." Mark pressed "Low," and a ceiling fan just above his head started to rotate lazily. He pushed "Off," and the blades began to slow to a stop.

"So what's the problem?" Mark asked.

"It's the reverse button. All our models except the CPRF-300 have a switch on top of the fan that allows it to be set to spin clockwise or counterclockwise. People who use the switch at all set their fans to blow air downward in the summer to make a room feel cooler, and they reverse the fan's motion to draw air upward in the winter to make the room feel warmer."

"And the CPRF-300 has it on the remote because . . ."

"The design team didn't want customers with high ceilings to have to drag a ladder out twice a year to use the feature."

"Makes sense. What's the problem?"

"The problem is that with the old design, the fan had to be stopped for an owner to be able to reach up and flip the switch. But the remote allows for the reverse feature to be engaged while the fan is running."

"What does that do?"

"Press 'High' and wait for the blades to cycle up to speed." Mark did so. When the blades were a blur, Ann said, "Now push 'Reverse.'" When Mark did, there were several rapid clicks and a soft grinding sound as the blades lost speed. The noises stopped after a few seconds. The blades slowed, came to a stop, changed direction, and sped up again.

"Huh. Well, that's a pretty annoying sound, all right," Mark said, somewhat dismissively.

"True," Ann said. "It's what happens after doing that a lot of times that concerns me."

"Oh, come on; no one's going to do that a lot of times. If it makes that sound, people will remember to stop the blades before they hit reverse."

"Maybe. These buttons are close together, though. What if someone hits the reverse button by mistake?"

Mark grunted. "Just for the sake of argument, how many times would someone have to do that before starting to have problems beyond the noises?"

"At least fifty; maybe a hundred or more."

"Nobody's going to hit the wrong button a hundred times by mistake."

"What if it's somebody's kid, and the kid wants to make a game of it?"

Mark thought that over for a moment. "OK, go ahead. What happens if a kid makes a game of it?"

Ann pulled a file from a cabinet drawer and began to recite her findings. "We tested 50 CPRF-300s last week. All of them eventually failed after they were reversed from the high setting repeatedly. The first failed after 55 rounds, the average was 112, and the last one failed at 193 rounds."

Ann continued. "Forty-five of them simply ceased to operate without further incident. Three emitted sparks but did not start a fire. One started a fire. The last one threw out a half-inch piece of metal from the inner casing with considerable velocity."

"Define 'considerable velocity,'" Mark said.

"Well, not lethal velocity. But I was there—it hit the wall pretty hard. It was traveling fast enough to put an eye out, certainly."

"OK. The one that caught fire, it was a big fire?"

"Not at the point when we extinguished it, but it would have spread, yes."

"Ugh," Mark said. "This is terrible timing. We're pushing hard for that new big account. That could double our business."

"Yes," Ann agreed.

Mark pursed his lips and thought for a moment. "What do you recommend?" he asked Ann.

"Well, the first thing has already been done. I've talked to the designers about redesigning our future models to automatically kill the power until the blades are stopped anytime the reverse button is engaged."

"That's good."

"As for the CPRF-300s, they're not safe. We could recall them, but because of the way they're put together, there isn't a cheap fix for the mechanical problem. I'm not sure what to say about how to handle them."

"OK. Thanks, Ann," Mark said. He turned to Ernie. "Get all the numbers and meet me in my office at 3 o'clock."

"Sure thing, boss," Ernie said.

## Manager's Office

"Here are the numbers," Ernie said. "We've sold 50,000 CPRF-300s to date. We've had no reports of malfunctions, fires, or any other problems from our customers, retailers, or the government. I mean, seeing is believing—there is a potential problem with the CPRF-300—but nobody has reported an actual problem, at least so far."

"Did you talk to Lawyer Dave and Jimbo?"

"I did. Lawyer Dave estimated legal costs at probably $20,000 to $200,000 per incident, with no upper limit on a worst-scenario case in which someone dies in a fire or is disabled by flying debris. 'Manufacturers usually get hammered in those kinds of cases no matter what happened,' he told me.

"Jimbo said it would be cheaper to replace the fans than to try to repair them, especially with shipping costs factored in."

"OK." Mark scribbled some notes. "What about that recall we did in '05? How many buyers took us up on that?"

"About 15 percent. We'd probably have fewer accept this one because a lot of them won't want to take down and remount a fan if the problem is not something they see as an issue. If we send every purchaser a warning not to reverse while running at high speed and offer to replace the fan free, I'd estimate that about 10 percent of them will actually accept. Most would be parents with small kids. If we offer to replace their remotes with new ones that don't have a reverse button, maybe we can get down to replacing only 5 percent of the fans."

Mark did some rapid calculations. "Still," he said, "that's maybe a million, a million-and-a-half bucks."

"True enough."

"So, just talking dollars and cents, we'd have to have a lot of real-world problems to add up to the cost of a recall."

"Unless someone is killed in a fire, and then all bets are off."

"Then there's the whole matter of, ah, timing. The contract we're up for could set the company up for years. I hear it's a five-year project. Even if we decide to recommend a recall, I don't want to saddle the executives with this now."

"I know."

"That deal will probably be done in a month. Six weeks, tops."

"Yeah."

Mark tapped his pen on his paper. "What's your gut tell you, Ernie?"

## What Do You Think?

1. If you were in Mark's position, would you recommend a recall today? Why or why not? Would you be following the principle of egoism or the principle of utility?

2. If you were in Mark's position, would you recommend a recall in two months, after the deal will have been completed? Why or why not? Would you be following the principle of egoism or the principle of utility?

3. Do the Cooper Fan Company's customers have a right to be warned about the defect? Does the company have a duty to warn them?

4. How can Mark best follow the golden mean?

5. Ann's testing showed 6 percent "bad" results (sparks) and 4 percent "really bad" results (fire and thrown metal). Would your answers to Questions 1 and 2 change if Ann's testing had shown 18 percent "bad" and 12 percent "really bad" results? What if it had shown 6 percent "bad" results but no "really bad" results?

# Summary

This chapter describes five ethical principles agreed on by most people. Two of them define ethical actions in terms of consequences, the effects or results of what a person does. The egoism principle maintains that the most ethical action is the one that has the best consequences for a person. The utility principle argues that the right thing to do in any situation is the action that produces the most good or happiness for the most people.

Three other widely shared ethical principles are the principles of rights, duties, and virtues. The principle of rights maintains that an action is moral when it respects the rights of others and immoral when it violates another's rights. The principle of duties maintains that people should do what is ethically right purely because they have a moral obligation to do so. The principle of virtues states that ethics is based on being a good person, that is, on incorporating ideal character traits into one's life.

# Key Terms and Concepts

**Match each definition with a key term or concept.**

_____ 1. The idea that an action is considered moral when it respects the rights of others and immoral when it violates another's rights

_____ 2. The method of defining virtues as perfect balances between opposite and undesirable extremes

_____ 3. An ethical obligation that one individual has to others

_____ 4. The idea that ethics is based on being a good person, on incorporating ideal character traits into one's life

_____ 5. An ideal character trait that people should try to incorporate into their lives

_____ 6. The idea that it is wrong to use other people in ways that harm them for one's own benefit

_____ 7. The idea that the morally right action is the one that produces the best consequences for everyone involved, not just for one individual

_____ 8. The idea that people should act as they would want others to act in the same situation

_____ 9. The idea that people should do what is ethically right purely because they have a moral obligation to do so

_____ 10. The effects or results of what people do

_____ 11. The idea that the right thing for a person to do in any situation is the action that best serves that person's long-term interests

_____ 12. A term used to describe how an individual is entitled to be treated by others

_____ 13. A way of viewing ethical right and wrong, often unique to an individual, a culture, or a subculture

a. consequences
b. duty
c. egoism principle
d. golden mean
e. principle of duties
f. principle of rights
g. principle of virtues
h. respect for persons
i. right
j. universality
k. utility principle
l. value system
m. virtue

# Review

1. True or false: A person who always acts in such a way as to maximize his or her own long-term interests is following the principle of utility.

2. Match each ethical principle with the correct application.

   ———— egoism principle

   ———— utility principle

   ———— principle of rights

   ———— principle of duties

   ———— principle of virtues

   a. Kay donates to a flood relief fund because she has an obligation to help people in need.

   b. Lin is careful with sensitive information because her clients are entitled to privacy.

   c. Gina arranges time off for employees who volunteer because everyone benefits.

   d. Jay admits a mistake because he's an honest person.

   e. Jen calls in sick because she'd like a day off.

3. List one strength and one weakness of each ethical principle discussed in this chapter.

4. Explain the principle of duties according to Immanuel Kant in your own words. Include the concepts of universality and respect for persons.

5. According to Aristotle, what is the golden mean? Explain in your own words.

# Critical Thinking

6. Toshi has a part-time job as an aide in the mayor's office. Yesterday a large, beautifully wrapped box was delivered to the office. Inside the box were dozens of expensive watches, gifts to the mayor's staff from the Tik-Tok Watch Corporation. A card attached to the box read, "Dear friends at City Hall: We at Tik-Tok are excited that we may soon be building a new factory in your community. We appreciate whatever

help you can give us in getting the zoning laws changed. Please keep the watches as a token of our goodwill and friendship."

Toshi knows that for the past few weeks, the city government had been debating a change in local zoning laws. Changing the laws would allow Tik-Tok to save millions of dollars when purchasing land for a new factory. Local officials, business leaders, and citizens are bitterly divided over the issue.

a. Whose rights are at stake in this situation?

b. How might Toshi's actions violate another's rights?

c. What moral duties does Toshi have that are relevant to this situation?

d. What action seems most consistent with those duties?

e. What moral virtues are relevant to Toshi's situation?

f. What action by Toshi would seem to promote the most virtues?

## Applications

7. Nina has an old car that barely runs. She wants to get rid of it. Her neighbor, Gabrielle, knows very little about cars. Nina is thinking about trying to con Gabrielle into buying the car. Nina knows she will have to lie about the condition of the car; otherwise, Gabrielle won't consider buying it. What is Nina likely to do if she tries to follow the concept of universality? Explain your answer.

8. Give an example of a recent movie that deals with ethical issues or in which the characters have to make important ethical decisions. Which principles from the chapter do the characters use? Does the movie portray some principles as being better than others? If so, do you think those principles really are better?

## Digging Deeper

9. Think of three universal ethical principles that are not mentioned in this chapter. It may not be as easy as you expect. What are your guiding principles that should *always* be followed? You can do some research first if necessary.

## The Bottom Line

10. Evaluate your feelings toward the main ideas presented in this chapter. Rank them from 1 to 5, with 1 being the idea that is most important to your own decision making and 5 being least important.

\_\_\_\_\_ principle of egoism

\_\_\_\_\_ principle of utility

\_\_\_\_\_ principle of rights

\_\_\_\_\_ principle of duties

\_\_\_\_\_ principle of virtues

# Personal Ethical Development

Three common questions about personal ethics are how people develop perceptions of right and wrong, how moral maturity can be measured, and what determines whether a person will act ethically. This chapter presents two important theories of human moral development and ethical behavior.

## Objectives
- Describe Lawrence Kohlberg's justice model of personal ethical development.
- Explain James Rest's Four Component Model of moral behavior.

## Key Terms and Concepts

moral development, p. 33
justice, p. 33
social contract, p. 36
moral sensitivity, p. 39
ethical judgment, p. 39

ethical motivation, p. 40
ethical character, p. 41
inner conflict, p. 41
fear of change, p. 42

Will has a summer job working for the local electric company. He has been assigned to the warehouse, where the company stores all the parts and equipment used to maintain the power lines and to keep electricity running. His job is to help load and unload the trucks; to keep the shelves stocked; and to run occasional errands for the warehouse supervisor, Mr. Walker.

The atmosphere is tense around the power company this summer. The union and management have been fighting over a new contract, and from what Will can tell, management seems to be winning. The employees are angry and bitter.

While completing a parts inventory one day, Will notices that many of the shelves are bare. A lot of equipment seems to be missing. When he reports his findings to Mr. Walker, the supervisor tells Will not to worry.

"I've seen this kind of thing before. It's just the line workers' way of getting even with management. If the workers don't get paid what they think they deserve, they make up for it by stealing equipment from the warehouse and off the trucks. It's not really right, but frankly, I'm on their side. The company is not being fair. So we'll ignore the missing materials and keep the workers out of trouble. With a little luck, the contract negotiations will be over by the time the company catches on to what's happening."

Will doesn't want to make his supervisor angry, but he is uneasy with looking the other way. Will found this job through a good friend of his mom's—Ms. Davidoff, a company vice president—a fact he has kept from Mr. Walker. He considers reporting what he knows to her, but he is reluctant to cause trouble for Mr. Walker and his coworkers.

## {**WHAT** Do You Think?}

**What should Will do? Why?**

# ■ Kohlberg's Justice Model of Moral Development

For decades, researchers have been studying **moral development**, the process by which humans grow more ethically mature, or develop an understanding of moral right and wrong. Several competing theories have been proposed to explain this process. One of the most important and influential is that of Lawrence Kohlberg (1927–1987), an American psychologist. Other theories have built on, or have been proposed in response to, Kohlberg's model. Kohlberg's theory is based on **justice**, which is impartial fairness, or equity. It uses an understanding of the concept of justice as the main criterion in measuring a person's moral maturity.

Kohlberg studied and interviewed thousands of children from many different nations, cultures, and religious groups. Typically, Kohlberg would present each child with a case study of a character facing an ethical dilemma. He would ask the child what the character should do in the situation and why. Kohlberg believed that the answer to the *why* question held the key to understanding the child's moral reasoning and, thus, his or her level of moral development. Kohlberg's research led him to identify six stages of human moral development.

## Stage 1—Punishment and Obedience

In Kohlberg's first stage (Figure 3-1), right and wrong are perceived in terms of the physical consequences of particular actions. Actions that lead to pleasant consequences are considered good, and actions that lead to unpleasant consequences are considered bad. Most children learn early in life that disobedience to authority figures (parents) leads to punishment, while obedience leads to praise. Soon morality comes to be thought of in terms of obedience to authority and avoidance of punishment.

Kohlberg found that many children understand that hurting others is wrong, but they often give different reasons when asked why. Typically,

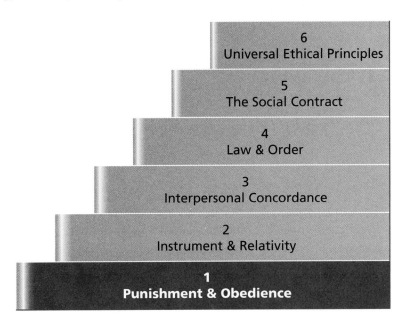

**FIGURE 3-1**

Kohlberg's justice model: punishment and obedience

children in Stage 1 think of the action as wrong because their parents have told them not to do it and because those who hurt others get punished. Notice that self-centeredness is at the heart of this way of reasoning. According to Kohlberg, children in this stage do not understand that other people have feelings and needs like their own; therefore, the children are not capable of sympathy or compassion. The only motivating force is avoiding punishment.

## Stage 2—Instrument and Relativity

A child in Kohlberg's second stage (Figure 3-2) has a more realistic view of others. Now other people are seen as having feelings and needs like the child, but the child is still motivated by self-centeredness. These children think of a "right" action as one can be used as an *instrument* to meet their needs and desires. In other words, moral actions are those used to meet personal needs. Stage 2 children can be manipulative, using the feelings and needs of others to get what they want. Morality is seen as *relative*, meaning it changes according to different situations.

For example, consider a young girl whose room is a mess. Her parents are expecting company soon and are anxious about what the visitors will think if the house doesn't look neat and clean. In Stage 2, avoiding punishment is less likely to be the reason the girl would clean her room. She is more likely to notice the stress and tension that her parents are feeling and to try to bargain with them, perhaps cleaning her room in exchange for money or some other reward.

**FIGURE 3-2**
Kohlberg's justice model: instrument and relativity

## Stage 3—Interpersonal Concordance

In Kohlberg's third stage (Figure 3-3), individuals feel a strong need to be liked, accepted, and well thought of by others. *Concordance* means "agreement or harmony." So, morally right actions are those that gain social approval. Wrong actions are those that bring social condemnation, embarrassment, or rejection.

People in Stage 3 are strongly influenced by peer pressure. The peer group may even replace parents as the primary moral authority. Consider a 14-year-old boy who starts smoking cigarettes because his peer group encourages him to do so. Stage 3 reasoning leads him to think that his actions are right because of the way the group treats him when he does what it expects. Unlike Stage 1 and Stage 2 children, he is willing to sacrifice his own physical self-interest to please the group and gain its approval.

**FIGURE 3-3**
Kohlberg's justice model: interpersonal concordance

## Stage 4—Law and Order

People in Kohlberg's fourth stage (Figure 3-4) have developed a mature view of the world. They understand they are part of a larger community, and they feel a moral duty to maintain its order and stability. An action that promotes the harmony and smooth functioning of society is seen as right. An action that interferes with the social order is seen as wrong. As a result, individuals in Stage 4 have a strong sense of citizenship, duty, responsibility, and obedience to the law (Figure 3-5 on page 36).

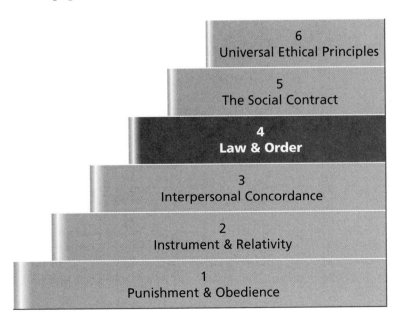

**FIGURE 3-4**
Kohlberg's justice model: law and order

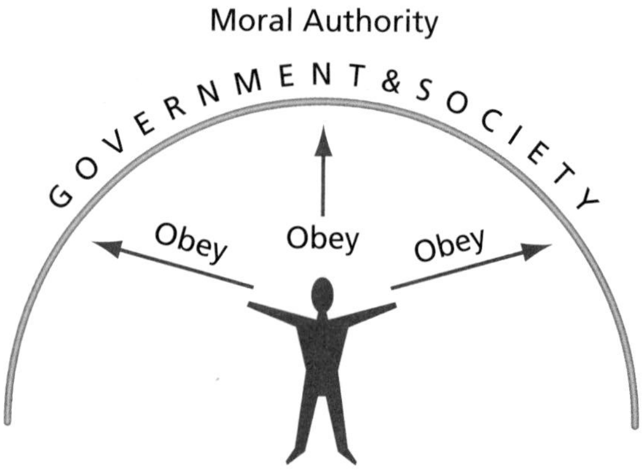

Moral Authority
GOVERNMENT & SOCIETY
Obey
Obey
Obey

**FIGURE 3-5**
Stage 4 thinking

**Ethics & Law**

Provide two examples of historic American laws that most people now believe were unjust or morally wrong. Provide one example of a current American law that some people argue is unjust.

**What is the ethical response for a person confronted with laws that he or she is convinced are unjust?**

You can probably see a potential flaw in Stage 4 reasoning. It can make it difficult for a person to understand the need to challenge abuses of authority or to protest unfair laws. Strict adherence to this level of development would have prevented the civil rights movement, for example.

## Stage 5—The Social Contract

Individuals in Kohlberg's fifth stage (Figure 3-6) view the government as a legal authority, not a moral one. They believe that there is a higher moral authority, the **social contract**, which represents the deepest values and beliefs of a society. The government's role is seen as serving the will of the people (Figure 3-7). When the government fails to live up to that responsibility, the role of citizenship is to question and challenge the government, perhaps by voting for candidates with a new point of view or by becoming politically active.

6
Universal Ethical Principles
5
The Social Contract
4
Law & Order
3
Interpersonal Concordance
2
Instrument & Relativity
1
Punishment & Obedience

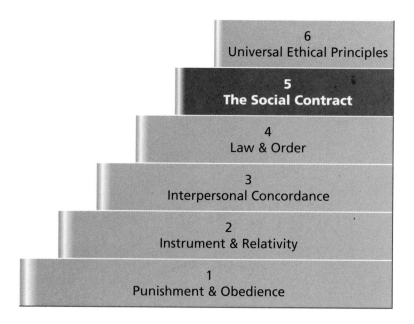

**FIGURE 3-6**
Kohlberg's justice model: the social contract

Stage 5 individuals view morality in terms of important social values. In the United States, those values might include beliefs in the equality of all people, the dignity and worth of the individual, human rights, and fairness. Other societies and cultures might have different values and beliefs and, therefore, may have different social contracts.

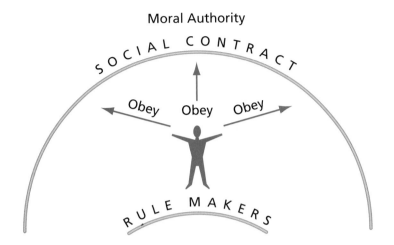

FIGURE 3-7
Stage 5 thinking

## Stage 6—Universal Ethical Principles

People at Kohlberg's highest level of moral development (Figure 3-8) view right and wrong in terms of universal ethical principles. These principles are self-chosen (no one forces a person to choose them) and universal (other people thinking rationally would have to agree that the principles are worthy). They could include some of the principles discussed in Chapter 2, especially dealing with justice or fairness to others, such as respecting the worth and value of human life, acting as you would want others to act, and believing in the importance of individual rights.

FIGURE 3-8
Kohlberg's justice model: universal ethical principles

People in Stage 5 might follow these principles also, but only if the principles are part of the social contract. People in Stage 6 would rely on these principles no matter what kind of society they found themselves in.

Kohlberg believed that few people ever reach this final stage of moral development. Those who do feel compelled by personal ethical principles to rise above the values and beliefs of their societies (Figure 3-9). They are willing to sacrifice their own needs, their interests, and sometimes their lives to try to pull their societies up to a higher moral plane. Kohlberg frequently mentioned Mahatma Gandhi and Martin Luther King, Jr., as examples of people demonstrating Stage 6 reasoning.

**FIGURE 3-9**
Stage 6 thinking

## CHECKPOINT 3–1

1. In your own words, write the main idea of each of Kohlberg's stages of ethical development. Use a separate piece of paper.

2. Return to the opening scenario. If Will decides to report what he knows, assess his level of ethical development.

3. If Will chooses to keep quiet, assess his level of ethical development.

4. Kohlberg assumed that a person's ethical maturity is based less on the person's ethical behavior than on how he or she thinks or reasons about right and wrong. Do you agree? Why or why not?

# ■ Rest's Four Components of Moral Behavior

James Rest (1941–1999) was a leader in research on personal ethical development. While he agreed with much of Kohlberg's work, he thought that more than moral judgment was involved in the process of making ethical decisions. Rest argued that for people to behave morally, three additional psychological processes must also take place.

## Moral Sensitivity

Imagine your family awards a scholarship at a local high school annually in memory of your father, who taught there. This year, your aunt (your father's sister) expects you to give the scholarship to her grandson, who is a senior at the school. You recognize that you can't consider her grandson for the scholarship because of the implication of favoritism, but she doesn't sense that choosing him would be wrong.

**Moral sensitivity** is the ability to recognize the presence of ethical issues, questions, and temptations and how your actions could affect the people involved. Moral sensitivity is not something to be taken for granted; not everyone has it. In the business world, it's not unusual to see someone's career end for an ethical misdeed that he or she didn't recognize as a matter of right or wrong.

According to Rest, the first component of moral behavior is to have the sensitivity to recognize an ethical problem when you see one (Figure 3-10). Still, that's not enough, is it? A person can realize that he or she is dealing with an ethical issue and still not know what to do about it.

**FIGURE 3-10**
The four components: moral sensitivity

## Ethical Judgment

**Ethical judgment** is the ability to decide on the best or right course of action—to be able to make a responsible ethical assessment. If you're honest with yourself, you don't usually have to think too hard to know what's right and wrong. You generally know right away. For instance, people shouldn't lie, cheat, or steal, and they should try to help others in need. Of course, some decisions are more complicated than that. What if lying is the only way to protect your company? Does a person's duty to help others in need mean that he or she should give a ride to a stranger standing on the side of a dark highway?

Rest's second component of moral behavior is this ability to determine the most ethical course of action in a situation (Figure 3-11). Like moral sensitivity, though, ethical judgment alone is not sufficient. Many times in life, people know the right thing to do; they just don't want to do it.

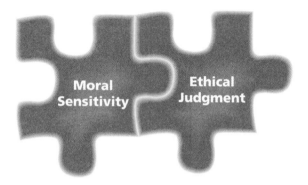

## Ethical Motivation

According to Rest, moral behavior also requires **ethical motivation**, that is, the personal disposition to do the right thing (Figure 3-12). You must have a strong inner desire to be a good person and to live a good life. Your ethical values must be more important to you than all your other values, such as the desire to have good grades or to be financially successful. You can probably think of examples of the lack of this quality. One example is an employee who exaggerates her accomplishments and takes credit for other people's work in order to get a promotion.

One additional component makes the model complete. Sometimes people recognize an ethical temptation, know the right thing to do, and want to do what's right—but still end up doing what they know is wrong. The fourth component is ethical character.

> To see what is right
> and not do it is
> cowardice.
>
> —CONFUCIUS

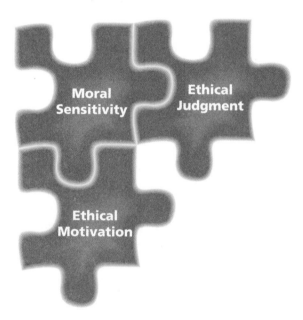

## Ethical Character

**Ethical character** consists of a group of qualities such as self-discipline and courage that enable you to follow through in difficult situations and do what you know you should, even under extreme pressure. Sometimes life isn't fair, and people can end up in difficult situations. Do you have the courage to report a group of fellow employees who are stealing? Do you have the self-discipline to go to work instead of taking a sick day even though you were up studying until late at night and you're exhausted? Figure 3-13 illustrates the complete Four Component Model.

**FIGURE 3-13**
The four components

## Conclusion

Rest and Kohlberg had much to say about personal ethical development, but many other thinkers have presented their own models. For example, Sigmund Freud argued that a person's ethics were shaped largely by childhood experiences. Erik Erikson believed that a person continues to develop throughout life, and he developed a model of personal development based upon stage of life. This chapter focuses on the well-developed and studied work of Rest and Kohlberg, but many other theories exist.

## An Interesting Footnote: Opposing Forces

Two opposing forces are at work in the process of personal ethical development (Figure 3-14). In most developmental theories, it is normal and expected that people will keep striving to move from one stage or step to the next. Therefore, some inner force must be involved, constantly pushing people toward higher stages of ethical reasoning. This force is **inner conflict**.

When something about a person's present stage isn't working well for him or her, the person is left with a sense of frustration or anxiety. That inner conflict motivates the person to look for different ways of thinking. That is why most people can look back over their lives and see that the difficult

> If there is no struggle, there is no progress.
>
> —FREDERICK DOUGLASS

times were often the times they grew the most. It also explains why people don't grow as much when their lives are comfortable and easy.

However, if inner conflict was the only force at work, everyone would get to the highest levels of ethical reasoning. After all, life provides many difficult times for everyone. So there has to be another competing force that prevents people from moving up. That second force is **fear of change**.

Many humans fear change more than almost anything else in life. That fear has a paralyzing power. Haven't you seen or heard of instances in which someone was in an unbearably bad situation, but he or she stayed in it because the fear of change was stronger than the misery of the person's circumstances?

So when things are going well and people's lives are comfortable, inner conflict remains subdued and fear of change outweighs it. Therefore, people stay where they are. In difficult times when a person's current way of thinking is inadequate, his or her inner conflict escalates. If it becomes stronger than the person's fear of change, he or she starts to grow and mature.

We cannot learn without pain.

—ARISTOTLE

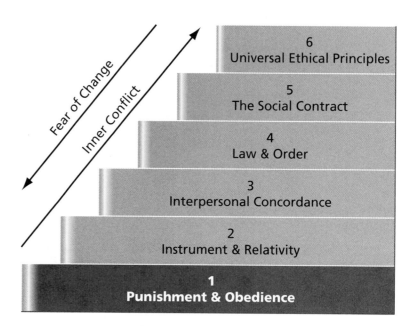

**FIGURE 3-14**
Opposing forces

## CHECKPOINT 3–2

1. In your own words, summarize the meaning of each of Rest's four components of moral behavior.

2. In your opinion, which component is the easiest to develop? Why?

3. In your opinion, which component is the hardest to develop? Why?

4. Which components do you see as strengths of yours? Which components do you see as weaknesses of yours?

5. Think back to Will's scenario at the beginning of the chapter. Explain how each of Rest's components could affect how Will perceives the situation and what Will might do about it.

6. Of Sigmund Freud and Erik Erikson, which believed that personal ethical development continued throughout life?

# ETHICS@WORK

This chapter has presented two models, one for describing personal ethical development and a second for determining ethical behavior. The following scenario is your chance to apply the models to a business situation. Answer the questions about the scenario, and be prepared to respectfully argue for your point of view in class.

## Main Issue and Options

**Issue:** Should Alan try to sell the service plan to his customers in the ways that Morty suggests?

**Options:** Alan can change his standard sales pitch, or he can keep doing what he has been doing.

## Microinsurance

### Monday at Noon

Alan punched in his code above the door handle, heard a faint click, and opened the door with the "Employees Only" sign. He left the showroom and headed up a staircase to the second floor of Big Al's Electronic Emporium. He passed a security room where a bored guard watched customers through one-way glass on the floor below.

"Any action today?" Alan asked him. The guard turned slowly, shook his head, and turned away. Alan passed two managers' offices and came to the break room, which also offered a view of the first floor through one-way glass.

"Kid!" Alan was enthusiastically greeted by a man in a plaid blazer. A gold name tag on his coat pocket read "Morty" in large capital letters and "25 years' service" in smaller letters below. "Siddown!" Morty patted the chair beside his, and Alan wandered over to it. "How are ya, kid?"

"Fine, Mr. Johnson."

"Morty! How many times do I have to tell you it's Morty?"

"Fine . . . Morty."

"There you go!" Morty took a heroic bite of a ham sandwich. A small dab of mustard was left clinging to his lower lip. "So, kid. How's business today?"

"It's good, Mr. . . . Morty," Alan said. "I sold a refrigerator and two HDTVs this morning."

"Say, that's great! How big?"

"The TVs? Ah . . . 46 inches."

"Not bad! What kind?"

"Sony."

"Sony!"

"Yeah. I think I'm starting to get the hang of this. One of the women told me that her friend bought a TV from me last week and that she ought to . . ."

"Yeah, referrals are great, kid," Morty interrupted. He trailed off and took another bite of his sandwich. Alan decided not to continue with his story and ate in silence.

"Hey, kid. Lemme ask you a question."

"OK, sure."

"How long do you want to work here?"

Alan paused and gave a quick glance at the "25 years" part of Morty's name tag. "Um . . . well, I guess at least until I graduate. I'm a sophomore now. The money's pretty good, and it would be nice to take out smaller loans. I . . ."

"I was talking to Big Al about you a couple days ago."

"You were?"

"Oh, sure. Big Al and I have been tight from the beginning. I was the third person he ever hired, you know. We talk about everybody."

"Wow. So, what did he say?"

"He likes you, kid. He thinks you're a natural with the customers. He told me that you move a lot of merchandise for a new guy."

"Hey, that's good. Good to hear."

"Yeah. You've got a problem, though."

"I do?"

"Yes, you do, and you won't last six months if you don't fix it," Morty replied. "You want to know what your problem is?"

"Yes. Definitely."

"OK. When you sold that fridge today, did you sell 'em an extended service plan?"

"No," Alan admitted. "No, I offered it, but they just didn't want it."

"Uh-huh. What about the two HDTVs? Service plan for either one?"

"Ah . . . no. They didn't want one, either."

"Do you realize that Big Al makes most of his money from service plans?"

Alan thought about that for a while. "Really?"

"Really."

"But, those things are cheap compared to . . . practically everything we sell."

"True, but practically everything we sell is sold nearly at cost." Morty settled back in his chair. "Big Al has to compete with Walmart and Best Buy. His prices have to stay at least in the neighborhood of their prices, so he marks up a TV that costs him $900 to maybe $939, but probably not even that much."

"Wow."

"Yeah, but the service plan, that's almost pure profit. We sell a big TV for $939 and sell them a service plan for $99 on top of that if we can, right?"

"Right."

"Now do that 100 times. That makes for about $10,000 in service plans. Morty looked at Alan, who nodded that he understood. Now, out of the 100 customers, maybe one guy has a problem we have to cover where his set has to be replaced. The manufacturer's warranty covers a lot of replacements because if a new set doesn't work at all, it's usually because it was defectively made. Sometimes one gets broken in a way that we have to pay for. So we're out $900 on that one."

"I got it." Alan had forgotten his lunch altogether.

"OK, so maybe five out of the hundred have a repair of some kind that we have to cover."

"Only five?"

"Maybe a few more, but people—most people—take good care of their big TV. It's their baby! So anyway, a few repairs—say another grand down the drain, total. That leaves Big Al with $8,000 out of the $10,000 extended service plan money in his pocket. So Big Al . . . can you do the numbers, kid?"

"He makes $39 from the TV and $80 from the service plan," Alan said.

"Bingo! He gets it!"

"Wow. I had no idea."

"Now you know." Morty finished his sandwich in two huge bites, dusted off his hands, and threw the paper wrapper into the trash can. Then he poured himself a large cup of coffee. "So you see, the amount of merchandise you sell is OK. It's about average. But you're only making a third of each sale, because you almost never sell somebody on the service plan."

"That's true. I mean, I always offer it the way they said to in training, but . . ."

"What do you say when you offer it?"

"Well," Alan thought. "I guess I just ask if they want the plan and give them a price."

"Oh, kid," Morty said, shaking his head. He checked his gold watch. "Look, I've got 15 minutes left on my break. How about a crash course in selling those plans?"

"Oh, I don't know, Morty. I mean . . ."

"Kid, this is a limited-time offer. I'm trying to save you here—you've got to sell those plans."

"I appreciate it. It's just . . . " Alan hesitated. "Is it fair to charge them . . ."

"Oh! Moralizing on me! Is this what they're teaching in college these days?"

"Well, actually, I am taking an ethics class this semester. I've got this guy Bredeson—he's really goofy-looking, but the class . . ."

"Yeah, they've got lots of bright ideas at colleges. Look, do you want the advice or not?"

Alan looked through the one-way glass at the customers below. His focus shifted, and he studied his own reflection in the glass for a moment.

"OK, Morty," he watched himself say.

1. If Alan chooses to take Morty's advice, is he acting with ethical character? Why or why not?

3. What is the largest amount that Big Al, the owner of the store, can ethically charge for his service plan? Circle the appropriate amount.

   $20   $40   $60   $80   $100   $125   $150   $250
   whatever people will pay

2. Suppose Alan chooses not to take Morty's advice. Assess his level of ethical development using Kohlberg's justice model.

## Later That Day

Alan sold three more HDTVs that afternoon. All three customers initially declined when he offered them an extended service plan. Alan talked them into buying the service plans in the following ways.

### Customer 1

The first customer was a woman with two small children. As she and Alan were talking about the extended service plan, one of her children bumped into a display table and nearly knocked it over. Alan remarked, "You know, if he knocked the TV over and it broke, the service plan would buy you a new one." This was a true statement. Earlier, Morty had told Alan, "Most of the time when we have to cover a broken set, somebody's kid has knocked it over or thrown a ball at it or something like that."

### Customer 2

When the second customer declined the service plan, Alan said, "These new 1080p sets have a lot of pixels. Sometimes one freezes up or goes dark—makes it kind of irritating to watch, especially sports. You said you'd be watching a lot of sports on this set? The service plan would fix or replace your TV if anything like that happened." This statement was also true. The customer thought for a moment and then agreed to buy the service plan.

Morty had said to Alan, "I've only had one guy who ever had a frozen pixel, and that was five years ago. The TVs we sell are rock-solid by the time the manufacturers get done testing them. Still, customers will buy the idea that one little spot might fail, and you're not lying when you tell them the service plan would cover that kind of problem, even though it's a thousand-to-one odds that it happens to them."

### Customer 3

When the third customer declined the service plan, Alan made the same sales pitch that he had to the second customer about the TV freezing up or going dark. The customer asked, "Does that happen very often?" Alan replied, "I don't know—I just started working here."

4. Does Alan's statement to each customer demonstrate ethical judgment? Why or why not? For each statement, assess Alan's level of ethical development under Kohlberg's justice model.

# Summary

This chapter outlines two theories in personal ethics. Lawrence Kohlberg's model of moral development identifies six stages in the process of growing ethically and uses an understanding of the concept of justice in measuring a person's moral maturity.

1. Obey authority and avoid punishment.
2. Act in ways that meet your own needs and get you what you want.
3. Act in ways that get you social approval.
4. Conform to established rules, laws, and policies.
5. Follow the ethical principles and values of your society or culture.
6. Follow your own personal, but universal, ethical principles.

James Rest's Four Components Model identifies four psychological processes that must occur for people to behave morally: moral sensitivity, ethical judgment, ethical motivation, and ethical character.

Many other theories of personal ethical development exist. In most of them, people normally strive to move from one stage or step to the next. Two inner forces that heavily influence how fast and how far a person progresses in ethical development are inner conflict and fear of change.

# Key Terms and Concepts

**Match each definition with a key term or concept.**

| | |
|---|---|
| _____ | 1. Impartial fairness, or equity |
| _____ | 2. The ability to recognize ethical issues, questions, and temptations and how your actions could affect the people involved |
| _____ | 3. The ability to determine the morally right or best course of action |
| _____ | 4. The inner desire to do the right thing |
| _____ | 5. A group of qualities such as courage and self-discipline belonging to a person |
| _____ | 6. The internal force that motivates people to move up toward higher levels of ethical thinking |
| _____ | 7. The internal force that holds people back from ethical growth |
| _____ | 8. The process by which people develop an understanding of right and wrong |
| _____ | 9. The deepest values and beliefs of a society |

a. ethical character
b. ethical judgment
c. ethical motivation
d. fear of change
e. inner conflict
f. justice
g. moral development
h. moral sensitivity
i. social contract

# Review

1. Kohlberg's highest stage of moral development was

   a. instrument and relativity.

   b. universal ethical principles.

   c. the social contract.

   d. interpersonal concordance.

2. The fourth component of personal ethical judgment is ethical

   a. sensitivity.

   b. judgment.

   c. character.

   d. motivation.

3. At which of Kohlberg's stages is peer pressure especially important?

4. In the social contract stage, what is the role of government, and what is the role of citizens?

5. In Rest's model, the Four Components are related. How? Why, in Rest's view, is each essential, but not sufficient on its own?

6. True or false: During difficult times in their lives, people are less likely to experience ethical growth.

# Critical Thinking

7. Last Saturday, five people were arrested for trespassing during a protest rally at a plant that manufactures parts for nuclear weapons. Each protestor gave a statement to the police. From their statements, identify the stage of Kohlberg's justice model and provide an explanation.

   a. Erin: "This business violates every principle our country stands for! This is not what America is about. The government is wrong to allow companies like this to exist. We are going to stand up for what America believes in and protest until the government passes laws to make this kind of business illegal!"

   Erin is at Stage _____ because

b. Danielle: "I'm really sorry about what happened, but it's not my fault. The leader of this group is vicious and dangerous. I had to go along with him, or I would have gotten into trouble. He might have hurt me."

Danielle is at Stage _____ because

c. Jquaan: "Look, all my friends belong to this protest group. I couldn't let them down. What kind of person would they think I am if I didn't climb the fence with them? I don't want my friends thinking I'm a coward!"

Jquaan is at Stage _____ because

d. Olivia: "I'm not really one of the protesters. Some guy paid us $50 each if we would make the crowd look bigger for the television cameras. I'm just out for myself here. I'll even testify against them if you drop the charges against me and pay me a little something for my trouble."

Olivia is at Stage _____ because

e. Christopher: "I cannot stand by silently while a company violates important principles that I believe in deeply. Human life is at stake. Prosecute me if you have to, but I'm standing by my principles."

Christopher is at Stage _____ because

8. Jean is a senior. To have enough credits to graduate, she must pass her composition class. To pass, she has to earn an A on the class research paper due in two days. Jean has not picked a topic or started her research. She has been too busy catching up in other classes. Now she's beginning to panic.

Jean's friend Molly had the same class last year. Molly kept her paper, on which she received an A. She offers to sell it to Jean for $50.

How would Jean reason through her decision according to Kohlberg's model? What will she do at each stage? Record your answers in the table.

| KOHLBERG'S JUSTICE MODEL | | |
|---|---|---|
| Stage | What is Jean thinking? | What might Jean do? Why? |
| 1 | | |
| 2 | | |
| 3 | | |
| 4 | | |
| 5 | | |
| 6 | | |

# Applications

9. Think of a movie or television show you saw recently that contained ethical themes. At what stages of moral development, according to Kohlberg's model, were the villains? the heroes? Did any characters show changes in moral maturity during the story? Answer these questions on a separate piece of paper.

10. Apply Kohlberg's model of moral development to yourself. Identify your current level. At what level would you like to be?

# Digging Deeper

11. Go online and find an article about someone behaving badly at work. It can be an executive, an employee, or anyone at all. On a separate piece of paper, assess the wrongdoer's behavior using Rest's model. Which of the four components (you can identify more than one) seems to be a weakness for the person who made poor choices?

12. Go online and research Erik Erikson. Summarize his stages of ethical development and compare his work to Kohlberg's. Which ideas seem most sensible to you?

# The Bottom Line

13. Evaluate your feelings toward the two models presented in this chapter.

### Kohlberg's justice model

NOT AT ALL USEFUL          EXTREMELY USEFUL

1     2     3     4     5     6     7

### Rest's Four Components of Moral Behavior

NOT AT ALL USEFUL          EXTREMELY USEFUL

1     2     3     4     5     6     7

# Shareholder Theory and Stakeholder Theory

A fundamental question in business ethics is, What is the purpose of a corporation supposed to *be*? Should the leaders of a company focus solely on maximizing profits, or do they have broader obligations? This chapter examines two theories that address the issue.

## CHAPTER 4

## Objectives

- Distinguish between the shareholder and stakeholder models.
- Identify a company's key stakeholders.

## Key Terms and Concepts

shareholders, p. 53
stock, p. 53
profit maximization, p. 53
shareholder model, p. 54
stakeholder model, p. 55

turnover, p. 55
supplier, p. 56
distributor, p. 56
philanthropy, p. 57

Assume that Kensington Reiss is a U.S. drug company. In recent years, it has made an average profit of $1 billion. This year, it launched a wildly successful new antidepressant, and profits doubled to $2 billion. Kensington Reiss's leaders are debating what to do with the "extra" billion dollars. Five items are under consideration. Some members of the board of directors favor taking none of the actions and retaining everything for Kensington Reiss's owners.

**1** Kensington Reiss makes several drugs that are a highly effective therapy for patients with HIV. They can help delay the onset of AIDS for years and in some cases for decades. The board is discussing starting a program that would make the medicines available to HIV patients in Africa at extreme discounts.

**Expected cost: $40 million (4 percent of the unexpected surplus)**

**2** One of Kensington Reiss's popular over-the-counter drugs can be used as an ingredient in manufacturing "Midnight," an illegal street drug that has gained immense popularity in recent years. Kensington Reiss has quietly paid for a study that shows that up to 15 percent of this drug's sales are made to buyers who will use it to make Midnight. Although few deaths have been linked to Midnight, there has been an increase in crime in the neighborhoods where Midnight is most often abused. Kensington Reiss does not operate a plant in any of the 20 metro areas in which Midnight is most commonly a problem.

Kensington Reiss's research and development leaders have studied ways the drug could be reformulated. They believe it can be made in such a way that it would remain effective as a cold remedy, but would no longer be useful to illegal drug manufacturers. The reformulation would, of course, come with a price.

**Expected cost: $20 million (2 percent of the surplus)**

**3** The company's leaders are also considering funding expanded parks programs in Detroit, St. Louis, and Philadelphia. The company has a large manufacturing plant in each city. The new open spaces would likely be used frequently by some employees, but they would be public parks open to everyone.

**Expected cost: $5 million (one-half of 1 percent of the surplus)**

**4** Kensington Reiss is in a highly competitive industry, and top executives in the field are paid very well. The board is concerned that several top executives will leave the company because Kensington Reiss's salaries for officers have not kept pace with industry averages. The board is considering significant raises, particularly for the chief executive officer and chief financial officer.

**Expected cost: $20 million (2 percent of the surplus)**

**5** The board has long been aware that the wages of clerical staff and line workers at the manufacturing plants lag behind industry averages. It is considering rewarding loyal employees by giving an across-the-board 10 percent raise to lower-paid workers who have been with the company for at least two years.

**Expected cost: $10 million (1 percent of the surplus)**

## ■ Shareholder Ethics

**Shareholders** own corporations. They purchase shares of **stock**, a financial instrument used to raise capital for a corporation. Some investors buy shares of specific companies, such as Apple, Harley-Davidson, and Polo Ralph Lauren. Many more people have money "in the market," but do not select individual stocks. They invest in mutual funds, which in turn own pieces of many companies. If you have any kind of retirement account that was set up by your employer, odds are quite high that a large portion of it is invested in corporate stocks.

Even if you have no investments, your life is still impacted by the stock market. When stocks increase in value, investors have a tendency to feel wealthier and to spend more money, especially if their gains are sustained for a long time. When consumers buy more products and services, companies hire more workers and unemployment stays low. Wages tend to increase well when workers are in demand. When the market falls or is too unpredictable, the opposite is usually true. More people put off purchases that are not essential. When demand for products and services falls, companies lay off workers and unemployment rises.

Profitable companies are good for the economy and good for workers. Are profits, however, the only game in town? Are corporate leaders responsible only for **profit maximization**, or do they have obligations to people who are not shareholders?

### Purpose of a Corporation: History

What is the purpose of a corporation supposed to be? The way this question is analyzed has changed over time. In a noteworthy 1919 lawsuit, Henry Ford was sued by the Dodge brothers and other major shareholders of Ford Motor Company. The shareholders were upset because, despite fabulous profits, Ford paid them essentially no dividends. The shareholders especially complained about Ford's use of corporate profits to support humanitarian and charitable works. The Michigan Supreme Court ruled in favor of the shareholders because corporation laws at the time required corporate boards to put shareholders first. The Dodge brothers won enough money to start their own car company, which still exists as part of Chrysler.

Companies were obligated to follow the **shareholder model** until the decade after the close of World War II—they were legally required to maximize shareholder wealth. In the late 1940s and early 1950s, however, the attitude of many powerful politicians toward corporations changed. There existed a powerful conviction that American companies had contributed mightily to stopping the Nazis. Many believed that, but for the ability of American corporations to turn out a massive volume of planes, bombs, ammunition, and other items essential to the Allies fighting in Europe, Hitler might have been victorious. There was a feeling that corporations were not mere legal entities, but instead were an essential part of society.

Many politicians wanted corporations to be able to participate more fully in society. They softened restrictive language in incorporation laws, and in the end it became legally acceptable for companies to "do good deeds." Such action was not and is still not required, but it is allowed.[1]

## Shareholder Model: Justification

The noted economist Milton Friedman was a leading advocate of the shareholder model. Friedman believed that corporations have two primary responsibilities. First, they must comply with the law. Second, once they have complied with the law, they must make as much money as possible for shareholders. If shareholders compete head-to-head with anyone else, Friedman argued that the company should act in the best interests of the shareholders. He asserted that only the shareholders have put their own money on the line and that they should therefore be given preference over others. Friedman characterized acting in any other way as "imposing a tax" on shareholders.

Every executive will treat employees well if he or she believes that doing so will lead to increased productivity and increased profits. Every executive is in favor of donating money to charity if the donation improves the company's image and leads to increased sales that exceed the amount of the donation. Such win-win cases are not ethical dilemmas, however. In a true dilemma, a company considers an action that would not increase the shareholders' return in any certain or measurable way. In such cases, the shareholder model advises, "Don't spend the shareholders' money."[2]

### CHECKPOINT **4-1**

1. Return to the opening passage on Kensington Reiss, and reexamine the five proposals. Which alternative(s) reflect the shareholder viewpoint?

2. Describe your reaction to this statement: *The purpose of a corporation is to make money for the shareholders.*

[1]From Bredeson. *Applied Business Ethics*, 1e. © 2012 South-Western, a part of Cengage Learning, Inc. Reproduced by permission. www.cengage.com/permissions.
[2]Ibid.

## CHECKPOINT **4-1** continued

3. Were company leaders permitted to do "good deeds" that failed to maximize shareholder wealth in 1919?     Yes // No

4. Are company leaders permitted to do "good deeds" that fail to maximize shareholder wealth today?     Yes // No

5. Describe Milton Friedman's two core beliefs about the purpose of a corporation.

# ■ Stakeholder Ethics

In recent decades, many have argued that corporations should consider more than shareholders alone in their decisions and actions. The basic notion of stakeholder ethics is that even if a company will make less profit for shareholders, it must care for a range of stakeholders if it is to behave ethically (Figure 4-1).

Almost no one contends that the owners of a corporation should be ignored—shareholders are among the stakeholders in a firm. Many assert, however, that a company must also look out for (among other groups) its employees, its customers, and the communities in which it operates. Some take a very broad view and argue that society and the environment ought to be considered as stakeholders. A great many Fortune 500 companies put the **stakeholder model** into practice by going beyond legal requirements and actively considering the needs and concerns of one or more groups described in this section.

## Direct Stakeholders

The following groups of stakeholders interact directly with a company. Firms that follow the stakeholder model will frequently take all of them into account when making difficult decisions.

### *Employees*

How a business treats its employees tells much about the values and character of those who run the company. Some employers treat employees as little more than tools to be used up and replaced. When companies treat their employees badly, the morale of workers suffers. Employees can feel used, even exploited. They do not experience pride in their company or fulfillment in their jobs. As those attitudes become pervasive, employees quit in large numbers and **turnover** becomes an expensive problem. Recruiting, interviewing, hiring, and training new employees can be a very costly process.

### *Customers*

A company that ignores its customers will not be in business for long. Customers provide the income necessary for companies to pay expenses and make a profit. Pleasing customers and keeping them satisfied are top priorities for most companies. Many large companies employ customer relations specialists to address the concerns of buyers. Without repeat business, most companies stagnate.

### Business Partners: Suppliers and Distributors

Most companies have suppliers, and many utilize distributors. A **supplier** is a business that provides a particular service or commodity that other businesses require. A plastics manufacturer needs chemicals and machines to make its products. It purchases those items from a number of different companies.

A **distributor** is a company that sells products manufactured by others to retailers. The distributor purchases the product at a wholesale price, a discount offered when a customer buys goods in large quantities for the purpose of reselling them to others. For example, a company that makes cat food dishes does not usually sell them in its own stores. Instead, it sells them in large quantities to other businesses that distribute the products to retail stores that, in turn, sell the dishes to cat owners.

| KEY STAKEHOLDERS | |
| --- | --- |
| **Direct Stakeholders** | **Indirect Stakeholders** |
| Employees | The environment |
| Customers | Society |
| Business partners: suppliers and distributors | |
| Communities | |
| Stockholders | |

**FIGURE 4-1**
Direct and indirect stakeholders

Wholesalers and retailers employ many people. Imagine a company that has used the same suppliers and distributors for many years. This year, its leaders discover they can reduce costs and increase profits slightly by changing partners. Does the company have any ethical obligation to remain loyal to its long-standing suppliers and distributors? What if hundreds or thousands of workers at its partner companies will be laid off if a switch is made?

### Communities

Organizations operate in the real world, and they impact the communities in which they build their factories and office buildings. Individuals have an ethical duty to be good neighbors. Similarly, many argue that businesses are obligated to be good neighbors as well.

Companies benefit from stable communities. If crime rates are low, if talented people are available for hiring, and if customers are abundant, companies tend to do well. Does this mean organizations must "give something back"? Many business leaders think so.

Businesses can be good neighbors by showing consideration for the needs and interests of the community, taking leadership roles in helping to resolve community problems, and sharing some of their wealth with community members who need help. Many corporate leaders understand that company profits can create unique opportunities to improve quality of life and to assist people in need. Examples of corporate **philanthropy** are everywhere. A local plumbing company sponsors a youth soccer team. The area McDonald's restaurants coordinate their efforts to sponsor a Ronald McDonald House to help the families of sick and injured children. An attorney donates money each year to provide scholarships for graduating seniors at a local high school. A restaurant gives extra food at the end of every business day to a neighborhood shelter. A large corporation underwrites a community theater that presents plays and concerts. A local shopping mall provides holiday presents for underprivileged children.

Many business leaders believe they have a responsibility to their community. They invest time and money in improving the quality of life there. The positive public relations they receive in return often lead to higher employee morale and productivity and may attract additional business from the community.

### Stockholders

Of course, a company's stakeholders include the stockholders who wager their own money on the business's success. Companies have a legal and ethical obligation to try to produce a profit for their investors. The stakeholder model does not require a company to be unprofitable. It merely calls for the needs of shareholders to be balanced with the needs of other stakeholders.

## Indirect or Abstract Stakeholders

Some followers of the stakeholder model want corporate leaders to consider stakeholders beyond those with whom they interact directly. Two of these indirect stakeholders are the environment and society.

### The Environment

All companies must comply with the law. Environmental laws, however, are frequently minimalist: they ban some kinds of bad behavior, but do not require much good behavior. Companies can often go far beyond legal requirements when it comes to protecting the environment.

Besides fulfilling their legal obligations, companies may demonstrate a concern for the environment through their decisions and actions with respect to other stakeholders. Employees, community members, and consumers can all be impacted by environmental issues. A commitment to the natural world can go beyond considering outcomes for these direct stakeholder groups, however. In effect, the environment becomes another stakeholder and is protected for its own sake.

Many consumers are very aware of which companies commit to sound environmental practices. Strong environmental policies can lead to higher profits and greater corporate success.

> We make a living by what we get, but we make a life by what we give.
>
> —WINSTON CHURCHILL

What if profits and protecting the environment, however, do not go hand in hand? What if a company could do more to reduce pollution or waste, but doing so would mean increasing the cost of the product? Should business leaders spend money to help the environment if it means less profit for the business and shareholders?

## Do the RIGHT THING

In 1976, a former British schoolteacher, Anita Roddick, decided to open a small cosmetic store in Brighton, England. She gave it a simple name—The Body Shop. Her commitment to social justice and animal rights issues quickly set her business apart, and it grew rapidly. In an industry in which the norm was to test products on animals, Roddick took a principled and very risky stand. She declared that her stores would never sell any products that had been tested on animals. In addition, Roddick established a strong recycling program and created corporate policies to promote environmentalism and social justice. Her business grew to become one of the largest chains of cosmetics stores in the world. Roddick became one of the wealthiest women in Great Britain and received many honors and awards, including selection to the United Nations Global 500 Roll of Honour.

Roddick chose to protect a new type of stakeholder: animals. Do you believe companies generally owe an ethical duty to animals? Why or why not?

### Society / "All Mankind"

The previous section discussed the many people who are direct stakeholders in a firm: its employees, employees of suppliers and distributors, customers, members of communities in which a business operates, and shareholders. But what about others who have no direct relationship with a firm but could be benefitted or harmed by its decisions and actions? Think again about the opening scenario. Assume a company makes a drug that is effective in treating HIV. Is the company ethically obligated to make the drug available at extreme discounts to patients around the world who are not its customers? What if no one else makes a similar drug? Does the obligation change?

## CHECKPOINT 4–2

**1.** Return to the opening scenario, and reexamine the five proposals. Which alternative(s) reflect the stakeholder viewpoint?

**2.** List a company's key direct stakeholders.

**3.** List a company's key indirect stakeholders.

**4.** Rank the stakeholders you listed in Items 2 and 3 from 1 (the one you consider most important) to 7 (the one you consider least important).

**5.** Describe the stakeholder you chose as most important. Why did you select it over the others?

**6.** Are you aware of a company that follows the stakeholder model? Name the company, and describe how it follows the model.

*Johnson & Johnson — Credo Appears this*

# ETHICS @ WORK

This chapter has compared the shareholder and stakeholder models. As with most ethics questions, neither model is necessarily "right" in the sense that everyone agrees with it or that the law requires following either set of ideas. Countless companies have adopted each model.

The following scenario is your chance to apply the models to a business situation. Which makes the most sense to you? Why? Answer the questions about the scenario, and be prepared to respectfully argue for your point of view in class.

## Main Issues and Options

**Issues:** As a business owner, does Alan owe obligations to his workers, his community, or anyone other than his shareholders? If so, what are the obligations, and how should they be met?

**Options:** Alan is legally free to follow either the shareholder model or the stakeholder model in his decision making.

## The Winds of Change

### Friday Afternoon

Alan Dawson sat in his office and watched the local weather report.

A reporter spoke with some difficulty from South Beach. "The winds are starting to noticeably pick up out here, and with landfall of this strong Category 3 storm less than 24 hours away, this is only the beginning," she said. The camera swung around and focused on an unsettled ocean beyond. Alan sighed.

"Mr. Dawson," said a man as he knocked softly. Alan didn't look up, and the man knocked louder. "Sir? Mr. Dawson?"

"Huh? Oh, Reggie," Alan eventually replied. "I'm sorry . . . I was woolgathering."

"Yes, sir, and I don't blame you. How's the storm?"

"Still Category 3, still headed straight for us. Sometime tomorrow, they say."

"Ah," Reggie replied softly. "Well, I came up to say that we've done what we can do. The windows are boarded, and everything that can be tied down is tied down. The last of the inventory went out this morning. We're as ready as we can be."

"I appreciate your efforts, Reggie. Give my thanks to everyone, will you?"

"Yes, sir."

"And send everyone who hasn't left already home. Get somewhere safe, Reggie."

"Yes sir. I'll be back as soon as it's over to start cleaning up."

"I know you will, Reggie."

"Goodnight, Mr. Dawson."

"Goodnight."

Dawson sat watching TV for a long while. Eventually, he turned it off and stepped through his side office door to a platform that overlooked his factory below. Gold DAWSON COMPUTERS logos boldly stood out on the light gray floor and the darker gray workstations. Silver conveyor belt rollers gleamed dully in the auxiliary lights and snaked endlessly from one assembly area to the next. Alan Dawson surveyed the plant he had created.

He smiled as he thought back to when he had started the company, assembling computers in his parents' garage 15 years earlier.

A strong gust of wind rattled the factory's metal roof. Frowning, Alan collected his things, locked up his office, and left.

## Monday Morning

A blue BMW 750i with a license plate that read DAWSON 1 slowly navigated tree limbs and other debris at the edge of the factory parking lot. It came to a stop in a relatively clear parking spot, and Alan Dawson emerged from it. He looked slowly around and let out a long, low whistle.

One wall was partially collapsed. Another had a hole in it the size of a school bus. The roof was just . . . gone. Broken glass, insulation, and chunks of metal were everywhere.

The parking lot was nearly empty of cars, but Dawson did see a familiar green Toyota. He smiled and thumbed "Bldg. Super." on his phone's touch screen. His call was answered on the first ring.

"Hello?"

"Reggie."

"Mr. Dawson. Where are you, sir?"

"I'm out in the parking lot. I saw your car. How's it look in there?"

There was a long pause. "It's bad, Mr. Dawson. Real bad."

"I'm coming in. Can you meet me at the back loading dock in five minutes?"

"Yes, sir. Be careful coming in."

Dawson grunted an acknowledgement and ended the call. He started to put his phone in his pocket; then he hesitated and thumbed "COO."

"Alan?" a voice answered.

"Hey, Carol. Look, don't bother coming down here."

"That bad?"

"Yeah. Yeah, it is. I think we're looking at a total loss."

"Oh, Alan."

"I'm going to look around for a while, but, ah . . ." he trailed off. "Any word from Coral Gables?"

"Yes. The call center is fine. No flooding, no major damage—they even have power."

"Wow. OK, well, let's use that for our base of operations. E-mail the manufacturing folks. Tell them they have two paid weeks off and that we'll follow up with them soon about what happens next."

"Will do. Alan?"

"Yeah?"

"What does happen next?"

"Not sure yet. I want to take a couple of days to think about it and take care of my house—we lost a couple of the big palms out back. Let's meet at the call center on Wednesday. Noon?"

"Noon it is."

## Wednesday

An assistant brought in two large coffees.

"Ah, terrific," Dawson said. "Thanks a lot."

"No problem, Mr. Dawson."

"Close the door on the way out, will you?"

"Sure thing." The assistant left Dawson and his chief operating officer alone in the call center's main conference room.

"So," Dawson began.

"So," she replied.

"I want to start putting together our basic strategy for what we're going to do about our factory. That's really it for today."

"OK."

"I talked to our insurance guy yesterday, and we're fully covered. He's been by the plant, and he agrees that it's a total loss. We'll get the full $100 million sometime this month."

"That's good."

Dawson sipped his coffee and stared out a window for a moment. "I want to rebuild here in Miami," he said.

"I thought you'd say that," Carol said.

"The insurance money will pay for a new top-of-the-line facility. We can be up and running again in six months—nine months, tops—and our output will be better than before."

"Right . . . or we could build a facility in China and operate it for half the labor costs we've had here," Carol replied. "This is a golden opportunity to do what all our competitors have done already."

"Some of these people have been with me for 14 years. They built this company. What about them? They can't relocate to China."

"They'll find other jobs."

"But not equivalent other jobs. Where is Reggie going to earn a six-figure salary? And the assembly line workers—most of them have a high school education, and some of them less than that. Where are they going to earn $20 an hour? They have families to support."

"They can retrain and start again somewhere else."

"I don't accept that."

"The shareholders won't like it," Carol responded. "They're getting a 4 percent return from us, and they want the 8 percent that most of our competitors are returning."

"I don't care."

"We've gone public, Alan. This isn't your company anymore."

"I'm the CEO, and I'm the chairman of the board!"

"You won't be either for long if this company doesn't make more money. The shareholders will replace you."

"I started this company!"

"They won't care. At least not for long."

Dawson sat in silence for a while. "Are you playing devil's advocate, or is it what you really think?"

"Does it matter?"

Dawson thought about that. "No. No, I guess it doesn't. I'm sorry, Carol. I'm not myself . . ."

"I know, boss. All of this is awful."

"Yeah. Yeah, it is." Dawson finished his coffee. "It's just that . . . I mean, personal feelings aside, unemployment is bad. The country needs to stop losing jobs. Where does it stop? Somebody has to protect the jobs."

"It's the government's job to set the rules of the game to protect American jobs . . ."

"I disagree. I disagree with that."

"Fine, but it is absolutely your job to look out for the shareholders."

"Maybe. Maybe so," Dawson said quietly. "I need to think about this."

"I know."

"Let's talk about it again on Friday morning."

"OK, Alan."

## What Do You Think?

1. Should Dawson push to rebuild the plant in Miami? Why or why not?

2. If you were in Dawson's position, and if your organization was a private company that you owned yourself (as opposed to a corporation owned by shareholders), would you rebuild the plant in Miami or relocate to China?

3. To what degree do you agree with Carol's idea that it is the government's job to create and protect American jobs and that it is a CEO's job to create wealth for shareholders?

STRONGLY DISAGREE      STRONGLY AGREE

| 1 | 2 | 3 | 4 | 5 | 6 | 7 |

## Friday Morning

(Back in the call center conference room)

"I'm firmly decided. We're rebuilding here."

"I'm glad, Alan," Carol said.

"So you were playing devil's advocate," Dawson smiled.

"That's what I get paid for. Part of it, anyway."

"True enough. I think with expanded capacity, and with tax incentives for a new, environmentally friendly plant, we can be very competitive right here."

"I'm 100 percent behind you, boss."

"I also want to pay our workers their wages while the plant is being rebuilt."

Carol paused. "You're kidding."

"No."

"OK, I'm not playing devil's advocate now." Carol leaned across the table, looking intently at Dawson. "We can't do that."

"We have to do that. The majority of them live paycheck to paycheck, and unemployment benefits won't cover half of what they earn."

"Alan! There's no work for them to do, and there won't be for months."

"Even so, these are loyal workers."

"These are grown-ups who need to save money for emergencies."

"Most people don't do that."

"Well . . . they certainly should."

"Maybe so, but they don't. If we don't pay them, they'll fall behind on their mortgages. They'll lose their homes."

"I admire your concern, but we can't ask the shareholders to foot the bill for wages when no value is being added to the company."

"We pay pensions to retirees. They're not working for us anymore."

"That's different!"

"In some ways," Dawson said. "I'll be giving up all my pay for the rest of the year to help foot the bill."

"That will cover only 10 percent of the costs."

"It's a start."

"The shareholders won't stand for it. They'll oust you, Alan."

"Maybe. Maybe not—I'm betting a lot of them will trust me and appreciate that we're taking care of the people that make money for them."

"I urge you to reconsider. I mean, if you want to pay a handful of irreplaceable people, I can see a benefit, but most of the assembly line workers' positions could be filled by any number of people, and they could be trained in a few weeks."

"Everybody. We have the lowest turnover in the industry, and our customers have the fewest problems in the industry because of it. Having a happy and stable workforce matters."

"We also have the lowest profit margins in the industry. We're going to lose market share during our manufacturing downtime. We need to be more careful than ever with the money we have."

"There's more to business than profits."

"Not to the shareholders."

"They put me in charge of this company. I'm the coach, and I call the plays until they say otherwise. This is the right thing to do, and we're going to do it."

## What Do You Think?

4. Should the company's factory employees be paid during the several months of rebuilding? Would it be any more or less justifiable to pay only a handful of high-level, difficult-to-replace workers?

5. Imagine you owned $1,000 worth of shares in Dawson Computers. What would you think of the decision to rebuild the factory in the United States?

STRONGLY DISAGREE · · · STRONGLY AGREE

1    2    3    4    5    6    7

What about the decision to pay all workers while the factory is rebuilt?

STRONGLY DISAGREE · · · STRONGLY AGREE

1    2    3    4    5    6    7

# Summary

Many business leaders struggle with the fundamental question, What is the purpose of this company supposed to be? Some conclude that shareholders should be the primary or even exclusive focus of decision making. Others decide that additional stakeholders sometimes require special consideration. Direct stakeholders include employees, customers, business partners (suppliers and distributors), communities, and stockholders. Indirect stakeholders include the environment and society as a whole.

Neither side is always right or wrong. Countless businesses follow the shareholder model, and countless more follow the stakeholder model.

# Key Terms and Concepts

**Match each definition with a key term or concept.**

a. distributor

b. philanthropy

c. profit maximization

d. shareholder model

e. shareholders

f. stakeholder model

g. stock

h. supplier

i. turnover

_____ 1. The theory that a company's only obligation is to try to make as much money as possible for its investors and owners

_____ 2. The theory that a company has ethical responsibilities to many people affected by the decisions and actions of the business

_____ 3. A business that provides a particular service or commodity that other businesses require

_____ 4. A business that sells to retailers a product manufactured by others

_____ 5. Efforts to improve the well-being of others through charitable donations

_____ 6. The number of employees a business is required to hire in order to replace workers who have left the company

_____ 7. A financial instrument the sale of which is used to raise capital for a corporation

_____ 8. A business practice that favors increasing shareholder wealth over all other objectives

_____ 9. The owners of a corporation

# Review

1. True or false: In the United States, corporations are legally required to maximize shareholder wealth.

2. True or false: Milton Friedman was a leading advocate of the shareholder model.

3. True or false: A business leader who believes that his or her obligation is to "maximize profits at all costs" is a follower of the shareholder model.

4. Kresge Manufacturing makes floor tile. Which of the following is a direct stakeholder in the company?

   a. its factory workers
   b. upper-level management
   c. the town where the factory is located
   d. all of the above

# Critical Thinking

5. Sometimes businesses face situations in which the interests of stakeholders are in conflict. To do what is best for employees or customers might harm the interests of investors. Producing a maximum return for investors could mean cutting salaries or raising prices. How do you think companies should resolve such conflicts? How should the stakeholder groups be prioritized? At what point do you believe that stockholder interests interfere with shareholder interests?

# Applications

6. Imagine you own a business. Write your own company credo, identifying your stakeholders and detailing the specific obligations you have to each group.

7. Assume you are an administrator for a large company that has decided to invest money in programs to improve the quality of life for people in your community. You have been placed in charge of the Social Responsibility Project. In a paragraph, explain one program you would recommend, how it would work, whom it would help, and how it would benefit the community.

## Digging Deeper

8. Find a business that participates in some form of philanthropy. Interview someone at the company in person, by phone, or by e-mail. Learn more about what the company does, why the company does it, and what benefits the programs bring to the company.

## The Bottom Line

9. Evaluate your feelings toward the two models presented in this chapter.

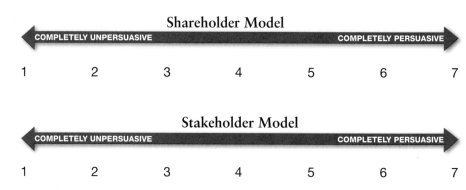

Shareholder Model

COMPLETELY UNPERSUASIVE    COMPLETELY PERSUASIVE

1        2        3        4        5        6        7

Stakeholder Model

COMPLETELY UNPERSUASIVE    COMPLETELY PERSUASIVE

1        2        3        4        5        6        7

Why did you rate each model the way you did?

# Ethical Selling, Marketing, and Advertising

## CHAPTER 5

Companies go to great lengths to sell their products and services. Because the free speech rights in the First Amendment of the U.S. Constitution apply to businesses, they have a great deal of freedom in deciding how to communicate with customers. Do companies ever go too far? Should more be done to protect children and other vulnerable customers?

## Objectives

- Identify and explain common ethical problems and ethical standards in advertising.
- Identify and explain key ethical problems and principles of honest and ethical selling.

## Key Terms and Concepts

false advertising, p. 69

puffery, p. 70

bait and switch, p. 71

telemarketing, p. 71

code of ethics, p. 71

substantiation, p. 73

warranty, p. 74

testimonial, p. 74

price gouging, p. 76

false prizes, p. 76

commission, p. 76

straight commission, p. 76

**HARD CHOICES**

Imagine the following television commercial:

A woman sits on her couch at night watching a horror movie. On her TV, a woman screams as a knife-wielding madman menaces her. The movie cuts to a commercial break. The woman heads to her kitchen for more popcorn. She hears a sound, turns around quickly, and spots a knife-wielding burglar at her back door. He gets the door open and says menacingly, "Come 'ere."

The camera zooms in on the Betapi Security Service box next to the back door. The "enter code" light is flashing. The burglar takes a step toward the woman and then another. She shrinks back in fear. The camera shifts to the security box. The yellow "enter code" light blinks off, the red "alarm" light blinks on, and a loud siren blares.

The burglar stops. He hears a dog barking outside and then a neighbor's voice. He grimaces, turns, and runs.

The woman's phone rings. She says, "Hello?" shakily.

"Mrs. Smith, this is Betapi Security Service. Are you OK?"

"No. Someone just broke in, but he ran off," she replies.

"I'm notifying the police now, Mrs. Smith."

"Thank you," she says. She slumps against her counter as the commercial ends.

In the zip codes where the ad is shown, the odds of a home burglary with forced entry happening in any given year are 500 to 1. The odds of such a burglary when a homeowner is in the house are 2,500 to 1. The odds of a burglary resulting in an assault against the occupant are 8,500 to 1.

## {**WHAT** Do You Think?}

1. Do you think television ads are usually informative or deceptive?
2. Is there anything wrong with the Betapi Security Service ad?

# ■ Ethics in Advertising

In the movie *Crazy People*, actor Dudley Moore plays the role of an advertising executive who, suffering from an attack of conscience, resolves to create only truthful ads. Examples of these honest ads include the following:

| | |
|---|---|
| An airline: | "Most of our passengers get there alive." |
| A cereal: | "Does this cereal taste great? Who knows? But at least the box is cute." |
| A cigarette: | "Pulmonary cancer? Perhaps . . . Flavor? For sure!" |
| A life insurance company: | "We know you love him. But if he happens to die, we give you two Mercedes and a summer home. Wouldn't that be nice, too?" |

The ad executive's employers conclude that he has lost his mind and send him to a mental institution. As a coworker puts it, "We can't level [with people]; we're in advertising!"

Advertising is the practice of attracting public attention to a product or business for the purpose of increasing sales. Contrary to the implications in *Crazy People*, most people in the field of advertising act ethically and serve an essential function in business. How can people purchase a product if they don't know about it? There is a fine line, though, between encouraging people to buy a car and manipulating people into buying a car. What constitutes ethical—and unethical—behavior in advertising?

## Ethical Problems in Advertising

The First Amendment to the Constitution guarantees the right to free speech. Individuals enjoy the strongest protection. The Supreme Court has decided, however, that in many important ways, free speech rights apply to organizations, including corporations.

Because constitutional rights are above any other kind of law, the government is limited in the types of restrictions that can be placed on advertising, which amounts to "corporate speech." Regulations can attack fraudulent ads that make claims that are flatly false. Ads for dangerous products, like cigarettes, can be curbed. Still, to a large extent, businesses are free to run many kinds of ads that are manipulative. Several common types of deceptive ads are discussed next.

### *False Advertising*

Sellers sometimes lie (and often, when they lie, they violate the law—see the Ethics & Law feature). **False advertising** is the practice of making statements about products that the advertiser knows are not true. The claims can be about how the product works, how it is made, or how it will affect people who buy or use it. For most of the nation's history, tobacco companies lied to the public regularly about cigarettes. The tobacco companies claimed that their cigarettes were healthier than their competitors' brands, often citing

The Federal Trade Commission (FTC) regulates advertising in the United States. According to the FTC's Policy Statement on Deception (1983), an advertisement is considered deceptive (and illegal) based on the following criteria:

1. *The advertisement contains "a representation, omission, or practice that is likely to mislead the consumer."* Examples include products that do not work as claimed, bait-and-switch advertisements for products not in stock, and failure to fulfill warranty obligations.
2. *The representation or practice must be considered from the perspective of a reasonable consumer.* For instance, a commercial shows a customer floating in the air with joy after buying a car. A reasonable person is not likely to conclude that purchasing the product would enable him or her to fly. However, a reasonable person might be misled by deceptive claims about gas mileage.
3. *The representation, omission, or practice must be material.* This means that the representation, omission, or practice is likely to influence a consumer's decision to buy a product. It is information that is important to consumers.[1]

**Should the government go further in regulating ads? If so, create a fourth rule to add to the three listed here.**

research done by scientists they employed. At one time, some companies even made the claim that cigarettes were good for people!

Besides being unethical, false advertising isn't even smart—at least in the long run. Consumers eventually figure out the truth, and the backlash can be severe. Many tobacco companies have lost millions of dollars in lawsuits filed by former customers (or their families) who contracted cancer from smoking the "healthy" cigarettes. In a society in which lawsuits are common, false and deceptive advertising is unwise and expensive.

### Puffery

**Puffery** is a term used to describe statements that are not outright lies, but merely exaggerations. Is anything wrong with a chewing gum claiming to be "the best taste your mouth ever had" or an amusement park claiming to provide "the best time you'll ever have in one day"? After trying the products, some people might agree with the statements; however, others would not. Is puffery unethical? Should puffery claims be illegal?

The FTC allows puffery, defining it as "exaggerations reasonably to be expected of a seller as to the degree of quality of his product, the truth or falsity of which cannot be determined."[2] For an advertising claim to be considered puffery and not false advertising, the average consumer must be able to see easily that the claim is an overstatement.

### Bait and Switch

An appliance store places a newspaper advertisement offering a top-of-the-line refrigerator for $200. The next morning, lines start forming early and continue to lengthen. By the time the store opens, hundreds of customers are lined up to take advantage of the offer. The advantage, however, turns out to belong to the store. It has only ten of that particular model in stock, and those refrigerators are gone in minutes. The vast majority of the customers find only apologetic salespeople offering to show them other refrigerators that cost much more.

[1]Federal Trade Commission, "FTC Policy Statement on Deception," October 14, 1983, 1–2.
[2]"In the Matter of Better Living, Inc., et al.," 54 F.T.C. 648 (1957), affirmed, 259 F.2d 271 (3rd Cir. 1958).

**Bait and switch** is the practice of advertising a product at a low price while intentionally stocking only a limited number in hopes of luring shoppers to buy more expensive items. This practice is illegal, but can sometimes be difficult to prove. Generally, there is no legally mandated minimum number of products that must be kept in stock. However, businesses that advertise discounted prices on a product in short supply are usually required either to state the number of products in stock or to offer rain checks to customers who request them. Rain checks are written guarantees that customers can have the product at the discounted price when more are delivered to the store.

### Advertising to Children

Children are especially vulnerable to deceptive advertising. They are generally trusting and believe what adults tell them. Young children can be naive, often believing that claims on TV or in the newspaper are true. In addition, children often have difficulty differentiating between fantasy and reality. If a superhero can become invisible in a cartoon, children may believe that the action figure will do the same once it is in their home.

Because of children's vulnerabilities, laws have been passed to protect them from deceptive ads. One such law prohibits creators and producers of a children's cartoon from advertising products related to the characters of that program during the broadcast.

### Telemarketing and Spam

**Telemarketing** is the practice of selling directly to individuals through unsolicited phone calls, e-mails, or faxes. Innovations in technology have made this practice more common. Computers can dial hundreds of phones, send thousands of faxes, and deliver millions of unwanted spam e-mails. Customers are often left feeling frustrated and powerless to stop the deluge. The unsolicited ads can waste customers' money (through use of paper, toner, and minutes on cell phones) and time. Telemarketers make very little money per call, e-mail, or fax, but so many ads are sent out that a few eventually result in sales.

Political leaders have noticed the growing sense of frustration—even outrage—in the general public regarding telemarketing. Laws have been passed allowing people to sign up for "do not call" lists. Telemarketing firms that continue to deliver unsolicited ads to people on the lists can face fines or other sanctions. Senders of spam are supposed to allow people the option of removing their e-mail addresses from the sales lists. In addition, some states prohibit the use of automatic calling programs.

## Ethical Standards in Advertising

As mentioned earlier, most people in the field of advertising act professionally and do not resort to unethical tactics. As professionals, they have a vested interest in setting, promoting, and maintaining high ethical standards for themselves and their peers. Professional organizations generally publish such standards in a **code of ethics**, a written set of principles and rules intended to serve as a guideline for ethical behavior for individuals under the organization's authority.

> If it's not done ethically, advertising won't be trusted. If consumers don't trust it, advertising is pointless.
>
> —JEF I. RICHARDS

The American Advertising Federation (AAF) created a set of "Advertising Ethics and Principles" in 1984 (Figure 5-1). It defines professional standards and provides a way to evaluate the ethics of advertisers. Several key provisions are discussed below.

## AAF ADVERTISING ETHICS AND PRINCIPLES

**Truth**

Advertising shall tell the truth, and shall reveal significant facts, the omission of which would mislead the public.

**Substantiation**

Advertising claims shall be substantiated by evidence in possession of the advertiser and advertising agency, prior to making such claims.

**Comparisons**

Advertising shall refrain from making false, misleading, or unsubstantiated statements or claims about a competitor or his/her products or services.

**Bait Advertising**

Advertising shall not offer products or services for sale unless such offer constitutes a bona fide effort to sell the advertising products or services and is not a device to switch consumers to other goods or services, usually higher priced.

**Guarantees and Warranties**

Advertising of guarantees and warranties shall be explicit, with sufficient information to apprise consumers of their principal terms and limitations or, when space or time restrictions preclude such disclosures, the advertisement should clearly reveal where the full text of the guarantee or warranty can be examined before purchase.

**Price Claims**

Advertising shall avoid price claims which are false or misleading, or saving claims which do not offer provable savings.

**Testimonials**

Advertising containing testimonials shall be limited to those of competent witnesses who are reflecting a real and honest opinion or experience.

**Taste and Decency**

Advertising shall be free of statements, illustrations or implications which are offensive to good taste or public decency.

*Source: American Advertising Federation (www.aaf.org).*

**FIGURE 5-1**
AAF code of ethics

### *Truth*

*Advertising shall tell the truth, and shall reveal significant facts, the omission of which would mislead the public.*

Ethics generally starts with truth and fairness. In the case of advertising, truth and fairness go hand in hand. Lying about a product is unfair to customers, who are cheated and exploited by the dishonest claim. So the foundation of ethical advertising is that ads should tell the truth.

Notice the two parts of this principle. All statements made should be truthful, of course. There is more to honesty than just truthfulness, however. Intentionally choosing not to reveal important facts about a product is a form of dishonesty, too.

## Substantiation

*Advertising claims shall be substantiated by evidence in possession of the advertiser and advertising agency, prior to making such claims.*

An advertisement for a pain reliever claims that the product relieves twice as much pain as competing products in half the time. Suffering from a headache, you go to the pharmacy and buy a bottle of these wonder pills. After taking a couple of doses, you decide the claims are not true. This particular pain reliever works no better than other products you have taken for headaches. So you call the company's consumer hotline and complain. The representative's reply is that the claims are not false advertising because the company believes they might be true. Ethical advertising requires more.

**Substantiation** is the validation of advertising claims with objective data from independent research. The burden of responsibility is on the advertiser to be able to prove that all claims are true.

## Comparisons

*Advertising shall refrain from making false, misleading, or unsubstantiated statements or claims about a competitor or his/her products or services.*

You live in a small town that has two roofing companies—Jaecar's Roofing and Jill's Roofing. One day you see a newspaper ad for Jaecar's Roofing that is full of negative statements about Jill's Roofing.

- Jill uses inferior nails!

- Jill's shingles aren't waterproof!

- Jill's employees steal lawn furniture!

To make false claims and comparisons about competitors is unethical, and it is also illegal. A firm making such claims may be sued for libel.

## Guarantees and Warranties

*Advertising of guarantees and warranties shall be explicit, with sufficient information to apprise consumers of their principal terms and limitations or, when space or time restrictions preclude such disclosures, the advertisement should clearly reveal where the full text of the guarantee or warranty can be examined before purchase.*

After weeks of searching, you buy your first car. It is a used car, but only a few years old. One reason you buy it with confidence is that the dealer offers a bumper-to-bumper warranty. The salesperson promises that if anything goes wrong during the first year, the dealer will make repairs at no charge.

Only a couple of weeks after you buy the car, two items break—the cup holder snaps off, and the rear-window brake light goes out. When you take the car back to the dealer for repairs, you are told that those items are not covered under the bumper-to-bumper warranty. The cup holder is considered

The big print giveth and the small print taketh away.

—TOM WAITS

an accessory, and the lightbulb is considered a regular maintenance item. You leave the dealer $117 poorer, feeling disappointed and cheated.

A guarantee is an assurance attesting to the durability or quality of a service or product. A **warranty** is a written promise to repair or replace a product if it breaks or becomes defective within a specified period of time. One problem with guarantees and warranties is that they are often explained in complex legal language, with important information hidden in small print. The car dealer probably gave you a booklet containing the warranty details. Always take your time and carefully read the details of warranties and guarantees.

### Price Claims

*Advertising shall avoid price claims which are false or misleading, or saving claims which do not offer provable savings.*

You see an ad claiming a jewelry store will lower its prices by 70 percent on Saturday. Once you arrive, however, you learn that only select items are included in the sale. Furthermore, when you look closely at the sale pieces, you see that the presale prices are unrealistically high. A bracelet you thought would sell for about $60 has an original price of $200. When the 70 percent discount is applied, the sale price drops to the $60 the price should have been in the first place. You leave the store feeling your time has been wasted.

### Testimonials

*Advertising containing testimonials shall be limited to those of competent witnesses who are reflecting a real and honest opinion or experience.*

A **testimonial** is an endorsement of a product by someone claiming to have benefited from its use. Advertisements often feature celebrities and experts touting the wonders of various products. Over the years, this practice has proven to be a very effective sales technique—many actors and athletes earn far more money pitching products than making movies or playing their sport. There are some ethical limitations, however, on how testimonials can be conducted. For example, what if an athlete endorses a product that he or she does not use? Is this acceptable, or is it deceptive?

### Taste and Decency

*Advertising shall be free of statements, illustrations or implications which are offensive to good taste or public decency.*

On the surface, it appears that producing offensive ads would risk alienating the very audience a company is trying to reach. The real world, however, is more complex. For example, a company may be trying to connect with an audience that reacts positively to material that offends others. Ads that are broadcast on some cable channels may include material that offends viewers of more conservative programming.

Edgy ads, though, can have unintended consequences. For instance, many special interest groups closely monitor advertisements in publications and broadcasts aimed at minors. When such groups find material they deem offensive or inappropriate, they may try to organize boycotts against the sponsors or the networks that ran the offending ads.

### Limitations of the Advertising Code of Ethics

While professional codes of ethics benefit both members of a profession and the public, they have limitations. For instance, you may have noticed that the language of the AAF standards is somewhat ambiguous. Vague rules are easier to bend, if one is so inclined.

A second problem with a professional code of ethics is that it is not enforceable. Membership in trade groups such as the AAF is voluntary. Unlike professions such as law and medicine, no one has to be licensed to be able to make a living in advertising. The AAF has no authority to revoke someone's license to advertise for violating the code. Conformity to the principles of the code is strictly voluntary.

## CHECKPOINT 5–1

1. Return to the opening scenario on Betapi Security Services. Does the example present any of the specific ethical problems described in this section?

2. Consider the opening scenario again. How might the ad be changed to follow the ethical standards described in this section?

3. In your own words, explain the criteria the FTC uses to determine whether an advertisement is deceptive.

4. What three specific ideas in the advertising code of ethics do you consider most important? Do you think most advertisers follow them?

5. Describe one current ad you believe to be unethical. Now, describe one you find to be ethically sound.

## ■ Ethics in Selling

The last section of the chapter examined advertising. This section addresses ethical issues that arise when people sell goods and services directly.

# Ethical Problems in Selling

When a person's income is based on his or her ability to sell products, temptations can arise. If the only goal is to make a sale, a person may begin to think that the end justifies the means—that anything that helps to make the sale is permissible. Many salespeople are honest individuals, but the actions of a small number of dishonest salespeople have created negative public perceptions. Several dishonest sales practices are described below.

## Price Gouging

**Price gouging** is the practice of pricing a product far above the normal market value on the assumption that consumers have no other way to buy the product. For example, some lumber stores have drastically raised the price of home repair products after destructive storms. When electricity goes out, bags of ice may sell for $20; electric generators may triple in price overnight. Supply and demand can sometimes run amok.

Price gouging is illegal in most states and, fortunately, seems to be occurring with less frequency. Law enforcement officials and the news media monitor stores carefully after disasters. They watch for any signs that unscrupulous businesses might try to profit unfairly from the suffering of others.

## False Prizes

A common sales technique—**false prizes**—seeks to trick potential customers into thinking they have won valuable prizes such as cash, cars, and cruises. Sometimes the lure of a prize is used to get customers to listen to a sales pitch about a different product, and the prize is awarded after the sales talk.

It is illegal for a business to promise a customer something and then break that promise. Those who utilize the false prize technique have found creative loopholes in the consumer laws, however. The loopholes are often explained in very small print. The "free cruise" may not include a variety of charges, taxes, and tips that add up to the price of a regular ticket. The "free vacation" may be a few days in a low-quality motel that you would never stay in otherwise. The "free piano" may turn out to be a toy keyboard.

A good rule of thumb in life is that if something sounds too good to be true, it usually is. Many people become excited at the thought of winning a prize, however, and unethical salespeople count on that.

## Commissions vs. "Straight" Commissions

Why do some salespeople resort to unethical sales techniques? The short answer is because of money. Many businesses pay their sales staff on **commission**. This means that, in addition to paying a salary or hourly wage, the company rewards salespeople with a percentage of the money from the sales they make. The more employees sell, the more they earn. Ethical lapses are most commonly driven, though, by the practice of offering salespeople a **straight commission**. This means employees get no salary or hourly wage; their income is based entirely on what they sell.

Being paid on commission motivates people to work hard to sell products. Many companies believe that paying their salespeople this way produces more sales and higher revenue for the business. On the other hand, the practice also can encourage deceptive and dishonest sales techniques, especially when a straight commission is paid.

## Principles of Ethical Selling

The good news is that selling does not have to be manipulative, deceptive, or disrespectful to be effective. Most people in most professions are honest and honorable. Many people make excellent incomes in sales while treating their customers with integrity and fairness. So how do salespeople think and act differently to sell products honestly and ethically?

# Do the RIGHT THING

Nurses do the right thing, at least in the opinion of people who participated in a recent survey. Each year, Gallup surveys Americans on their perceptions of the honesty and ethics of workers in different professions. Here are some of the results of one recent poll. The number beside each profession is the percentage of people who ranked that profession's ethics as "very high" or "high."

Nurses (81%)

Newspaper reporters (22%)

Druggists or pharmacists (71%)

Local officeholders (20%)

Medical doctors (66%)

Lawyers (17%)

Police officers (57%)

Business executives (15%)

Judges (47%)

Advertising practitioners (11%)

Auto mechanics (28%)

Members of Congress (9%)

Bankers (23%)

Car salespeople (7%)

*Adapted from "Honesty/Ethics in Professions," Gallup, Nov. 19–21, 2010, http://www. gallup.com/poll/1654/honesty-ethics-professions.aspx.*

1. Why are some kinds of workers perceived highly and others not?

2. What can advertisers and car salespeople do to improve the image of their professions? Or can nothing be done?

### *Think Long–Term*

The majority of unethical business actions and decisions are based on short-term thinking. People sometimes think in terms of acquiring money immediately, which can lead to cutting corners and taking shortcuts. They do not consider the long-term consequences of their actions. These people may make more money at the moment, but they will have repercussions to deal with as a result of their actions.

A merchant can fool customers into buying a poorly made, defective, or overpriced product. What happens after the sale, though? Cheated customers are not likely to buy from that store in the future, and they are very likely to tell their friends and family about the negative experience. Honest, ethical selling requires mature, long-term thinking. It makes far more sense (and results in higher profits) for a merchant to satisfy a customer and to generate repeat business.

### Elevate the Goal

The goal of many sales calls today is not simply to sell a product to a customer, but to create a mutually beneficial relationship. This focus changes everything about the conversations between salespeople and customers. There is no reason for manipulation or lying. People are not viewed as wallets to be exploited, but relationships to be built and nurtured.

Recall Immanuel Kant's principle of respect for persons. Kant said that it is always wrong to exploit other people—to use them in ways that harm them for one's personal benefit or gain. Ethical selling means acting in the customers' best interests, not merely trying to get their money.

### Learn to Listen

The traditional model of selling involves memorizing the key points of a sales talk, presenting that information to consumers, and hoping the sales pitch will convince some listeners to buy. Questions asked of consumers are often designed to lead them to a decision to purchase. Unsolicited questions from consumers are considered distractions. The process of selling is canned and planned. Is that the kind of conversation you want to have when you go shopping? Do you want to listen to someone talk about a product, or would you rather have someone listen to what you need? Which approach would be more likely to win your business?

## CHECKPOINT 5-2

1. Of the ethical problems in selling that were discussed, which do you believe to be the most common? Which is the most serious?

2. Which two principles of ethical selling do you believe to be most important? Do you think salespeople usually follow them?

3. Do you agree with the assessments of different professions in the Do the Right Thing feature? Rate the professions listed yourself. Which do you believe have "high" or "very high" ethics?

# ETHICS @ WORK

This chapter has presented many ethical issues that arise in sales and advertising. The following scenarios are your chance to apply the ideas to specific situations. Answer the questions that follow the scenarios, and be prepared to respectfully argue for your point of view in class.

## Main Issue and Options

**Issue:** The ads in the following scenarios are all legal. The question is, Should the companies that run them choose to take them off the air?

**Options:** Each company is free to run or hold back the ads.

## Five Commercials

### Ad 1

A very well-dressed businesswoman sits at an outdoor table at a coffee shop. She sips coffee from a paper cup with a large "Smith Bros." logo and smiles at the camera.

"Stopping at Smith Brothers Coffee Traders is the best part of my day," she says. "After the rush of early morning meetings, it's the perfect getaway, and with 24 downtown locations, there's probably one near your office." She sips from the cup again and then turns to another camera.

"Nothing's better than perking up and planning for the rest of the day with a warm cup of Smith Brothers, and with less caffeine than a bottle of soda, I know I'll be calm enough to handle anything that comes up."

At this point, for one second, the words "5 oz. serving size Smith Bros. original roast vs. Super Turbo Cola 20 oz. size" flash by. Although Smith Brothers does have a five-ounce cup, that size is not on the menu, and almost no one in the history of Smith Brothers has ever ordered a 5-ounce coffee. The original roast is the blend with the lowest level of caffeine served at Smith Brothers. Several more popular blends have as much as double the caffeine of the original roast. Super Turbo Cola has one of the highest caffeine levels among soft drinks, and the 20-ounce bottle is the largest personal serving size of the beverage. The bottom line is that an average can of an average soft drink contains about 40 milligrams of caffeine, and an average cup of an average Smith Brothers coffee contains 250 milligrams of caffeine.

### Ad 2

Senator Smith is up for reelection, and he has spent millions on campaign ads. They have, for the most part, trumpeted his accomplishments. With only two months to go before the election, he is surprised to find himself trailing in the polls. He switches strategies and starts to run the following ad. Jan Jones is his opponent.

A male narrator speaks in a deep and menacing voice, while a series of black-and-white photos is shown on the screen. "It's a dangerous world," the voice-over says as a picture of soldiers in Iraq is shown. "Anything can happen at any time," it continues as the image changes to show the twin towers of the World Trade Center, which were destroyed in a terrorist attack in 2001. "It's an uncertain world . . ." The picture changes to a shot of the floor of the New York Stock Exchange. Stressed-looking traders are focused on the "big board" (a large display board), which reads "-403.67" ". . . and families are hurting." The next image shows a man reading a letter with "Notice of Foreclosure" stamped across the top in large letters.

Now the images begin to repeat. "Jan Jones has never dealt with any of these problems. She has never been elected to a public office. She has never run a business.

She is not qualified to handle the serious issues facing our nation today. We need proven leadership and a steady hand in these tough times."

Now the screen shows Senator Smith for the first time. He is well dressed and surrounded by his family. "I'll continue to fight terrorists and support our troops. I'll continue to fight for lower taxes for small businesses and for help for those who are struggling to find a job or make ends meet."

Senator Smith's campaign logo is superimposed on the screen, and the ad ends.

## Ad 3

A woman in a conservative nightgown and a sleeping mask rests on her bed. A silly-sounding voice says, "Amanda!" The voice is vaguely recognizable. The voice actor has done work for several cartoon shows.

The woman stirs slightly. The voice is heard again, louder this time: "a-MAAAN-da!!" The woman snorts, takes off her sleeping mask, and says (comically alarmed), "Who's that?"

"Down here," says the cartoonish voice.

The woman looks around her room. "Down where?"

"In your mattress!"

"Huh?!" the woman says. As she squints, the camera zooms in and shows a cartoon bug. He is multicolored and disgusting-looking, and he is surrounded by dozens of smaller bugs. They are dancing under a disco ball.

"It's just us, Amanda!"

"Bugs! In my mattress?" She exclaims.

"Just us dust mites. Millions of us!!" The camera zooms out and shows legions of bugs.

"Humph!" Amanda says. She walks to her closet and pulls out a wand with a large "Super Light" logo on the handle. With a determined look, she returns to her bed, strips off the sheets, and turns on the Super Light. She then directs a dim beam of violet light onto her mattress and moves it slowly back and forth. The bottom third of the screen reads, "Super Light kills 99.9 percent of dust mites."

The perspective shifts back to the cartoon bug world. The disco-dancing bugs look skyward and shade their eyes from the violet light. Then they start to scream. One by one, they explode into little puffs of smoke. The disco ball crashes to the mattress and shatters, and the music comes to a halt.

Shifting back to the real world, the screen shows Amanda turning off the Super Light, nodding with satisfaction, and walking away.

Mattresses do have dust mites, and many do in fact have many of the microscopic bugs. They are indeed creepy-looking when examined under a microscope. Dust mites can trigger allergy symptoms and asthma attacks in some people. The light does kill almost all dust mites.

## Ad 4

A man brushes his teeth. When he spits into his sink, he notices a light pink color to what he spits out. "Honey," he says, "it happened again."

"Your gums?" she says from off camera.

"Yeah. I thought I was done with this."

His wife enters the bathroom. She holds a new toothbrush in its original packaging. "Try this," she says, handing it to him. "I got this for you last time, remember?"

"Oh, I guess not," he says, sheepishly.

"Well, you should use it. Your old toothbrush is too harsh—it's no wonder your gums are bleeding. Comfort toothbrushes are made a new way, with a new kind of bristle. It cleans your teeth without irritating your gums."

"Huh. OK, I'll try it."

"You'll be glad you did."

Sometimes, bleeding gums are indeed caused by abrasive toothbrushes or by people exerting too much pressure while brushing. They are also sometimes a sign of periodontal disease or a nutrition deficiency.

## Ad 5

[Aside: A gun firing makes a sound of 145–155 decibels. The space shuttle, at launch, registers at 165–175 decibels. A meteor impact near the Tunguska River in Russia in 1908 weighed in at a world-record 300–315 decibels and has been rated as the loudest event in recorded history.[3] *The character in this ad might be even louder.]*

As familiar guitar licks from an 80s-era hair band play loudly, the camera zooms in on a ripped spokeswoman. She is standing opposite a life-sized cardboard cutout of herself from when she weighed twice her current weight.

"THIS USED TO BE ME!" she shouts, gesturing at the cutout and flexing tremendous biceps. After nodding to the camera, she rears back and punches the cardboard hard enough to send the head flying a dozen feet into the background. "THEN I HEARD ABOUT THIN NOW!"

She picks up a quart-size bottle of an orange drink with a distinctive "THIN NOW!" label, upends it, and chugs it down. "AAAHH—THAT'S GOOD!" She crushes the bottle and throws it after the cardboard head. "THIN NOW GAVE ME THE ENERGY I NEEDED TO LOSE 140 POUNDS! THANK YOU, THIN NOW!"

The following statement flashes across the screen: "Real user—not an actress. Atypical result." There is a half space between the *A* and the *t* in *Atypical*. It is hard to say whether the text reads "Atypical," meaning not typical, or "A typical." The message quickly disappears.

"BUY THIN NOW TODAY AT THESE FINE RETAILERS!" Grocery and drugstore logos fill the screen. "BE LIKE ME! GET THIN—NOW!"

## What Do You Think?

1. Rate the five ads.

| | COMPLETELY UNACCEPTABLE | | | | COMPLETELY ACCEPTABLE | |
|---|---|---|---|---|---|---|
| Ad 1 | 1 | 2 | 3 | 4 | 5 | 6 | 7 |
| Ad 2 | 1 | 2 | 3 | 4 | 5 | 6 | 7 |
| Ad 3 | 1 | 2 | 3 | 4 | 5 | 6 | 7 |
| Ad 4 | 1 | 2 | 3 | 4 | 5 | 6 | 7 |
| Ad 5 | 1 | 2 | 3 | 4 | 5 | 6 | 7 |

2. Focus on your two "worst" ads. Specifically, what makes you react negatively?

3. What ethical standards in advertising or principles of ethical selling could be followed that would make the ads you identified in the last question more acceptable?

4. Focus on your one "best" ad. Specifically, what makes you react positively?

5. What ethical standards in advertising or principles of ethical selling are followed that make the ad you identified in the last question more acceptable?

[3]"Top 10 Loudest Noises," Listverse, November 30, 2007, http://listverse.com/2007/11/30/top-10-loudest-noises/.

# Summary

Ethical issues relevant to the advertising profession include false advertising, puffery, the practice of bait and switch, concerns about advertising to children, and proper use of telemarketing tools. The AAF code of ethics attempts to establish an ethical standard for the field. Its provisions include truth in advertising, substantiation of claims, fairness in comparisons with competitors, clarity and full disclosure in guarantees and warranties, fair and honest price claims, proper use of testimonials, and compliance with accepted standards of taste and decency.

Several ethical issues and concerns are relevant to the profession of selling. They include price gouging, false prizes, and straight commissions. Most unethical actions and decisions stem from short-term thinking and the pressure to make immediate sales by any means necessary.

Principles of ethical selling include thinking long-term, building relationships with customers, and listening carefully to the needs and concerns of potential buyers. Selling products with honesty and integrity is more likely to lead to increased customer loyalty and repeat buyers.

# Key Terms and Concepts

**Match each definition with a key term or concept.**

a. bait and switch

b. code of ethics

c. commission

d. false advertising

e. false prizes

f. price gouging

g. puffery

h. straight commission

i. substantiation

j. telemarketing

k. testimonial

l. warranty

_____ 1. A written promise to repair or replace a product if it breaks or becomes defective within a specified period of time

_____ 2. A written set of principles and rules intended to serve as a guideline for ethical behavior for individuals under an organization's authority

_____ 3. An endorsement of a product by someone claiming to have benefited from its use

_____ 4. The validation of advertising claims with objective data from independent research

_____ 5. The practice of advertising a product at a low price while intentionally stocking only a limited number in hopes of luring shoppers to buy more expensive items

_____ 6. A term used to describe statements that are not outright lies, but merely exaggerations

_____ 7. A sales technique that seeks to trick potential customers into thinking they have won valuable items such as cash, cars, and cruises

_____ 8. A method of compensation in which income is based entirely on what a person sells

_____ 9. The practice of selling directly to individuals through unsolicited phone calls, e-mails, or faxes

_____ 10. The practice of pricing a product far above the normal market value on the assumption that consumers have no other way to buy the product

_____ 11. A method of compensation in which salespeople are rewarded with a percentage of the money from the sales they make, in addition to a salary or hourly wage

_____ 12. The practice of making statements about products that the advertiser knows are not true

# Review

1. Which type of misleading advertising is always illegal?

   a. false advertising

   b. bait and switch

   c. puffery

   d. both A and B

2. Match each type of ad with an AAF standard.

   _____ 1. A pizza chain claims its main rival is always late on deliveries.

   a. warranties

   _____ 2. A drug company says its antacid acts 80% faster than competing brands.

   b. price claims

   _____ 3. A computer manufacturer guarantees to repair its laptops free of charge for a year after purchase.

   c. comparisons

   _____ 4. A movie star promotes a perfume.

   d. substantiation

   _____ 5. A dry cleaner offers $10 worth of free dry cleaning services, but charges three times as much as competitors.

   e. testimonials

3. Match each example with the correct unethical sales practice.

   _____ 1. An employee earns no salary, but is paid a percentage of the profits on each security system he sells.

   a. straight commission

   _____ 2. A company offers a free round-trip airline ticket for attending its financial seminar. It turns out that there are many restrictions on the ticket's use.

   b. price gouging

   _____ 3. In a major power outage, a hardware store charges three times as much as usual for batteries, flashlights, and portable generators.

   c. false prizes

   _____ 4. An employee is paid an hourly wage plus a percentage of each season ticket subscription she sells.

   d. commission

4. Learning to listen to customers involves

    a. giving a sales pitch.

    b. asking questions designed to lead the customer to buy.

    c. encouraging customer questions.

    d. all of the above

# Critical Thinking

5. What causes people to act unethically in the workplace? According to a survey by the American Management Association, the answer might surprise you. The researchers found that the most common cause of employee misdeeds is not greed, a desire to further one's career, or even an attempt to protect one's job. Instead, almost 70 percent of those surveyed blamed their ethical misdeeds on the pressure imposed by supervisors and administrators to meet unrealistic goals and deadlines. Corporate executives, under great pressure to succeed, often pass that pressure down the ladder to rank-and-file employees. Trying to further one's career came in a distant second.[4]

    List five specific things leaders can do to reduce ethical misdeeds at work.

# Applications

6. Deon is a new employee at an advertising agency. He is thrilled to have the job of his dreams so soon after graduating from college. His first assignment is to help create television ads for a national chain of steak house restaurants. Deon is a vegetarian and fervently believes that eating meat is wrong. If he participates in this project, he will be encouraging people to do something he is convinced they should not do. However, because this is his first project for the company, his superiors are watching him carefully. First impressions are important, and he wants to make a good one.

    What should Deon do? Support your answer with ideas from the chapter.

[4]American Management Association, "The Ethical Enterprise: Doing the Right Things in the Right Ways, Today and Tomorrow, A Global Study of Business Ethics 2005–2015," http://www.amanet.org/images/HREthicsSurvey06.pdf, p. 55.

7. Isabella is a salesperson for a retail electronics store. Because Isabella is paid a small hourly wage, she needs the commissions from her sales to support her family. Being an ethical person is very important to Isabella. She understands that her self-respect depends on that, and she wants to be a positive role model for her children.

   One problem Isabella has with her job is that it appears that the salespeople who receive the biggest paychecks are the ones using deceptive, manipulative sales techniques. They also are often the first to be considered for promotions. Isabella is discouraged. She knows she would sell more products if she used these underhanded tactics, and she is tempted to do so. She really needs the extra income to provide for her children. How can she teach them to be honest, though, if she isn't?

   What should Isabella do? Support your answer with ideas from the chapter.

8. Analyze the following hypothetical advertisements. Decide whether you think each example contains an ethical problem. If you think there is an ethical problem, explain what it is. If you don't think there is an ethical problem, explain why.

   a. Television commercials for "Commander Oort" action figures. The commercials, which run each Saturday morning during the "Commander Oort" cartoon, show the toys flying as Commander Oort does in the cartoon, although small print on the screen states that they don't actually fly.

   b. An ad for plastic surgery in a popular magazine for teenage girls.

   c. An ad for a dance studio in a magazine for senior citizens. The ad highlights several benefits of dance lessons, including companionship, improved health, and relief from loneliness.

d. Beer commercials that air during prime time on a popular cable TV music video channel.

e. Television and print commercials for a bank that issues credit cards, advertising a 0 percent interest rate for the first six months. No mention is made of what happens to the rates after that time.

## Digging Deeper

9. Use the Internet to research the Direct Selling Association's Code of Ethics. What selling practices are prohibited by the code? What standards are required? How are the rules and principles enforced? Answer these questions on a separate piece of paper.

10. Interview a business owner or an advertising professional about his or her views on ethics in advertising. Create your own list of at least three questions to ask. Share your findings in an oral presentation to the class.

## The Bottom Line

11. Do you believe most companies follow ethical practices in selling and advertising?

| ABSOLUTELY NOT | | | | | | ABSOLUTELY |
|---|---|---|---|---|---|---|
| 1 | 2 | 3 | 4 | 5 | 6 | 7 |

# Technology, Testing, and Workplace Privacy

Companies have a wide variety of tools that can allow them to keep tabs on workers' activities, both at and away from the office. In many cases, "snooping" is entirely legal, but is it the right thing to do?

## CHAPTER 6

## Objectives

- Identify the reach of privacy protection in law.
- Discuss ethical issues associated with drug testing.
- Discuss ethical issues associated with polygraph, or lie detector, testing.

## Key Terms and Concepts

right to privacy, p. 90
judicial restraint, p. 90
judicial activism, p. 90
statute, p. 91
drug and alcohol abuse, p. 92
pre-employment drug testing, p. 93
post-offer drug testing, p. 93
random drug testing, p. 93
Employee Polygraph Protection Act, p. 94

# {HARD Choices}

Jim greeted Abby, took off his overcoat, laid it across the back of a chair, and sat down. Seven packets bound with paper clips were spread out along one side of the conference table. Each had a photograph placed on top with a name written beneath in blue marker: *Anderson, Baker, Cooper, Daniels, Evans, Franklin,* and *Gordon.* Dale had already interviewed the finalists. Now it was up to him, once he'd heard from Abby, to make the final decision.

"OK," Abby begins. "I did what you asked me to do. No aggressive data mining. I just looked at their social network pages, microposts, and things like that. I didn't try to use any sneaky back doors to get around privacy settings; I only looked at stuff they posted that anyone can see."

"Excellent."

"Starting with Anderson. Nothing much. Some party pictures with friends. Several show her with alcohol. She's 22 now, and in a few of the shots she might be under 21. Nothing wild. Some poetry, quotes from movies, that kind of thing. She seems nice."

"Dale thought so, too. He ranked her fifth out of the seven. 'Pleasant in person, decent grades, resume a little thin,' he told me."

"OK, moving on," Abby replies. "Baker had, ah, substantially more party pictures. Lots of booze. Bonging beers. Chugging whiskey."

"Interesting. He has a 4.0 grade point average."

"Huh."

"Any drugs in those photos?"

"Not that I saw. Cigarettes, yes. Alcohol, tons. No drugs."

"OK," says Jim. "Dale ranked him fourth overall. Decent interview and weak internship to go with the GPA."

"On to Cooper. More party shots than Anderson, fewer than Baker. The only new thing with him was that he posted this photo." She hands a printout to Jim, who looks at it briefly.

"He had a series of photos labeled 'New Orleans Road Trip.' Looks like a Mardi Gras trip."

"Is the woman in the background?" Jim asks.

"No, she's the only thing in the picture."

"Might she be underage?"

"She doesn't appear to be."

"OK," Jim says. "He had a great internship. Dale ranked him third."

"Next we have Daniels. No party pictures, nothing controversial. One micropost worth mentioning. She posted this an hour after her interview with Dale."

Abby hands Jim a printout with the following highlighted: "Just interviewed with giant bald dork at Smith and Morian. Think the loser liked me. We'll see. Hope I get an offer from Tess Brothers. Can't imagine working for that guy."

Jim fights it and then cracks a smile. "This really isn't funny," he says.

"No," Abby agrees. They both laugh.

"I mean, we're Plan B for her, and she's talking about her potential boss behind his back."

"Yep," Abby says.

"Well, Dale didn't like her much either. He ranked her sixth. What about Evans?"

"I think Mr. Evans might have . . . an anger problem."

"Oh," Jim is taken aback. "What makes you think so?"

"Several things. He posts angry song lyrics. He talks a lot about his guns on his social network page. One of his photos shows him holding a pistol. He says derogatory things about his girlfriend, and she looks . . . really sad in every picture of her on his page."

"Anything specific? Anything to indicate he uses guns inappropriately, hits his girlfriend, or anything like that?"

"No."

"He passed our standard background check. No criminal record. But your gut says 'bad guy.'"

"I could be wrong."

"Dale ranked him second. Really liked him." Jim pauses. "OK. I appreciate your candor. What about Franklin?"

"Ah. Now Franklin does have a specific issue."

"Dang! Dale ranked him first—he thought Franklin was terrific. What is it?"

"On his social network page, one of the pictures shows Franklin without a shirt from behind. He has a tattoo around his right shoulder blade . . ."

"Abby, lots of kids who interview with us probably have tattoos. If it's not visible when he's in a suit, I really don't see . . ."

"It's not a regular tattoo, or I wouldn't make a big deal about it."

"Ah. Hey, I'm sorry for interrupting you. It's just—Dale was so keen on this guy."

"That's OK. The tattoo is very distinctive. It seemed as if I'd seen one like it somewhere, maybe on TV. I looked around on the Internet and eventually found it."

"What is it? Devil worship or something?"

"It's a hate group."

"A hate group," Jim repeats. He takes off his glasses and rubs his eyes. "Whom do they hate?"

"Jewish people. The group started in Europe and has spread over here."

"Are you sure it was a match? I mean, might he have a similar tattoo?"

"The coloring, design, script, and motto were identical. This isn't something generic he got out of a catalog at a tattoo parlor."

"And they're really bad?"

"They're very into Hitler."

"I see."

"Look," Abby says. "Maybe he got it without knowing much about the group. Maybe he just saw the design and thought it was cool. Maybe he doesn't know what it represents."

"Possibly, I suppose. Are there any anti-Semitic statements on his page?"

"No. No links to anything, either."

"You're positive it's him in the picture?"

"Yes."

"Is the picture still up, do you think?"

"I looked yesterday, so probably so."

"I want to look at it myself." Jim scribbles a note on his pad. "Let's do the last one, ah . . ."

"Gordon."

"Gordon, right. What's the scoop on her?"

"There is none. She's not on any of the popular social networking sites. Nothing. She hardly comes up if you search for her. Very low profile online."

"*I* don't have any social networking stuff."

"You're 45. She's half that. I'm not saying it's a bad thing, but she is the only one in this group without a substantial online presence. Might be a loner."

"Or she might just interact with humans in person. Or really value her privacy."

"Maybe so."

"OK. Well, Dale was noncommittal. Ranked her seventh overall. 'Bland personality, bland resume,' he told me. She does have good grades."

"Seems about right. Well, that's all of them. It's up to you now."

# {**WHAT** Do You Think?}

1. **Is it reasonable for employers to screen applicants by searching social networking sites and microposts?**

COMPLETELY REASONABLE ⟵———————————⟶ ABSOLUTELY UNFAIR

1    2    3    4    5    6    7

2. **Which of the applicants (if any) should have Abby's report held against him or her? In other words, which applicants (if any) should have at least a somewhat lower chance of being hired? Why?**

# ■ Privacy Law

People tend to be very sensitive about "privacy rights." Almost everyone, on some basic level, cherishes the right to be left alone. But does the law really offer this kind of protection?

## Origins

The **right to privacy** is probably the most controversial of all constitutional liberties. Loosely stated, it is the legal idea that there are certain areas of one's life that should be free of government regulation and that the government should not have the ability to influence certain decisions.

The Supreme Court first weighed in on the right to privacy in the 1965 case *Griswold v. Connecticut*. Before this case, a Connecticut state law made it illegal to use birth control or even to give others advice about the use of contraceptives. The state of Connecticut prosecuted an employee of Planned Parenthood (Griswold) who had counseled couples on methods of contraception. The Supreme Court reversed the conviction of Griswold, reasoning that the state law violated the privacy rights of Griswold and those seeking information from her.

An interesting point about the Court's decision is that the Constitution does not directly mention a right to privacy. Other constitutional liberties are mentioned by name—one can find specific mention of free speech in the First Amendment, due process in the Fifth Amendment, and the right to be free from cruel and unusual punishment in the Eighth Amendment. However, the Supreme Court has accepted the idea that when the Constitution is viewed as a whole, it creates certain "zones of privacy."

Not all Supreme Court justices have agreed. Justice Potter Stewart notably called the Connecticut law "silly," but he also thought that it was acceptable to have such a law under the Constitution. The controversy about the existence and reach of the implied right to privacy continues to this day.

The 1973 case *Roe v. Wade* put the right to privacy on the map. Before this case, most states had laws that banned most or all abortions. The Supreme Court accepted that the plaintiff's decision to seek an abortion was protected by privacy rights, and it voided the state laws. No decision in the last 50 years has sparked more debate.

Other controversial applications of privacy law abound. Should a private club be allowed to have only men as members, or only white

## Ethics&Law

Supreme Court justices are human beings, and each has his or her own idea of how laws should be interpreted or applied. The media often call certain judges "liberal" or "conservative," but such labels can be misleading. "Conservative" judges often agree with Republicans on issues, but they sometimes do not. By the same token, "liberal" judges often agree with Democrats, but not always.

A much more accurate and useful way of thinking of judges is as "literalist" or "not literalist." Some judges believe that the Constitution, statutes, and any other laws they review should be applied exactly as written. These judges (often called "conservatives" or practitioners of **judicial restraint** by the press) hold the general belief that privacy is a weak, or even a nonexistent, legal standard.

Others (who are often called "liberals" or practitioners of **judicial activism** by the press) believe that it is important to consider the purpose of a law, and they are sometimes willing to go beyond the specific language in a law when they apply it to a case. Such judges tend to favor a stronger and broader application of privacy rights.

**Go online and find an article that refers to a judge as a judicial activist. Why was the label attached to the judge? Do you approve or disapprove of the judge's actions?**

members? Should a newspaper be able to print the name of a minor who has committed a crime? Should the government be permitted to listen in on telephone conversations? Should a state be able to regulate the sexual behavior of consenting adults? Should the government be allowed to take a thermal image of one's home to look for evidence that marijuana is being grown inside?

At the time of this writing in 2010, a suspected terrorist had recently attempted to blow up a commercial jet headed for Detroit with explosives smuggled on board in his underwear. The government was debating whether to require airline passengers to submit to a preflight full-body scan that would enable security agents to see through their clothes. Many privacy groups had expressed concern at these plans.[1]

## The Right to Privacy at Work

Moving from national and social issues to business issues, should companies be able to look through employee e-mail or monitor the Web sites that employees visit? Should they be able to require workers to submit a urine or hair sample for a drug test or take a lie detector test?

In the end, a private company is legally allowed to do most of these things because the constitutional right to privacy does not apply to private companies in the same way that it does to the government. Constitutional liberties protect people from government tyranny, but they usually do not protect people from other people or from private organizations. If the police tell you to shut up, for example, you have a good free speech case. If your boss tells you to shut up, you don't.

Often, privacy rights at work must come from **statutes**, which are laws passed by Congress. In many key areas, there are no statutes, so many privacy issues fall solely within the realm of ethics. The "snooping" on social network pages in the opening scenario is entirely legal.

---

## CHECKPOINT 6–1

**1.** Return to the opening Hard Choices scenario. The rankings Dale gave each applicant appear in the left column below and on the next page. In the blank column to the right, give your assessment of how Jim should rank the candidates, taking the information from Abby's report into account. (The top three will be made offers.)

| Dale's rankings | Jim's rankings should be . . . |
|---|---|
| 1. Franklin | *1. _____ |
| 2. Evans | *2. _____ |
| 3. Cooper | *3. _____ |
| 4. Baker | 4. _____ |
| 5. Anderson | 5. _____ |

[1]From Bredeson. *Applied Business Ethics*, 1e. © 2012 South-Western, a part of Cengage Learning, Inc. Reproduced by permission. www.cengage.com/permissions.

| Dale's rankings | Jim's rankings should be . . . |
|---|---|
| 6.  Daniels | 6. _____ |
| 7.  Gordon | 7. _____ |

**2.** Assume now that the seven people listed above already work for the company in the scenario and that Jim is given the same information. Should he discipline or fire any of them if they are current employees who are doing a good job?

**3.** How reasonable would it be for a university to screen applicants this way, by searching social networking sites?

COMPLETELY REASONABLE ← → ABSOLUTELY UNFAIR

| 1 | 2 | 3 | 4 | 5 | 6 | 7 |

**4.** Describe the importance of the cases *Griswold v. Connecticut* and *Roe v. Wade.*

**5.** Does the constitutional right to privacy apply to workplaces? Why or why not?

# ■ Drug Tests and Polygraph Exams

Many employers require employees to undergo random drug testing. Some others require that employees occasionally submit to a polygraph, or lie detector, exam. This section examines legal and ethical concerns that surround each type of testing.

## Drug and Alcohol Abuse

In a recent survey, company leaders were asked to list the most troublesome ethical problems their industries faced. The list included many issues that were not surprising, including employee theft, lying on job applications, and environmental concerns. One of the most bothersome issues according to those surveyed was **drug and alcohol abuse** by employees.[2] It is a major concern for many reasons:

[2]"The National Survey of CEOs on Business Ethics," Center for Ethics and Corporate Responsibility, J. Mack Robinson College of Business, Georgia State University, and Robert J. Rutland Institute for Ethics, Clemson University, http://robinson.gsu.edu/files/ethics/2008CEO_Survey.pdf, 2008, p. 10.

- It is a leading cause of lost production due to employee sick time.

- Drug and alcohol abuse is a primary cause of employee accidents and injuries.

- It has a dramatic effect on employee turnover. When employees quit or lose their jobs, companies must pay to recruit, hire, and train replacements.

- Substance abuse drives up the costs of insurance that companies provide to their employees. In fact, some companies now have their workers drug-tested in order to obtain discounts on health and life insurance rates.

Figure 6-1 lists some recent facts about drug and alcohol use at work.

---

### SUBSTANCE ABUSE AT WORK

- In a recent year, 19.3 million U.S. adults were users of illicit drugs, and 12.9 million (66.6 percent) of those people worked.

- Eight percent of full-time and 11.5 percent of part-time workers were illicit drug users.

- Of 57.4 million adult binge drinkers, 74.4 percent were employed.

- Of 16.6 million heavy drinkers, 74.9 percent were employed.

- Seven percent of employees reported observing substance abuse on the job.

*Sources: U.S. Department of Health and Human Services, "Results from the 2009 National Survey on Drug Use and Health: Volume I. Summary of National Findings," pgs. 2, 33; Ethics Resource Center, "2009 National Business Ethics Survey," p. 34.*

**FIGURE 6-1**
Workplace substance abuse is a serious problem

---

## Drug Testing of Employees

Requiring employees to be drug-tested raises important ethical issues, but usually no legal issues. Private companies are generally allowed to give drug tests if they wish, because no federal statute exists that gives workers specific rights to resist drug testing.

**Pre-employment drug testing** is designed to screen out job applicants who may abuse certain illegal drugs. One testing company has reported that, in 2009, 3.4 percent of job applicants failed these screening exams.[3] To save money, some businesses require **post-offer drug testing**, meaning that they don't test every applicant, but only those who are offered jobs. Many companies have policies for testing only employees who display symptoms or signs of drug abuse. It is also routine for employees to be automatically tested after on-the-job injuries.

The most controversial type of drug testing is **random drug testing**; it subjects all employees to being tested with little or no advance notice. In other

---

[3] "Drug Testing Index," Quest Diagnostics, September 16, 2010, http://www.questdiagnostics.com/employersolutions/dti/2010_09/dti_index.html.

words, employees who do not abuse drugs, who do not display any signs of impairment, and who may have exemplary job histories must still endure the invasion of personal privacy required for drug tests. Even critics of random testing concede that there are occupations in which across-the-board testing could be justified on the grounds of public safety (for example, airline pilots, train engineers, police officers, and school bus drivers). Can random testing of restaurant dishwashers or telephone operators, however, be justified on the same basis?

A closely related question is what should be done with employees who do test positive for using illicit drugs. Should they be fired, or should companies offer to help those employees who want to overcome their addictions? There are voices on both sides of that debate, but the railroad industry presents an interesting case study.

Not so many years ago, the general policy was that railroad employees determined to be abusing drugs or alcohol were automatically fired. The result was that rather than seek help, employees with substance abuse problems tried to hide their addictions, which often made the problem worse. At some point, administrators noticed that the policy was not preventing drug and alcohol abuse as much as driving it underground, and a new guideline was established. Employees who failed drug tests would be fired, but those who self-reported their substance abuse problems would be offered medical assistance and counseling. As a result, instead of hiding their problems to keep their jobs, employees were more likely to ask for help, dramatically improving their chances of rebuilding their lives and becoming productive employees and citizens again.

## Polygraph Examination of Employees

Another frequently debated issue is whether to make use of polygraph exams. Almost everyone has seen a lie detector. Lie detectors have been featured in a number of reality TV shows and a hilarious Ben Stiller movie, *Meet the Parents*. Polygraph testing at work may seem exotic, but more than 2 million private sector workers took a lie detector test at work in a recent year.[4] Many companies have turned to this device for help in finding an employee who has stolen money, equipment, or intellectual property. Some have even used it to detect crimes before they occur.

Polygraph exams are limited somewhat by a statute called the **Employee Polygraph Protection Act** (EPPA). Under this law, most private companies can use lie detectors only after an event demanding an investigation has taken place. Banks are a notable exception—they can use lie detectors whenever they wish—and a few types of companies can test prospective employees. EPPA also requires that workers be given advance written notice before being subjected to a polygraph exam, and it gives them the right to bring a lawyer to the exam. In addition, workers cannot be fired if the only

---

[4]"Lie Detector Testing," American Civil Liberties Union of Florida, http://www.aclufl.org/take_action/download_resources/info_papers/4.cfm?print=true.

evidence of a misdeed is a failed exam. Supporting evidence must be found before an employee can be subjected to negative consequences.

The central idea of polygraph science is that most people cannot control certain body responses when they lie. Polygraph machines measure such responses, typically heart rate, blood pressure, respiratory rate, and the amount of sweat on the fingertips. Even people who are smooth liars, people who can look a person in the eye and tell a lie that seems believable, can't usually control physical reactions like blood pressure.

Independent tests have found polygraphs to be 80 to 90 percent accurate in the sense that from 80 to 90 times out of 100, the machine correctly identifies whether a person is being truthful or deceptive.[5] Polygraph science is labeled as "junk science" by some critics, however. The Supreme Court has called polygraph evidence unreliable, and the results of polygraph exams usually cannot be introduced as evidence in court.[6]

## CHECKPOINT 6–2

1. Name three ways in which drug and alcohol abuse increase employer expenses.

2. True or false: Most people who are addicted to illegal drugs are unemployed.

3. In your own words, describe the following types of drug tests:

   a. pre-employment drug test

   b. post-offer drug test

   c. random drug test

4. List the key provisions of the Employee Polygraph Protection Act.

5. Why are random drug tests and polygraph tests controversial?

[5]"Lie Detector Tests: Do They Tell the Truth?" Nolo, http://www.nolo.com/legal-encyclopedia/lie-detector-tests-tell-truth-29637.html.

[6]From Bredeson. *Applied Business Ethics*, 1e. © 2012 South-Western, a part of Cengage Learning, Inc. Reproduced by permission. www.cengage.com/permissions.

# ETHICS@WORK

This chapter has presented issues related to privacy in the workplace. The following scenario is your chance to apply the issues to a business situation. Which make the most sense to you? Why? Answer the questions that follow the scenario, and be prepared to respectfully argue for your point of view in class.

## Main Issue and Options

**Issue:** Should the CEO take action against any of the five workers described at the end of the scenario?

**Options:** The CEO is legally free to take any course of action he wishes, including firing any or all of the workers.

## Trouble at Greentown Bank

### ER Waiting Room

Marty, a manager at Greentown Bank, rushed through the double doors and absent-mindedly brushed the snow from his hair as he looked around the emergency room. He soon spotted a coworker and walked over to her.

"Is Carl . . ." he began.

"OK, I think. The doctor came out a few minutes ago and said he's awake."

"Thank God. What happened?" When his coworker didn't reply, he added, "It wasn't . . ."

She nodded. "I think it was."

Marty slapped his gloves into an empty hand and exhaled heavily. Not knowing what else to do, he sat down to wait.

### Marty's Office

Three days later, Marty was sitting in his office, the door slightly open, when he heard a knock. The chief operating officer ducked his head around the door.

"Got a minute?" the COO asked.

"Sure."

The COO walked in, closed the door, and sat down. He cleared his throat. "Hey, Marty, I wanted you to hear this first from me."

"OK."

"I let Carl go."

"He just got out of the hospital . . ."

"After another overdose."

"We don't know if that's why . . ."

"He admitted it, Marty. He admitted it. I'm sorry."

"Ah. Cocaine?"

"Yep."

"He promised me," Marty said. He still couldn't quite believe it. "Promised me, after last time . . ."

"I know. I'm sorry. It gets worse, though."

"How so?"

"When we knew he was back in the hospital, and we guessed why he was there, we took a look at the records. A close look."

"And?"

"Carl's been supplementing his pay."

"What do you mean?"

"Marty, he stole almost $50,000 from us."

"What!"

The COO sighed. "When we confronted him with the evidence, and we have a lot of it, he broke down crying. He blamed it on the drugs and begged us not to go to the cops."

"No." Marty sat silently for a moment. Then he asked, "Are we? Going to press charges?"

"That's not my call."

"Ah."

"Listen, Marty, I know you really tried to get him back on track. Sometimes things just don't work out."

"Yeah, I guess they don't."

The COO checked his watch. "Sorry, but I've got a meeting."

"Sure, sure. Hey, thanks for coming by."

"You bet, Marty." The COO shook Marty's hand and left.

## Greentown Bank's Executive Conference Room

The next day, a furious CEO sat at the head of the long conference table.

"We will never, I repeat, never allow something like this to happen again. We will never place our customers' and shareholders' money at risk. We will never again risk our reputation. We got lucky this time and nothing showed up in the papers, but next time we might not be so lucky. I am instituting two policies, effective immediately.

"First, beginning in 60 days, we will implement a random drug testing program. Every employee, including me, will be asked to submit a urine sample several times per year. The tests will not be announced ahead of time. This will be a zero tolerance policy, and the penalty for failing a test or refusing to take one will be immediate termination.

"I have decided on a 60-day delay because I want any of our workers who have a problem similar to Carl's to have a last clear chance. I am told that urinalysis tests can usually detect drugs for only about 30 days after they are used. The message is, 'If you want to keep working here, knock it off right now!'

"Second, when we start drug testing, we will begin asking all our employees to take a quarterly lie detector exam. We have retained the services of a licensed polygraph examiner. Anyone who fails an exam or refuses to take one will be dealt with harshly, but our lawyers and I are still working on specific sanctions. No one is ever going to steal $50,000 from us again because we'll catch him before he is able to carry out his plan.

"These policies will go out to all employees later today. That's all, everybody."

## Marty's Office

"Got a minute, boss?"

Marty looked up from his monitor. "Sure thing, Ernie. Come on in."

"Thanks. I just read the new policies, and I'm not happy."

"I knew you wouldn't be."

"I've been here for 30 years. I've never used drugs, and I've never stolen a penny."

"I know that, Ernie."

"Look, we're all sorry about Carl, but I'm not going to be held under suspicion."

"I feel your pain, Ernie, I really do," Marty replied, "but it's the new policy."

"I won't do it."

"You have to."

"No, boss, I mean I really won't do it. I've got enough to retire, if it comes to that. I won't be treated like a criminal."

"Ernie . . ."

"Look, boss, I'm just letting you know. I'm going to refuse to take both tests. If I get fired, I get fired."

"I hope you'll reconsider," said Marty. "I'd hate to lose you."

"I'd hate to go, but I won't take those tests."

## Vacant Office

The polygraph examiner had set up his equipment in an empty office. Marty sat on a stool with straps and wires dangling from his chest, upper arm, and fingertips.

"Is your name Marty?" the polygraph examiner asked.

"Yes." The polygraph's needles softly scratched across a scrolling page.

"Are you originally from Antarctica?"

"Yes," Marty replied. The needles scratched swift, angry arcs. Marty chuckled.

"Have you ever stolen money from Greenville Bank?"

"No."

"Are you wearing a white shirt?"

"Yes." Marty was.

"Do you have any plans to steal from Greenville Bank in the future?"

"No."

"Is today Monday?"

"Yes," said Marty. It was.

"Are you aware of any plan by anyone else to take money from Greenville Bank?"

"No."

The questions continued. Although he was always truthful, beads of sweat began forming on Marty's brow.

## CEO's Office

A week later, the CEO's assistant called Marty and asked if he could come down to the CEO's office right away. Marty arrived a few minutes later and was seated. Two files lay on the CEO's massive desk. The CEO consulted one of them and then looked over his glasses at Marty. "I asked you to stop by because I want input from my managers before I make any final decisions."

"Yes, sir."

"I am considering—just considering, for now—softening my position on failed tests. It seems we have, ah, more than a few."

"Yes, sir."

"Five of your subordinates are on my lists."

"Five." Marty could think of nothing else to say.

"Don't worry, Marty. Other managers have about the same numbers." Marty was somewhat relieved. The CEO continued. "Anderson tested positive for marijuana. Bates tested positive for cocaine. Cooper failed the lie detector test on the 'have you ever stolen from Greenville' question. Daniels failed the lie detector test on all three key questions. And then there's the guy, what's his name . . ."

"Ernie?"

"Right, him. He wouldn't even take the tests. Either one."

"Good grief."

"Look, Marty, these are your people. You know them. Carl was one of yours, too, which makes me particularly interested in what you have to say, since he started all this. What would you do if you were in my shoes?"

## What Do You Think?

1. Did the CEO overreact when he implemented the drug testing policy, or was his decision appropriate?

2. Did the CEO overreact when he implemented a policy of giving polygraph exams to all employees, or was his decision appropriate?

3. How should Anderson and Bates be disciplined, and should they face the same punishment?

4. How should Cooper and Daniels be punished?

5. How should Ernie be punished?

# Summary

Companies sometimes have an interest in monitoring employee behavior at and away from the office. The Supreme Court has interpreted the U.S. Constitution as guaranteeing a right to privacy, but it usually prohibits only the government—and not private companies—from taking various actions.

Companies often choose to subject workers to certain kinds of drug tests. Employees with addiction issues can be costly in several ways. Some companies also make use of polygraph exams. When any of these tests are failed, companies face difficult dilemmas in deciding on consequences for workers.

# Key Terms and Concepts

Match each definition with a key term or concept.

_____ 1. A law that sets ground rules for companies and workers when companies ask workers to take a certain kind of exam

_____ 2. A major concern of employers, according to a recent survey

_____ 3. Drug testing of job applicants

_____ 4. A law passed by Congress

_____ 5. Drug testing that may be administered to any employee with little or no advance notice

_____ 6. Drug testing of applicants who are offered jobs

_____ 7. A constitutional liberty first recognized in the cases *Griswold v. Connecticut* and *Roe v. Wade*

_____ 8. The conservative approach to interpreting laws that calls for applying laws literally

_____ 9. The liberal approach to interpreting laws that calls for considering their purpose

a. drug and alcohol abuse

b. Employee Polygraph Protection Act

c. judicial activism

d. judicial restraint

e. post-offer drug testing

f. pre-employment drug testing

g. random drug testing

h. right to privacy

i. statute

# Review

1. True or false: Constitutional rights like the right to privacy usually apply to private corporations.

2. True or false: In most key areas, statutes provide privacy rights at work.

3. List two reasons why companies see substance abuse as a serious problem.

4. Which is the least costly type of drug testing? the most controversial?

5. EPPA requires companies to

   a. give notice to employees before a polygraph exam.

   b. allow employees to being a lawyer to a polygraph exam.

   c. both A and B

   d. none of the above

# Critical Thinking

6. Suppose someone steals $500 from a business. The company has a polygraph examiner test each of its 101 employees. His assessment is 95 percent accurate, which means that of the 100 people who are innocent, the exam will correctly identify 95 as truthful. However, it will be wrong 5 percent of the time and will incorrectly identify 5 as deceptive. The "bad guy" will most likely be correctly identified as deceptive.

   At the end of the day, the company's leaders will get a list of 6 names. One will probably be the thief's, but the other 5 will be names of employees who did nothing wrong but were merely the victims of a "usually accurate, but occasionally incorrect" exam. In light of the problem just described, have your feelings about the usefulness of polygraphs changed? Why?

# Applications

7. Imagine you own a business and can create any drug testing policy you wish. Will you have one? Will you test everyone? If so, how often, and what will the consequences be for failing an exam? If you choose to implement a policy, write an outline for it.

8. Imagine you have your own business, and one day you discover an important file is missing. Will you consider bringing in a polygraph examiner if the file does not resurface? If so, what will the consequences be for failing the exam? Write an explanatory statement to your employees.

# Digging Deeper

9. Go online and find an example of a corporate drug testing policy for an occupation that interests you. Does the policy seem fair? Would you be comfortable if the company where you worked had a similar policy?

# The Bottom Line

10. Is looking at the social networking pages of job applicants a fair practice?
    Yes // No     Why?

    Is requiring employees to take drug tests a fair practice?
    Yes // No     Why?

    Is requiring employees to take polygraph exams a fair practice?
    Yes // No     Why?

# Ethics and Discrimination

Discrimination is more than morally wrong—it is illegal. To protect themselves from lawsuits, and to reap the benefits of a diverse workforce, many organizations go beyond minimum legal requirements by creating affirmative action programs and anti-harassment policies. If a company is considering adopting or modifying such policies, what are the most important considerations?

## CHAPTER 7

## Objectives

- Identify key principles of discrimination law and motivations for creating diversity programs.
- Distinguish between different types of sexual harassment cases.

## Key Terms and Concepts

discrimination, p. 103

Civil Rights Act of 1964, p. 103

diversity, p. 103

affirmative action, p. 104

reverse discrimination, p. 104

boycott, p. 105

sexual harassment, p. 106

quid pro quo, p. 106

hostile work environment, p. 106

Business 1 operates a factory with long and physically taxing shifts. It is adding a third shift and will be hiring 100 workers for its assembly line. As the hiring process is about to begin, the production manager makes a statement to the senior human resources team. Business 2 is a gym. The head personal trainer, Ally, is talking to the owner, Maria.

## Business 1

"When you're interviewing, think about whether the applicant will be able to work in a hot factory for an eight-hour shift five days a week. I'm not saying to knock out anyone with a specific disability that can be accommodated. What I'm saying is that if an applicant is, you know, excessively out of shape, then give a harder look at someone else, especially for the assembly line positions. We need to operate at peak capacity if this new shift is going to make money, and we need everyone to work at top speed.

"I'm not talking about someone who is a bit out of shape. Frank here is fine," the production manager says, gesturing to one of the HR people who is overweight but not obese. Some quiet laughs are heard around the table. "Frank plus 100 pounds is not OK. Are we clear?"

## Business 2

"He can bench-press more than anybody on our staff," Ally says.

"That may be so," Maria replies.

"He's really into it, too. He won't have a problem motivating anyone."

"That may also be true, but those aren't the only things to consider."

"If you're worried about him not being able to get through a workout, I think you're wrong," Ally insists. "I worked him out pretty hard, and he kept up fine. We're not hiring cardio people; we're hiring trainers for the weight room."

"I appreciate the fact that he impressed you, Ally. I just think we should pass on him."

"Because of his weight."

"Because of his weight, yes," Maria says. "He's not just a little overweight, Ally. He's at least 100 pounds overweight. He's obese."

"I think that's a little high . . ."

"It's not, and you know it. Look, we have an image to maintain. People pay us a lot of money to work them out, and they expect to be trained by someone who is fit. If our own employees are extremely out of shape, why will our customers expect our services to help them? I'm willing to let it slide a bit on the weight room trainers, but there's a limit. The answer is no. Find somebody else."

"All right, Maria," Ally says.

## {**WHAT** Do You Think?}

1. Is Business 1 doing anything wrong if it refuses to hire obese workers?
2. Is Business 2 doing anything wrong if it refuses to hire obese workers?

# ■ Discrimination

**Discrimination** is the illegal treatment of a person or group based on prejudice. Federal laws protect people from many types of discrimination.

## The Civil Rights Act

The first and most important of the discrimination laws is the **Civil Rights Act of 1964**. This landmark statute prohibits discrimination based on race or color, gender, religious beliefs, and national origin. Before 1964, it was generally legal for private employers to refuse to hire someone for almost any reason at all. The practice was never morally right, but no laws existed that allowed mistreated applicants to sue.

It is illegal to refuse to hire a qualified person based upon any factor covered by the Civil Rights Act. It is important to also note that while the law bans discrimination, it does not generally *require* diversity programs (discussed below).

## Other Laws

Since 1964, the federal government has taken action three times to pass statutes similar to the Civil Rights Act of 1964. Discrimination based on disabilities is illegal—employers must make reasonable accommodations for chronic "impairments" that affect "major life activities." The weight discrimination described in the opening scenario, however, is likely legal. Merely being overweight or obese may not be a sufficiently specific problem to impact a major life activity (such as seeing, hearing, or walking), and even if an overweight applicant qualifies as disabled, hiring the person may not be reasonable for the company for a variety of reasons.

Congress has banned age-related discrimination. Employers cannot discriminate against workers age 40 or over on the basis of age. Congress has also acted to prohibit certain uses of genetic information. An example of an illegal use of genetic information is denying an employee health insurance because of DNA data.

Other types of discrimination are not currently addressed by federal law. Some states and cities go further than the federal government, however, in prohibiting actions and extending protections to additional groups. Local bans on sexual orientation discrimination are fairly common, for example.

## Diversity Programs

Most successful business leaders have come to understand the intrinsic value of **diversity**, or the inclusion in their workforce of people who differ in culture, background, personality, and other ways. In business, diversity goals include recruiting, including, and incorporating people of all types and backgrounds throughout the company. Researchers have consistently found that active diversity programs can help companies attract and retain talented employees, limit the costs associated with lawsuits, motivate employees to be more efficient and creative, open access to new markets, improve customer service and satisfaction, and reduce employee turnover and absenteeism.

The dual goals of increasing diversity and avoiding discrimination lawsuits have led many businesses to embrace **affirmative action**, that is, to take active measures to ensure equal opportunity in hiring and advancement decisions. However, some critics have claimed that, over time, the practices have been extended to the point of creating **reverse discrimination**, the alleged practice of giving jobs and promotions to minority applicants at the expense of better-qualified members of majority groups. The courts have usually, but not always, ruled in support of affirmative action programs when reverse discrimination claims have been made.

## Do the RIGHT THING

Many companies express their commitment to diversity in affirmative action policies. In creating such policies, organizations seek to remind their current employees of the value of a diverse workforce and also to make applicants from all backgrounds feel welcome. Corporate leaders know that if they attract a broad pool of job seekers, they will be able to field the most competitive team possible. If Company A attracts, for example, only male applicants, and Company B attracts male and female applicants, then Company B will have a much higher chance of finding the best employee for each job opening.

American Honda Motor Company has created a typical policy statement. In it, the corporation promises to hire and promote without discriminating and based "solely upon an individual's qualifications and interest." It also promises to refrain from discriminating when making decisions about compensation, layoffs, and eligibility for special programs like tuition assistance for employees who continue with their education.[1]

Are affirmative action policies more important for corporations or universities, or are they of equal importance in both places? Why?

## Equal Opportunity

A cornerstone of contemporary business is the idea that all people should have equal opportunities to get jobs and promotions. U.S. laws and people's shared ethical principles require it. In the real world, however, things are sometimes not so simple.

---

[1]"Affirmative Action Policy Statement," American Honda Motor Company, http://corporate. honda.com/careers/diversity.aspx?id=policies#aaps.

People are still discriminated against in hiring and promotion decisions because of their skin color, nation of origin, gender, religious beliefs, or age or because they have a disability. Some are denied jobs for which they are qualified. Others are hired but paid less than equally qualified coworkers. Some are denied equal opportunities for promotions and advancement in the company. Still others are left unprotected from unfair treatment and abuse by supervisors or fellow employees.

All these practices are illegal, and businesses found to have violated those laws can end up on the wrong end of very expensive lawsuits. While most of the lawsuits are filed and fought by individuals, in some cases, the suits are brought by groups of employees. One grocery store chain was forced to pay more than $80 million to female employees who the court ruled had not been given opportunities equal to those of their male coworkers.

As high as legal costs can be, damage done to a company's public image can be even more expensive. Consumers do not tend to support businesses they believe are discriminatory and unfair. Consumer groups and other special interest groups can organize **boycotts**, or agreements not to buy products or conduct business with certain companies to protest perceived injustices.

The Equal Employment Opportunity Commission (EEOC) is the federal agency responsible for enforcing antidiscrimination laws and investigating allegations of job discrimination. The agency is charged with protecting rights to a fair and nondiscriminatory workplace for all Americans working in all businesses and professions.

## CHECKPOINT 7–1

1. Return to the opening passage. Assess the actions of the two companies.

COMPLETELY UNACCEPTABLE       ENTIRELY REASONABLE

| | | | | | | | |
|---|---|---|---|---|---|---|---|
| Business 1 | 1 | 2 | 3 | 4 | 5 | 6 | 7 |
| Business 2 | 1 | 2 | 3 | 4 | 5 | 6 | 7 |

2. Did you rank one company's actions as more acceptable than the other's? If so, why?

3. Are the actions of the two companies legal?     Yes // No

4. What seven specific types of discrimination are prohibited by federal law?

5. Are diversity programs usually voluntarily created or legally required?

# ■ Sexual Harassment

A common form of employment discrimination is **sexual harassment**, which can involve sexual pressure from supervisors, sexually charged remarks, and other unwelcome behaviors. In the 1980s, the Supreme Court recognized sexual harassment as a form of gender discrimination that violates the Civil Rights Act.

Although the majority of plaintiffs in sexual harassment cases are women, it is important to understand that men can also be sexually harassed. Two specific categories of sexual harassment have been identified and prohibited by the courts.

## Quid Pro Quo Cases

**Quid pro quo** (a Latin phrase meaning "something for something else") harassment refers to situations in which sexual demands are directly tied to a person's keeping his or her job or receiving a promotion or another job benefit. A classic example is a supervisor demanding sexual favors from a subordinate, either by threatening the subordinate's job or by promising a raise or promotion in return.

There is no specific defense in a quid pro quo case. If the plaintiff has the evidence to prove that a claim is true, the company will lose the lawsuit and likely a great deal of money.

## Hostile Work Environment Cases

The other category of sexual harassment is referred to as **hostile work environment**. In these cases, supervisors or coworkers use embarrassment, humiliation, or fear to create a negative climate that interferes with the ability of others to perform their jobs. One company was found liable because loading dock workers posted sexually themed pictures around the workplace to intimidate female employees. Another company was forced to pay damages for not putting a stop to inappropriate jokes and cartoons that were passed around the office. A company may be held liable if an employee can demonstrate that the workplace environment has the effect of interfering unreasonably with his or her work performance or creating a hostile or intimidating workplace that affects the victim's psychological well-being.

Many companies have come to rely on a standard legal defense that the Supreme Court created for hostile work environment cases. If a company has a legitimate sexual harassment policy that encourages complaints to be filed internally, the company legitimately investigates the complaints that are made, and a plaintiff files a complaint with the Equal Employment Opportunity Commission without first following the company's internal policy, then the defense is generally met. In effect, companies can create a "last clear chance" to fix things in-house. It is worth stressing that this defense does not apply to quid pro quo cases.

# Can Companies Go Too Far in Combating Sexual Harassment?

Lawsuits have had a huge effect on sexual harassment in the workplace. Companies have paid millions of dollars in settlements and damages to victims. That has led other companies to invest in increased employee training to prevent future occurrences and limit corporate liability. A strongly worded policy that is vigorously enforced is often enough to change a corporation's culture.

A small, but not trivial, number of companies go even further. "Love contracts," for example, have become standard documents in some businesses. They require two employees who wish to become romantically involved to submit paperwork first. These contracts often require the workers to waive any legal rights to sue the company if their relationship goes wrong or at least to agree to take action against the company only in arbitration and not in court. Some firms have policies that ban supervisors from dating subordinates, but allow other coworkers to date provided both employees sign a similar agreement. Both types of policies are legal, and courts have backed up real companies that have fired workers for violating them.

Love contracts sometimes help a company avoid sexual harassment lawsuits. They can come with costs, however. Professionals, especially new professionals, often spend more waking hours at work than they do anywhere else. The office is a natural place to meet romantic interests. Placing strict prohibitions on dating can lead some workers to find employment elsewhere or simply to ignore the rules. As with any action that seeks to regulate the behavior of employees away from the office, some workers resent what they see as invasions of their personal lives.

Policies that define and discourage sexual harassment directly are always a good idea. Policies that require love contracts require careful deliberation.

## CHECKPOINT 7-2

1. Define hostile work environment sexual harassment in your own words.

2. Define quid pro quo sexual harassment in your own words.

3. Which of the two types of sexual harassment seems more serious? Which do you think is the most common?

4. What should a company do to minimize the likelihood of sexual harassment?

# ETHICS @ WORK

This chapter has examined issues related to workplace discrimination. The following scenario is your chance to apply the ideas to a business situation. Answer the questions that follow the scenario, and be prepared to respectfully argue for your point of view in class.

## Main Issues and Options

**Issues:** Is the kind of company policy described in the scenario appropriate? Is the employee under an obligation to follow the rule?

**Options:** Mike can obey the rule, openly challenge it, or secretly challenge it.

## Workplace Blues

### Lunchroom

A 40-ounce soft drink made Jim's lunch tray difficult to balance, but he did his best as he navigated the cafeteria. He spotted his friend Mike across the room. Actually, he noticed Claire, who was just getting up from a seat next to Mike. Then he noticed Mike. Jim hesitated for a moment, and when he was sure Claire was really leaving, he walked over to Mike's table. When he arrived, Mike didn't notice. He was watching Claire walk away.

"Mike?" No answer. "Mike? Hey, Mikie!" Jim said, raising his voice.

Mike slowly turned his head. After a second, he said lazily, "Oh. Hey, Jimbo. How are ya, buddy?"

"Not as good as you. May I join you, good sir?"

Mike replied with the same mock formality. "By all means, good sir." He gestured to an empty chair with a flourish.

Jim sat down. "Saw you talking to Claire."

"Ah, Claire," Mike said, grinning widely. "I," he said, "just asked her out. We're going to dinner. On Friday. How about that?" he asked, sitting back in his chair and grinning even more widely.

"Ah, that's great, buddy. Except, ah, you know . . ."

"Know what?" Mike looked suspicious. "She's not married or something, is she?"

"No, nothing wrong with Claire. You know, the other thing."

Mike's grin disappeared. "You're killing my buzz, Jimbo. What are you talking about?"

"Have you ever read the employee handbook?"

Mike grimaced. "Why would I read the employee handbook?"

Jim groaned. "Never mind. Short version: your contract says you agree to live by the rules in the employee handbook, and the employee handbook says that you can't date your fellow employees."

"You're a liar."

"No. Haven't you noticed that nobody really dates around here?"

"I don't hang out with anyone around here after work," Mike replied. "Except you. I have no idea who's hooking up around here."

"Well, nobody is—at least not with each other."

"Jim," Mike said, steering the conversation in another direction. "You've seen Claire."

"I have."

"How would you describe her?"

"As a happily married man who is not after her, I believe I can give an unbiased opinion."

"Which is?"

"She's hot."

"That is correct."

"Which doesn't change the fact that your contract . . ."

"Wait," Mike said, holding up a finger. "Let me finish."

"All right, Mike."

"How many hours a week do we work here?"

"I dunno. Fifty-five?"

"Ah," said Mike, "it must be nice to have some seniority, but a new employee like me puts in more like 65 or 70. And Jim, if I'm always here, then where else am I going to meet anyone?"

"Not sure. Bookstore?"

"Yes, yes, everyone knows you met your wife in a bookstore. I can't pull that off, OK? Everyone at the bookstore can tell that I don't read anything."

"So . . . somewhere else."

"No. I'm always here. I need to meet girls *here*. Surely anyone can see that."

"I sympathize with you, but here's another summary for you," Jim replied. "Four years ago, the company loses a big sexual harassment lawsuit and partners freak out. Three and a half years ago, the no-dating policy goes into the employee handbook. Three years ago, a fairly high-level guy and gal both get fired for taking a trip to the Bahamas together. Ever since, no one dates around here."

"That's outrageous!"

"I'm not saying it's a good policy," Jim responded, "but it is the policy."

"But I'm not harassing Claire!" Mike said with exasperation. "She wants to go out with me! If she didn't, I'd leave her alone."

"I know that, but they don't know that. Look, all the executives care about is that they do something to make sure that we don't lose $1.3 million in another sexual harassment lawsuit. The no-dating policy lets them show the board that they've done something. That's it. End of story."

Mike thought for a while. Then he said, "I don't care. I'm going out with her anyway. I'm not doing anything wrong."

"All right. I won't rat you out. But what if you guys get together? How long do you really think you can keep it a secret?"

"I don't know," Mike said, sullen.

"What will you do if you get caught?" Jim prodded.

"I don't know!" Mike was highly irritated now. "Find another job, if it comes to that."

"In this economy?" Mike was silent. Jim waited a moment and then continued. "And what about Claire? Will she find another job, too?"

Mike's expression turned icy. "You know, this is all really easy for a married guy to say."

Jim turned up his palms. "Hey, I'm on your side here. I just want you to think it through, that's all."

"Yeah, all right, I know. It's just that, you know, five minutes ago . . . man, Claire's just terrific. I couldn't believe she wanted to go out with me. Now . . ."

"I know. It's not fair. It's not fair at all."

The two ate in silence for a while. "Maybe I can," Mike said eventually, "ah, you know, talk to somebody in human resources. Explain everything. Maybe they'd give us an exception."

Jim frowned. "Yeah. Or, you could just wear a sign that says, 'I'm planning to violate company policy. Please fire me!'"

"So . . . bad idea."

"Doesn't seem good to me. Not if you want to try to get away with it."

Mike groaned. "So, what, I just tell the hottest girl who's liked me in . . . forever that I'm sorry, but we can't go out after all?"

"Not necessarily," Jim replied. "Look, man, I told you that I'm on your side. Anyway, the lawsuit happened four years ago. Everybody was hypersensitive about it right after it happened, but maybe everyone's kind of forgotten about it by now." Jim took a long sip and finished his soft drink. "Maybe you can keep it a secret. Or maybe Claire will hate you if you take her to dinner, and it will be a moot point."

"Thanks." Becoming less sarcastic, Mike then said, "Actually, thanks. For real. I had no idea about the policy. It's good to at least know about it."

"Yeah," Jim said, nodding. "You're welcome."

Mike looked at his watch. "Oh, man," he moaned. "I've got a meeting in five minutes." He stood, collected his things, and started toward the door. "I'll see you around, Jim, OK?"

"See you around, Mike." Jim pushed his tray away and watched as his friend left the cafeteria. He sighed.

## What Do You Think?

1. If you were in Mike's (or Claire's) position, would you find a way to go out, or would you cancel the date because of the company's policy?

2. If you would keep the date, would you ask the company to make an exception to the rule, or would you try to hide the relationship? If you would break the date, would that impact your ability to do a good job for the company?

3. In your opinion, are no-dating policies for coworkers reasonable? Do you think they make sexual harassment less likely?

4. Suppose you were in Mike and Claire's position, and your company had a policy that allowed employees to date if they signed an agreement not to sue the company if the relationship went wrong. Would you feel comfortable signing? If not, would you break the date, or would you try to hide the date from the company?

5. Assume your next job is with a company that has no policy on dating coworkers. Would you be reluctant to become involved with a coworker? Why or why not?

# Summary

Federal law protects employees from discrimination in hiring, advancement, and pay; unfair treatment; and abuse on the basis of race or color, gender, religious beliefs, national origin, disability, age (over 40), and use of certain genetic information. State and municipal laws frequently ban additional forms of discrimination. Because diversity benefits them, and to avoid discrimination lawsuits, many companies adopt an affirmative action policy.

Sexual harassment is a commonly misunderstood type of discrimination that is prohibited by law. Both quid pro quo and hostile work environment lawsuits can be filed in court. Two common methods that companies use to protect against litigation are employee training and a strongly worded policy that is vigorously enforced. Some companies go to great lengths to try to prevent sexual harassment cases, sometimes arguably go too far. So-called love contracts are an example.

# Key Terms and Concepts

**Match each definition with a key term or concept.**

_____ 1. The inclusion in a company workforce of people who differ in culture, background, personality, and other ways

_____ 2. A group agreement not to buy products or conduct business with a certain company to protest a perceived injustice

_____ 3. The alleged practice of giving jobs and promotions to minority applicants at the expense of better-qualified members of majority groups

_____ 4. The practice of taking active measures to ensure equal opportunity in hiring and advancement decisions

_____ 5. A type of harassment in which supervisors or coworkers use embarrassment, humiliation, or fear to create a negative climate that interferes with the ability of others to perform their jobs

_____ 6. A type of harassment in which sexual demands are directly tied to a person's keeping his or her job or receiving a promotion or another job benefit

_____ 7. Illegal treatment of a person or group based on prejudice

_____ 8. Unwelcome physical or verbal behavior directed at employees because of their sex

_____ 9. The most important federal law that addresses discrimination

a. affirmative action

b. boycott

c. Civil Rights Act of 1964

d. discrimination

e. diversity

f. hostile work environment

g. quid pro quo

h. reverse discrimination

i. sexual harassment

# Review

1. Which of the following types of discrimination is prohibited by the Civil Rights Act of 1964?

   a. race discrimination

   b. disability discrimination

   c. discrimination based on obesity

   d. both A and B

2. Which of the following types of discrimination is prohibited as a result of later laws?

   a. gender discrimination

   b. discrimination based on religious beliefs

   c. disability discrimination

   d. all of the above

3. Research shows that diversity programs can

   a. help companies retain quality workers.

   b. open access to new markets.

   c. improve customer satisfaction.

   d. all of the above

4. Which federal agency enforces antidiscrimination laws and investigates allegations of job discrimination?

5. At a company, employees tell off-color jokes and hang sexually suggestive posters in the break room even though some employees have reported being offended. This amounts to _____ sexual harassment.

   a. quid pro quo

   b. hostile work environment

   c. both A and B

   d. neither of the above

6. A supervisor implies that an employee has a better chance at a promotion if the employee will go out on a date with him. This amounts to _____ sexual harassment.

   a. quid pro quo

   b. hostile work environment

   c. both A and B

   d. neither of the above

# Critical Thinking

7. Julie works in the human resources department of a small business that manufactures specialty parts for bicycles. Business has been good lately, and the company is hiring more assembly line employees. Julie's close friend Bandu is out of work and is looking for a job. Julie suggests that Bandu apply at her company. "I know the owner and can put in a good word for you," she tells him.

    When Bandu's application comes through, Julie checks it over and sends it to the owner. The next day it is returned to her marked "Rejected." When Julie asks why, the owner seems uneasy. "What I'm about to tell you is confidential," he warns her. "This is a small company. We seem to be more comfortable and productive when we don't have too much diversity. That's been our policy in the past, and I don't see any point in changing things now."

    Although he has lived in America for several years, Bandu was born in India. Julie knows he is talented, smart, and hard-working. As Julie looks around the company, it dawns on her that there aren't many employees who are members of a racial or ethnic minority group.

    Has the owner of the bicycle company done something illegal, unethical, or both? Why?

# Applications

8. You work at a retail store in the mall. Your good friend Karen works there, too. Lately she has seemed unhappy and uneasy and has been missing work more than usual. You have tried to be supportive without being nosy, but it's obvious something is bothering her. One day at lunch, she breaks down and tells you that the store manager has been asking her to come to his apartment after work. Her family is going through a tough time financially, and they are depending on the money Karen earns. She makes you promise not to tell anyone. "The manager's just a creep," she tells you. "I won't give in to him, but I'm not going to quit because of him."

    What type of sexual harassment does Karen seem to be describing? Does she seem to have a good case? If she decides to go forward with legal action, what should she do first?

9. The Civil Rights Act of 1964 was passed to protect the rights of minority groups. Interestingly, if a law banning weight discrimination passed, it would protect a significant *majority* of people—about two-thirds of Americans meet the medical definition for being either overweight or obese.[2] Would you favor such a law? Why or why not?

# Digging Deeper

10. Go online and find an example of a corporate diversity policy. Now, draft a diversity policy of your own for an ideal company. What are its goals? How will it operate? Is it similar to the real policy you found online?

# The Bottom Line

11. Current federal law prohibits discrimination based on race, religion, gender (including sexual harassment), national origin, disability, age, and genetic information. Should the law go further and ban more types of discrimination, or is the current state of discrimination law about right? Why?

[2]"Obesity and Overweight," FastStats, Centers for Disease Control and Prevention, last updated June 18, 2010, http://www.cdc.gov/nchs/fastats/overwt.htm.

# Ethics for Employees

The last two chapters examined the treatment of employees by companies. This chapter looks at ethical obligations that workers owe their employers.

## CHAPTER 8

## Objectives

- Identify and explain common ethical misdeeds by employees.
- Define character traits of top employees.

## Key Terms and Concepts

honesty, p. 120

respect, p. 121

integrity, p. 122

industriousness, p. 122

loyalty, p. 122

whistle-blowing, p. 123

Moira recently graduated from college and landed her first corporate job. She works as an administrative assistant for a company that manufactures home decorations. On the job only four months, Moira is already starting to lose her idealism. She has heard of many instances of employee theft at her company and has even witnessed a couple of occurrences. She has observed employees coming to work intoxicated—even sneaking drinks at work. She has seen employees routinely arrive late for work and sneak out early. Fifteen-minute breaks and thirty-minute lunches often end up lasting twice as long. Employees routinely use their computers for sending and receiving personal e-mails, shopping online, checking horoscopes and the weather, even gambling—and all that is happening in just her department!

The department manager is very laid-back. Moira has tried to talk with him about the problems, but he seems unable or unwilling to confront them. It appears to Moira that he wants the employees to like him and that they are taking advantage of that. Moira is growing more and more frustrated. She prides herself on being a dependable, hard worker, and she took this job assuming that the other employees would be that way, too.

Moira is tempted to give up and join the other employees in getting paid for doing as little as possible, but she knows she wouldn't respect herself. She has considered going over her manager's head to his supervisor and reporting the problems, but that would almost certainly alienate her supervisor and the other employees. She has not been at the company long enough to request a transfer, and quitting her job after four months doesn't seem like a wise career move. She is sitting at her desk one afternoon, wondering what she should do.

## {WHAT Do You Think?}

1. If Moira came to you as a friend, what would you suggest she do? Why?
2. Would you seek to make others better employees? If so, how?

# ■ Ethical Violations by Employees

Ethics is a growing concern in today's workplace. Executives and managers in corporations across the country are emphasizing the need for their workers to be ethical people. Many businesses in the United States, from small companies to large corporations, have a code of ethics that workers are expected to follow. Many companies are also investing in resources such as ethics training programs and ethics hotlines to give employees guidance when facing tough decisions in their jobs. Why are businesses going to this much trouble?

One reason is that many businesses have found that unethical actions by employees can be expensive. U.S. companies lose billions of dollars in profits each year due to actions such as employee theft, abuse of sick time, and drug and alcohol abuse in the workplace. In addition, corporations are often held legally responsible for the actions of their employees. This means that companies can be sued when their employees behave badly in ways that harm others.

## Employee Theft

Each year, employee theft costs the average U.S. retail store more money than shoplifting does. An annual survey of retailers by the National Retail Federation found that in 2009, for example, U.S. employees stole $14.4 billion from their employers.[1] Employees have easy access to merchandise. They know more about store security procedures and ways to evade them. Employees may frequently be left unsupervised in a store, while customers rarely are.

In addition to merchandise, workers have been known to steal office supplies, equipment, cash, phones, computers, and even company vehicles. Employees who get caught usually face company discipline. Many people have lost their jobs (and even their careers) because they gave in to the temptation to take something that did not belong to them.

## Wasted Time

Over the past several years, surveys have found that the typical American worker spends a substantial amount of time each workweek intentionally doing nothing productive. A recent review of several studies showed that employees with PCs spent about five hours a week on their work computers doing personal business on the Web.[2] This didn't include time devoted to other nonproductive activities, such as personal phone calls, text messaging, and socializing with coworkers. At minimum, employees wasted almost an entire day each week. The practice can be viewed as another form of employee theft.

---

[1]Kathy Grannis, "Retail Fraud, Shoplifting Rates Decrease, According to National Retail Security Survey," National Retail Federation, June 15, 2010, http://www.nrf.com/modules.php?name=News&op=viewlive&sp_id=945.

[2]"The Top Ten Ways Workers Waste Time Online," 24/7 Wall St., Sept. 30, 2010, http://247wallst.com/2010/09/30/the-top-ten-ways-workers-waste-time-online.

How would you feel about the wasted time if you owned a business? Wouldn't you do everything you could to make sure your employees worked hard and remained productive? It has become routine for companies to monitor telephone calls their employees have with customers. Courts have ruled that phones, computers, and e-mails belong to the company, not the employee, so businesses are reading employee e-mails and monitoring the Web sites workers access. Some businesses even monitor computer keystrokes to measure worker productivity, allowing occasional timed breaks to go to the restroom. While the desire to maintain a high level of productivity is understandable, employee advocates have criticized some practices as extreme and dehumanizing.

## Misuse of Technology

A growing problem in the workplace is the misuse of computers, copiers, phones, and other equipment. One reason that many companies monitor employee phone calls is that too many employees make lengthy personal calls at work. Businesses complain that workers are using company copy machines for large personal copying projects in order to save ink on their home copiers.

Many companies describe their biggest problem as the misuse of company computers. In Chapter 2, you learned that one of the top online shopping days of the year is the Monday after Thanksgiving. In 2010, nearly half of the more than $1 billion in online sales generated that day came from Web sites visited on office computers.[3] Online shopping is far from the only culprit. Doing personal searches, writing personal e-mail, chatting, perusing online news sites, streaming sports broadcasts, and playing online games such as fantasy football are also common ways to pass the time at the office.

The growing use of social networking sites at work creates additional difficulties for employers. Several studies over the past few years have shown that a significant percentage of employees, nearly a quarter or more, visit social networking sites during work hours. A 2010 survey of more than 500 organizations found that nearly three-quarters "are concerned that employee behavior on social networking sites exposes their businesses to danger, and puts corporate infrastructure—and the sensitive data stored upon it—at risk."[4]

Online gambling is also a rapidly increasing phenomenon. For some people, the convenient access leads to addictive gambling, and they take the addiction with them to work. An even bigger problem for employers is online pornography. A survey by the Nielsen Company found that during one recent month, more than 21 million Americans—29 percent of working adults—accessed adult Web sites on work computers.[5] In addition to lost

[3]Nicholas Kolakowski, "Cyber Monday Spending Rose in 2010: ComScore," eWeek.com, Dec. 1, 2010, http://www.eweek.com/c/a/Desktops-and-Notebooks/Cyber-Monday-Spending-Rose-in-2010-ComScore-130227/.

[4]"Malware and Spam Rise 70% on Social Networks, Security Report Reveals," Sophos, Feb. 1, 2010, http://www.sophos.com/pressoffice/news/articles/2010/02/security-report-2010.html.

[5]Brian Montpoli (posted), "29% Accessed Porn on Work Computers Last Month," CBS News, April 23, 2010, http://www.cbsnews.com/8301-503544_162-20003319-503544.html.

productivity, employees visiting sexually explicit Web sites may create conditions that can lead to sexual harassment lawsuits.

## Disclosure of Confidential Information

Many companies don't manufacture anything. Virtually all their value is in the form of information, and information can be easy to lose.

Sometimes, the most costly employee lapse can be a failure to protect confidential information. A single inadvertently disclosed file can be far more expensive than the theft of everything in the petty cash drawer or the office supply closet. Many companies are in a constant race with competitors to secure patents or develop software. In a recent survey of more than 1,000 businesses in the United States and the United Kingdom, 12 percent of respondents reported that sensitive company information had been disclosed through employee use of social networking sites alone.[6]

Many other companies have legal obligations to keep customers' financial, medical, or educational data secure. Failures to protect the information can lead to costly lawsuits. Be sure to make yourself aware of your company's policies for handling confidential data.

While problems of employee misconduct are serious and more common than they should be, it is important to keep in mind that most workers are good, honest people. Most employees don't steal. They give an honest day's work, and they don't abuse drugs or alcohol. They treat their supervisors and coworkers with respect. Most companies are not overly concerned with some level of personal activity at the office, so long as employees are productive. The key is knowing your company's policies and abiding by them.

---

## CHECKPOINT 8–1

1. In your own words, explain what main issues are involved in the following employee misdeeds and why those issues are important to employers.

employee theft

wasted time

misuse of technology

disclosure of confidential information

---

[6]"Webroot Research Shows Half of SMBs Block Employee Access to Facebook," November 15, 2010, Webroot, http://pr.webroot.com/web-security/ent/research-shows-half-of-smbs-block-employee-access-to-facebook-111510.html.

2. Which of the ethical lapses described in this section have you engaged in yourself? Do you feel guilty about your actions?

3. Which of the ethical lapses described in this section have you seen others engage in most frequently?

# ■ Character Traits of Excellent Employees

You may remember from Chapter 2 that an *ethical virtue* is a character trait of a good person or a good life. Examples include honesty, generosity, caring for others, and courage. Business leaders look for those same character traits when making hiring and promotion decisions. Employees who consistently exhibit such qualities are often rewarded with increased responsibilities, promotions, opportunities, and raises. On the other hand, workers who lack those virtues may find themselves being disciplined or even fired, and they may spend their careers wondering why they can't seem to get ahead at work.

## Honesty

The core of personal ethics is **honesty**. People who are consistently honest are perceived as being trustworthy. Others recognize that these people can be counted on—that they can be entrusted with sensitive information. What is honesty? The best definition may come from the courts—"to tell the truth, the whole truth, and nothing but the truth." Interestingly, those three parts of the traditional legal oath are not quite the same and are perceived in different ways.

The honesty violations that are generally perceived as being most serious are related to the phrase *nothing but the truth*. People often refer to that kind of violation as *lying*. That means a person says that something is or was when, in fact, it is not or was not. An employee injured in a fall at home lies, claiming the accident occurred on the job, in the hope of getting better medical coverage or filing a fraudulent lawsuit. A manager tells slanderous lies about an employee to get that person fired so the job can go to the manager's friend. The consequences of that type of lying are usually severe because most people view that level of dishonesty as especially egregious.

The middle level of dishonesty concerns the phrase *to tell the truth*. These violations often involve a person not reporting something that he or she has an obligation to report. An employee becomes aware that the company is disposing of toxic wastes dangerously and illegally, but she doesn't disclose that information to anyone. A worker sees another employee being bullied and abused by a supervisor, but he keeps that knowledge to himself.

The level of dishonesty generally considered to be the least serious involves the third part of the oath, telling *the whole truth*. These violations are about not being forthcoming, about demonstrating a lack of openness. A police officer catches you speeding and pulls you over. When she tells you that she clocked you at 20 miles per hour over the speed limit, would you add that you also ran a red light? Should you? A coworker asks if you like his very expensive new suit. You reply honestly that you do, but should you also mention that the suit fits as though it is a size too small?

## Respect

**Respect** is consideration and appreciation for others. It means showing proper deference to a supervisor and consideration for coworkers and customers. Respectful people do not treat others abusively, dishonestly, rudely, or manipulatively. Being respectful means treating people as persons, not as tools, problems, or obstacles.

Being respectful also requires appreciating workers from different backgrounds. The workforce is continuously becoming more diverse, including more older workers and more members of minority groups. The U.S. Bureau of Labor Statistics predicts that by 2018, nearly one-quarter of the labor force will be age 55 or older. Hispanics will make up 17.6 percent, African Americans 12.1 percent, and Asians 5.6 percent.[7] Besides this general growing diversity, active diversity programs bring a high degree of diversity to many companies' staffs. An increasingly diverse U.S. population and globalization connect more employees with customers and business associates from other cultures.

Someone once said that respect is best demonstrated by how you treat people who you don't think can help you. It is natural, even clever, to act respectfully toward a supervisor who has the authority to fire or promote. But how many people go out of their way to act respectfully toward people who are lower on the corporate ladder?

## Do the RIGHT THING

Legendary businessman Sam Walton founded Walmart, the highly successful chain of discount retail stores that revolutionized American business and made him one of the wealthiest people in the world. Walton possessed many character traits that led to his success, but few traits endeared him to his workers as much as the respect with which he treated them. Walton often traveled from store to store, encouraging his employees, and it was said that he knew the names of all of his store managers, as well as the names of their spouses! Imagine a person that busy taking the time to learn the names of the people who work for him. That appreciation and respect for others was an important part of Walton's success.

Is there another company you are aware of (or that you have worked for) that strives to treat workers with respect?

[7]"Employment Projections: 2008–2018 Summary," Bureau of Labor Statistics, Dec. 10, 2009, http://www.bls.gov/news.release/ecopro.nr0.htm.

## Integrity

**Integrity** is faithful adherence to a strict personal ethical code. Integrity implies consistency. It means being the same good person through and through. It means sticking to the truth and sticking up for one's principles no matter what the consequences. On the other hand, if you have ever known anyone who seemed to be a different person when someone else was around, then you know what integrity is not.

Integrity sometimes has to be its own reward, for it is not always rewarded by others. Pressures from peers, coworkers, and supervisors to take the easier path can often be very strong. The consequences of that easier path may seem better, at least in the short term. People of integrity see a bigger picture, however, and have the strength of character to shrug off such distractions and to continue to stand up for what is right, true, fair, and just.

Not all employers seek employees who display honesty and integrity. Some managers and administrators, perhaps motivated by greed and short-term thinking, are less than ethical themselves and may prefer the same in their employees. That is one reason why employees should be just as selective about whom they choose to work for as employers are about whom they hire. Few workplace situations are as miserable as being a person of integrity trying to succeed in a dishonest company.

## Industriousness

To be **industrious** is to consistently demonstrate perseverance and hard work. If employers have an obligation to give a full day's pay for a day's work, then employees have the corresponding obligation to give a full day's work for a day's pay. Top workers demonstrate personal initiative, doing more than expected and looking for opportunities to do more.

This character trait requires a great deal of maturity and the wisdom to think long-term. It is not easy to keep working hard when others are doing much less—and may be getting paid the same or even more. For that reason, the workplace can sometimes seem unfair to industrious people, at least in the short term.

In the long term, though, the rewards of industriousness can be great. Hard work and dedication get noticed. Since those qualities are not as common as managers would like, industrious employees tend to become very valuable to their employers. There is an old saying that the cream always rises to the top, and industrious employees are often the first to be considered for new opportunities and promotions.

Sloth makes all things difficult, but industry, all things easy.

—BENJAMIN FRANKLIN

## Loyalty

**Loyalty** means faithful allegiance to a person, an organization, a cause, or an idea. Some people are loyal to their friends or family members. Some are loyal to their schools or teammates. Some demonstrate loyalty through devotion to their religious faith, country, or ethical principles. In the context discussed here, loyalty extends to a company or an employer.

This character trait of excellent employees is not a blind loyalty that ignores or covers up wrongdoing. It is not unquestioned allegiance to co-workers, a supervisor, or even a company president. This ethical virtue is not a matter of "my company, right or wrong." The loyalty is not to people, but to the highest values and principles of the organization.

## Do the **RIGHT THING**

Occasionally, workers find out that their coworkers or employers are acting unethically and even illegally. Those employees then face the difficult decision of whether to blow the whistle. **Whistle-blowing** is the act of reporting unethical or illegal actions by one's superiors or peers to authorities or the media. Blowing the whistle on one's own company requires a great deal of courage. Whistle-blowers are some-times viewed as traitors by their employers and coworkers. They are often punished or fired, even though state and federal laws protect whistle-blowers from retaliation.

Whistle-blowing cases can be difficult to resolve. Businesses often deny the charges made by whistle-blowers. The public is left unsure of whom to believe. After all, not all charges made by whistle-blowers are true. There have been cases in which angry employees made false alle-gations to embarrass their companies. Sometimes whistle-blowers sim-ply get the facts wrong and make inaccurate assumptions. However, in many cases, whistle-blowers' charges have proven to be correct.

Actions by whistle-blowers can force businesses to change their policies, admitting their actions were, in fact, unethical or illegal. Whistle-blowers have saved lives by revealing dangerous products. They have saved taxpayers billions of dollars by speaking out against corrupt practices between businesses and government agencies. They have brought wrongdoers to justice by courageously testifying against their own companies in courtrooms. Are those results worth risking one's job for? Many whistle-blowers think so.

1. Would you "blow the whistle" on illegal activity in your own company?


2. Do you think most people would?


There are many ways of developing ethical virtues and becoming a good person and employee. One of the most successful and reliable was explained by Aristotle (Chapter 2). A dishonest person can become an honest person by being honest just one time when it isn't easy to do so. The person must then commit to doing it again—and then again and again. Over time, honesty will become a habit. Once ingrained as a habit, honesty becomes part of an individual's character, of his or her personal identity. This process can work for all ethical virtues. It means deciding what kind of person you want to be and then acting that way until you're there. Like other kinds of change, it requires being patient with yourself when you experience setbacks. The only failure is to quit trying.

## CHECKPOINT 8-2

1. Explain what each of these employee virtues means to you.

   honesty

   respect

   integrity

   industriousness

   loyalty

2. Reconsider Moira's story at the beginning of the chapter. Assume you are hired to replace the current ineffective department manager. What three steps could you implement to improve the efficiency and morale of the department?

3. Which employee virtue do you see as your biggest strength? Which do you see as your biggest weakness? Explain how you could turn the weakness into another area of personal strength.

# ETHICS @ WORK

This chapter has presented both shortcomings of many employees and goals to which workers can aspire. The following scenario is your chance to apply the ideas to a business situation. Answer the questions that follow the scenario, and be prepared to respectfully argue for your point of view in class.

## Main Issues and Options

**Issues:** Is the company policy reasonable? Should the workers be disciplined for violating it?

**Options:** The manager is legally free to retain the workers, fire them, or assess any penalty he wishes.

## Don't Be a Hero

### Grocery Store Management Office—First Case

The store director pushed "play" on the console in front of him. The screen showed sharp black-and-white images of the home and garden department. "Here you are, correct?" he said as he gestured to an image of a man in a dark apron.

"Yes, sir," Hank replied. He looked nervous.

"The security guys spliced this together for me—they used footage from two different cameras. I just want you to talk me through how things seemed to you at the time."

"Yes, sir." On the screen, a man in a hooded sweatshirt approached a woman from behind, looked over her shoulder, and grabbed at the woman's purse. The strap caught on her arm, and the man pushed her to the ground and ripped the bag from her shoulder. "I was restocking the potting soil, and I heard a woman start screaming. I looked around and I saw this guy standing over her and yanking at her purse; it looked as if he was hurting her. So I dropped everything and started heading over there and shouting at the guy. He finally got her purse and took off." On the screen, the man ran out of the frame.

"And you took off after him?"

"Ah, yes, sir."

"Why didn't you stay with the customer? See if she was OK?"

"She was yelling, 'He stole my purse! Stop him! Stop him!' and she looked OK to me. It just happened so fast. I guess I just followed her orders."

"He could have been armed."

"Well, I guess so. It was kind of just instinct to try to help."

"OK, so then what happened?" The screen went blank for a moment and then shifted perspectives to show an image of the store's parking lot, shot from a new camera.

"Well, he took off out the side door, and I followed him out into the parking lot and shouted for him to stop. I ran halfway through the parking lot, but, ah, he was pretty fast, and I knew after a while that I couldn't catch him." The security tape confirmed Hank's story.

"And then?"

"Well, I went back to make sure the customer was OK, and then I helped her call the police. The cops asked me a lot of questions—helped me remember what I saw, you know? When I was chasing the guy, I got close enough to notice that he was wearing Levi's and that he had white Reebok shoes with a scuff mark on the left heel. They seemed glad to have that information."

The store director made notes as Hank talked. "Hank," he said, "you know we have a strict policy against doing this kind of thing, right? It's in the employee handbook, and it was part of your training, correct?"

"Ah," Hank looked even more nervous, "yes, sir. I just . . . I didn't have time to think of that. I mean, I was just minding my own business, and then . . ." Hank spread his hands. "It just happened so fast."

"What was your plan? If you caught up to him?"

"Well," Hank considered the question for a moment, "I mean, for sure I was going to get the lady's purse back." He shrugged his shoulders slightly. "I guess, ah . . . I hadn't really thought about it after that."

"OK, Hank."

## Grocery Store Management Office—Second Case

A week later, the store director rolled a new spliced-together video for another employee. "This is you?" he asked as he pointed to an image of an employee in the electronics department.

"Yes, it is," Blake answered.

"OK. This tape will show the incident from different angles. Just talk me through how things looked through your eyes."

"Will do. So this dude here," Blake said, pointing to the screen, "I'd seen him around before." Blake shook his head. "Never bought anything, just spent a lot of time looking at the iPads."

"OK."

"So the day all this happened, he comes in wearing a coat, and man, it was like 75 degrees that day. So I kept an eye on him."

"Did you notify Security?"

Blake rolled his eyes. "No offense, sir, but those guys are the laziest guys in the store. I mean, I didn't even bother, because I *have* called them before, and they never even show up for like an hour, and then they fill out a form, and that's it."

"OK." The screen showed the man in the jacket walk rapidly to the Apple display and then pull something from his pocket.

"So I notice that he's got something—looks like wire cutters to me—and sure enough, that's what he has! He cuts through the cable holding the iPad demo and slides the whole thing under his jacket." The surveillance tape clearly showed the theft.

"I walk over to him and say, 'Hey!' and he tries to take off." The tape now showed the shoplifter take three rapid steps away. "So then I tackled him."

The screen showed Blake making a nice clean takedown. When he saw the image, Blake smiled in spite of himself.

The store director noticed. "You seem amused," he said.

Blake's grin vanished but then returned. "Well, come on, it was a pretty good tackle."

"Hmph. So go on with the story."

"Well, as the tape shows, I just kind of sat on him. He struggled at first, but then he mostly gave up. Somebody must have called Security, and eventually the guys actually did show up, and they took him away."

Blake waited for the store director to say something. When he didn't, Blake added, "I got the iPad back, and it still worked! I ran a new cable through it, and it's still our demo."

"Yes. Blake, do you know how much an iPad costs us?"

"Ah, I don't know. We sell them for $499, so maybe $399?"

"That's about right. Do you know what a single lawsuit costs us? If a customer had been hurt in this scuffle, or if this guy sues us for false imprisonment?"

"It wasn't false anything! You saw him steal from us right on the tape!"

"That's not the point. A single lawsuit costs us tens of thousands of dollars in legal fees. More if we lose a case and have to pay a judgment."

Blake thought about that for a moment. "OK, but how much do we lose to shoplifting in a year?"

"That doesn't matter."

Blake pressed him. "Would you say it's more than $50,000?"

"Well, perhaps so . . ."

"I heard it's more like $500 a day. Maybe a couple hundred grand a year."

"That might be accurate."

"Sir, if more people acted the way I did, you'd have a whole lot less shoplifting."

## What Do You Think?

1. Rate the degree to which you find "don't be a hero" policies sensible in the following types of businesses.

COMPLETELY REASONABLE  COMPLETELY UNREASONABLE

| | | | | | | |
|---|---|---|---|---|---|---|
| bank | 1 | 2 | 3 | 4 | 5 | 6 | 7 |
| liquor store | 1 | 2 | 3 | 4 | 5 | 6 | 7 |
| grocery store | 1 | 2 | 3 | 4 | 5 | 6 | 7 |

2. Do you agree with this general criticism of "don't be a hero" policies?

*If robbers and shoplifters expected to be confronted by clerks, and perhaps by armed clerks, then there would be far fewer robbers and shoplifters.*

3. Should Hank be fired, disciplined without being fired, or commended? Should Blake be fired, disciplined without being fired, or commended?

4. If you had been shopping at the store when the incidents presented in the scenario unfolded, would you have wanted the clerks to act as they did, or would you have preferred them to do nothing?

5. Assume Hank and Blake are fired. If you saw a news report of the incidents and the firings, would you be angry at the store in either case? If you were a regular customer, would you be less likely to shop there?

# Summary

Employers are increasingly concerned about the ethics of their employees, partly because unethical actions by workers can be costly. Common ethical violations by workers include employee theft, wasted time, and misuse of company technology, especially computers. Employees who are guilty of those offenses often find the consequences to be very serious, including the loss of jobs and even careers.

Character traits of top employees include honesty, respect, integrity, industriousness, and loyalty. Employees exemplifying those qualities are often rewarded with increased responsibilities, promotions, opportunities, and better pay.

# Key Terms and Concepts

**Match each definition with a key term or concept.**

a. honesty

b. industriousness

c. integrity

d. loyalty

e. respect

f. whistle-blowing

_____ 1. The act of reporting unethical or illegal actions by one's superiors or peers to authorities or the media

_____ 2. The character trait of consistently demonstrating perseverance and hard work

_____ 3. The character trait of consistently telling the truth, the whole truth, and nothing but the truth

_____ 4. The character trait of maintaining adherence to a strict personal ethical code

_____ 5. The character trait of maintaining allegiance to a person, an organization, a cause, or an idea

_____ 6. The character trait of showing consideration and appreciation for others

# Review

1. True or false: For most U.S. retail stores, losses from employee theft exceed those from shoplifting.

2. List three examples of ways that employees waste time.

3. List three examples of ways that employees misuse office technology.

4. True or false: Breaches of confidentiality are usually deliberate.

5. Give a work-related example of each of the five ethical virtues described in the chapter.

# Critical Thinking

6. Zeke works for a large carpet-cleaning company. He and his partner, Estela, are dispatched by the company to businesses and residences. Zeke and Estela take a lot of pride in their work and professionalism. Customer evaluations score them very high in efficiency, quality of work, and courtesy. Even the pay is good. Their problem is with their supervisor.

   While Ms. Patterson treats Zeke well enough, she is consistently hostile and abusive toward Estela. The supervisor belittles and yells at Estela in front of other employees and customers. She has used words such as *stupid* and *useless* when talking about Estela to others. No matter what Estela does, she can't please Ms. Patterson.

   Zeke considers Estela a friend, and it's hard for him to watch her being mistreated. He tried to talk with Ms. Patterson once about the issue. "This is between me and Estela," she warned. "Unless you want to get on my bad list, too, you'd better mind your own business."

   Zeke is considering going over Ms. Patterson to report the matter to the vice president, but he isn't sure that would do any good, and it would probably make matters worse for him. Estela has talked many times about quitting, but she doesn't want to give Ms. Patterson the satisfaction.

   What should Zeke do?

# Applications

7. You are a supervisor managing seven employees. Layoffs are coming, and you must decide which employees to cut first. Rank the following employees from 1 (most valuable) to 7 (least valuable).

_____ Kia is talented and energetic, but uses crude and offensive language. Coworkers and customers have complained.

_____ Sam works hard, but has been caught taking office supplies and company products for personal use.

_____ Sumiko is one of the most honest people you've ever known, though not terribly talented. You have never known her to lie. You would trust her with your personal bank account number, but not with your most important sales account.

_____ Mantero is a follower. When others are working hard and being productive, he is doing the same. When others are wasting time or engaging in unethical conduct, though, Mantero joins in.

_____ Ana is an average worker with a lot of potential, but rarely seems to have much motivation. Although very smart and good with people, she is frequently late and has the most absences in your department.

_____ Patrick makes friends easily with coworkers and customers, but has a serious drinking problem.

_____ Maggie never seems to make a mistake. Reports and documents are painstakingly written and errorless. However, you recently caught her gambling online using a company computer.

8. Imagine you are ready to invest a lot of money to start your own business. You plan to hire five employees to help get the company off the ground. You know that your success or failure will depend, as much as anything else, on the quality of their work. First, list character traits you would want in these people. Then list traits you would consider unacceptable.

preferred traits

unacceptable traits

# Digging Deeper

9. Interview a business owner or executive in person, by phone, or by e-mail about employee ethical misdeeds. What types of employee behavior present the biggest problems? What consequences do those employees face?

# The Bottom Line

10. What is the most important characteristic of a good employee? What is the worst habit of a bad employee? Why?

# Ethical Lending and the "Great Recession"

At the time of this writing, the economy was in bad shape.
Lending practices contributed mightily to the downturn. Lenders
are entitled to make a profit, but when do they go too far?

## CHAPTER 9

## Objectives

- Identify key issues to consider when making loans.
- Discuss several specific ethical issues surrounding foreclosures.
- Apply universal ethical principles to financial issues.

## Key Terms and Concepts

usury, p. 134

usury law, p. 134

payday loan, p. 135

mortgage, p. 136

foreclosure, p. 136

deficiency judgment, p. 136

negative equity, p. 137

strategic default, p. 138

The company that Eric works for issues credit cards to millions of customers. Recently, it has been struggling. Eric's supervisor has charged him with finding ways to cut losses for the company and to create new sources of revenue. Eric spends the next two weeks doing research and analysis. At the end of that time, he tells his supervisor that he thinks he's found some answers. His supervisor listens and then arranges for Eric to present his ideas to the CEO, COO, and top management at a meeting.

"The obvious thing we can do is raise our interest rates and fees. Everybody else's are higher than ours, so we won't lose many customers if we do. Right now, our customers usually pay 15 percent interest. We can raise that to as high as 22 percent without a significant loss of customers, I think.

"To really turn things around, though, we have to do more. We have to figure out which of our customers are likely never to pay us back, and we have to stop lending them money. The thing is, we don't know who those customers are until they miss payments, go over their limits, or declare bankruptcy. By then it's too late. We have to better predict who is likely to be a problem for us before those people start missing payments.

"I've been analyzing mountains of data, and there are definitely patterns. For example, if you live in a zip code with a lot of home foreclosures, you are much more likely to default on a credit card in the next five years. The same is true if you spend a lot of money on clothes and electronics at high-end stores, and it's especially true if you work in an industry that has had a lot of layoffs lately.

"If we take all our customers in those groups—'high-foreclosure neighborhood,' 'big luxury spender,' and 'at-risk industry'—and if we cut their credit limit on our cards from, say, an average of $5,000 each to an average of $3,000

each, we cut losses. When they default on their debts, we lose less.

"The problem is that a whole lot of people in each group haven't done anything wrong. Most of them won't be laid off. Most of them will never default on their cards. They just happen to be in a demographic that has a larger-than-average number of people who will spend our money and never pay it back. If we go with this plan, though, everybody gets the same notice in the mail: 'Sorry, but your credit limit has been reduced.' When we reduce somebody's credit limit, that person's credit score goes down. It doesn't matter why we did it; the score drops just the same. That also means that, in addition to having less of a credit line from us, that person will have a harder time getting a new one from anybody else.

"OK, so credit cards aside, we need to consider going in new directions. Our infrastructure makes it fairly cheap for us to expand into other types of lending. I think we could make a fortune in payday loans.

"They're much riskier than our credit card operations. Tons more defaults. Since they are short-term loans, though, they are usually exempt from state laws that cap the interest rates we can charge on them. We can go as high as a $20 or $25 fee on a $100, two-week loan. That's on the order of a 500 percent return, so even if we have a staggering number of customers who never pay us back, so what? I think that payday loans alone could move us back to being profitable at least a year ahead of schedule, maybe more.

"Payday loans are controversial. Critics say they amount to usury. Still, if you have no money, you need money, and you can't get it anywhere else, then who's to say you shouldn't get a payday loan? If our customers are adults, and if the fees are worth it to them, I don't see the problem. Payday loans are a legal service, and many others offer them and profit from them."

# {**WHAT** Do You Think?}

1. Do you favor Eric's company raising the standard interest rates and fees on its credit cards? Why or why not?
2. Do you favor lowering credit limits for customers in "at-risk" demographics? Is there any difference between lowering the credit limit for someone whose personal behavior has placed him or her in an at-risk demographic and someone who is there for another reason? For example, is it fairer to cut the limit for somebody who buys a lot of luxury items than it is for somebody who is in a profession that has laid off a large number of workers recently?
3. Should Eric's company get into the payday loan business? Why or why not?

# ■ Ethical Issues in Lending

Access to loans can help people improve the quality of their lives and can help companies prosper and flourish. However, unethical actions on the part of financial professionals may result in serious harm to individuals, communities, and businesses.

## Banking

Some people think of banks primarily in terms of savings and checking accounts. Customers put their money in the bank, collect a little interest on it, and take the money out when they need it. However, there has been a revolution in banking practices and services over the past few decades. Contemporary banking is more about loans and credit cards.

The ability to borrow money allows people to purchase goods that are difficult, perhaps even impossible, to save for. How long would it take to save $25,000 for a car or $250,000 for a house? Car loans and home mortgages allow people to enjoy their purchases now and pay for them over time. Consumer purchases lead to prosperous businesses, higher employment, a healthy stock market, and a strong economy.

However, many people have learned the hard way that it is much easier to borrow money than to pay it back. Interest rates, finance charges, and temptingly low minimum payments can keep people trapped in debt for many years, particularly if new expenses arise. The car needs repairs, the refrigerator breaks, or the family wants a vacation. More money is borrowed. At some point, the borrower finds that he or she is barely able to make the minimum payments each month.

The pressure to maximize profits can lead lenders to ethically questionable behaviors. Some banks and credit card companies have been criticized for encouraging people to borrow more money than they can afford to pay back and for practicing **usury**, or charging excessively high interest rates.

## Credit Cards

After many years of record profits, the bottom fell out of the credit card industry in the fall of 2008. Too many cards were issued to consumers with a poor financial track record. Too many of these consumers spent more than they could ever realistically repay. When the financial meltdown hit, the results were disastrous. Credit card lenders wrote off about $45 billion as "uncollectible" bad debt in 2008 alone.[1]

A credit card lender is in a weak position when a customer can't pay a balance. Credit card balances are rarely secured, meaning there is no collateral for the debt. If a bank makes a loan that is used to buy a car or a house, the contract usually secures the loan with the purchased item. If payments are missed, the bank can eventually repossess the car or foreclose on the house. The car or house can then be sold, and the bank can get at least a reasonable amount of its money back.

If a borrower can't pay an unsecured credit card balance, the credit card company can't seize any property. It can sue, but lawsuits are generally more expensive than the unpaid bill. It can hire a collection agency to harass the customer, but if the person simply doesn't have the money, that is also ineffective.

Furthermore, when a consumer declares bankruptcy, credit card lenders typically receive 5 percent of their balances at the most. Unsecured lenders are near the bottom of the list used by bankruptcy courts to decide which creditors are paid first and last. So, the industry has problems collecting.

A positive for the industry is that credit card loans are less regulated than mortgage and car loans. There is more "wiggle room" in the law, which gives options to companies looking to increase revenue or cut costs.

States have **usury laws** that set maximum rates of interest. The law that applies to a credit card company, though, is that of the state where the company's headquarters is located, not the state of each individual credit card holder. It is easy enough for a headquarters to be placed in a "friendly" state. Credit card companies are generally able to charge high fees, raise their customers' rates for the smallest of reasons, and lower credit limits without violating the law.

The industry is often grilled by the press, by consumers' rights groups, and from time to time by Congress. *How can you charge 29.99 percent interest* and *how can you charge $35 late fees* are among the more commonly asked questions. Card issuers defend themselves with vigor. They argue that they

---

[1]Eric Dash and Andrew Martin, "Banks Brace for Credit Card Write-Offs," *The New York Times*, May 10, 2009, http://www.nytimes.com/2009/05/11/business/11credit.html.

are in business to make a profit and that lower rates and fees would make the industry unprofitable. They assert that no one is forced to make a late payment and that everyone can avoid interest altogether by choosing to charge no more than can be paid in full at the end of each billing cycle. They also argue that their customers are adults and that adults are fully capable of making reasonable financial decisions.

## Payday Loans

At the edge of the lending frontier are **payday loans,** which are usually due to be repaid on the borrower's next payday or two weeks down the road. A typical payday loan is for $300 to $500. When advertised, these loans are usually characterized as emergency loans. TV spots show an unhappy character with a broken-down car, a sick child, or some other problem. In the next scene, a clerk counts new $100 bills into the same character's hand. "Instant cash" and "no credit check" are promised.

The catch is the fee charged for the short-term loan. It is usually about $15 per $100 borrowed, which amounts to a staggering 400 percent annual rate of interest. Most states exempt payday loans from even the loose regulations placed on credit card loans. This makes charging 400 percent interest perfectly legal.

According to a consumer advocate testifying recently before Congress, an average person who takes out a payday loan "rolls it over" (renews it) 8 to 12 times per year.[2] A person borrowing $500, and paying a $75 fee 12 times, pays $900 to borrow $500 for 24 weeks. Some borrowers roll over their payday loans around the calendar and pay the fee 26 times per year.

Payday lenders maintain that the fees are necessary because their clients have a high default rate, and they must be profitable to stay in business. "We'll lend someone money when no one else will," they argue. This is perfectly true, but many remain skeptical of the industry.

---

### CHECKPOINT 9–1

**1.** In your own words, define each term.

usury

usury law

payday loan

---

[2]M. J. Ellington, "No Cap on Payday Loans," *TimesDaily,* July 25, 2010, http://www.timesdaily.com/article/20100725/NEWS/100729876?Title=No-caps-on-payday-loans.

2. In your opinion, do payday loans amount to usury? Why or why not?

3. Although a few states make high-interest payday loans illegal, the majority do not. Should Congress or state lawmakers in the other states set limits on the interest rates that may be charged? If so, what maximum annual rate of interest do you think is acceptable?

4. What specific practices, if any, should companies that issue credit cards change?

# ■ Special Issue: Mortgages and Foreclosures

A **mortgage** is a loan made for the purpose of purchasing a home. Mortgage lenders share special blame in starting the current recession. In 2007 and 2008, millions of homeowners became unable to make mortgage payments at about the same time, which led to a collapse in the housing market. Broader economic problems followed in short order.

**Foreclosure** is the process by which the holder of a mortgage repossesses a borrower's property and seeks to have the entire debt repaid promptly. Foreclosure usually happens as a result of a borrower's failing to make timely payments and usually results in a property being sold at auction to the highest bidder. If all goes well, the auction raises enough money to fully repay the loan. In fact, in occasional cases the auction raises more than the mortgage balance, and the surplus is returned to the borrower who has lost his or her home. Generally, however, an auction raises far less money than is owed.

## Why Foreclosures Are Bad for Borrowers

The most obvious downside to a foreclosure is that a borrower can no longer live in the home. At the time of this writing, some 3,000 families a day faced losing a home to foreclosure.[3] In addition, a problem that many people fail to anticipate can arise later. In the current housing market, a foreclosure auction usually generates less than the outstanding loan balance. In such a case, in the majority of states the mortgagee can seek a **deficiency judgment** against a borrower for the remaining amount.

Mortgagees have become increasingly aggressive in recent years as their losses from mortgage defaults have increased. Many routinely pull credit

[3] "Home Foreclosures Reach 1 Million," *The Christian Science Monitor*, Jan. 14, 2011, www.csmonitor.com/business/latest-news-wires/2011/0114/home-foreclosures-reach-1-million.

reports on defaulting borrowers to assess whether the borrowers have enough assets to make a deficiency judgment worth pursuing. Newspapers commonly feature stories on former homeowners who "thought they were done" when their homes were sold at auction and who express distress and surprise that they have to come up with additional funds to pay a deficiency judgment.

## Why Foreclosures Are Bad for Lenders

Foreclosures almost always lead to losses for lenders. The current housing market is depressed overall, and foreclosure properties tend to attract bids lower than the market value for similar houses in the area, often due to concerns that they have not been well cared for. The Mortgage Bankers Association estimates that a single foreclosed home generates an average of $50,000 in losses.[4]

A lender loses money in the form of missed payments. Often, lenders must continue to make tax payments on the property even if the occupier of the property is no longer making mortgage payments. If a borrower has abandoned a home, the lender has to pay for lawn maintenance and repairs. Homeowners' association fees and fees to collection agents sometimes come into play.

A lender may be responsible for other costs as well. Often, court fees must be paid. Auctioneers must be hired. In some states, laws require a sheriff to supervise a foreclosure auction, and sheriff's fees can be substantial.

Deficiency judgments can reduce losses. Often, however, borrowers who default on their loans either seek formal bankruptcy protection or have so little in assets that most losses cannot be recaptured.

## Negative Equity

**Negative equity** refers to a loan balance that is larger than the value of the asset for which the loan was made in the first place. It is not a new or uncommon phenomenon. Borrowers who finance most of the purchase of a new car, for example, almost always find themselves "upside down" for a time because the value of a new car tends to drop about 25 percent as soon as buyers take possession.

The unusual occurrence in the late 00s was the large number of homeowners who came to have negative equity in their homes. In the early years of the decade, many borrowers came to carry little home equity either because they put little money down on a new home or because they took out home equity loans to cash out the rising values of their properties. Then, when the housing market collapsed and values plummeted, many homes were left "underwater." At the time of this writing, approximately one in four homeowners was in this situation.[5]

---

[4]Craig Focardi, cited by Dona Dezube, "Heroic Homeownership," *Mortgage Banking*, June 2006, p. 82, from "Foreclosure Statistics," Federal Deposit Insurance Corporation, http://www.fdic.gov/about/comein/files/foreclosure_statistics.pdf.

[5]Ruth Simon and James R. Hagerty, "One in Four Borrowers Is Underwater," *The Wall Street Journal,* Nov. 24, 2009, http://online.wsj.com/article/SB125903489722661849.html.

## The Game: Borrowers and "Strategic Defaults"

The current recession has put substantial pressure on the finances of millions of households. For many, a breaking point eventually arrives and not all bills can be paid. If a person has only $2,000 available, but he or she has $3,000 in bills to pay, the person must prioritize some bills over others. This kind of choice has been characterized as a **strategic default**.

## Do the RIGHT THING

In the current economy, people who have seen the value of their home plummet and have been foreclosed on often have little recourse. Enter Boston Community Capital (BCC), a financial institution with a 25-year history of investment in building healthy communities. BCC identifies homeowners who have lost their homes but who would have been able to keep them if their mortgage and payments had been based on the house's current market value. Its clients are victims of predatory lending practices or fell behind in payments due to lost jobs, major illness, or other personal hardships. BCC negotiates with the bank or other entity that holds the mortgage, attempting to buy the property at or near the current market price. When it succeeds, BCC in turn sells the home back to the homeowner at market price plus 25 percent for protection against default.

To help ensure homeowners will be able to stay in their homes this time around, BCC sets up a 30-year, fixed-rate mortgage with a carefully structured payment plan. Applicants undergo a thorough and rigorous screening process, with less than 50 percent qualifying.

The BCC foreclosure relief program was profiled on a recent *PBS NewsHour*. At that time, BCC had purchased 90 homes and sold them back to their original owners with not a single default. The initiative has also attracted the interest of the U.S. Federal Reserve, which featured a presentation by BCC at a recent national conference on the impact of foreclosures and vacant properties on communities.

*Sources: Paul Solman, "Boston Firm Offers Homeowners a Second Chance After Foreclosure," PBS NewsHour, Oct. 29, 2010; "Boston Program Helps People in Foreclosure Buy Back Their Homes," Here and Now, June 2, 2010; Boston Community Capital Web site.*

1. What do you think of the featured program?

2. Do you think that it is a better approach than the alternatives presented earlier in the chapter? Why or why not?

A 2010 *U.S. News and World Report* article, "Forget the Mortgage, I'm Paying My Credit Card Bill," discussed a recent study by TransUnion, one of the three major credit reporting agencies. The study found that in 2009, the number of people who had fallen behind on their mortgage payments, but who were not behind on their credit card payments, had increased by more than 50 percent in a single year, from 4.3 percent to 6.6 percent of all Americans. The article offered several explanations for the shift, including the fact that credit cards are seen by some as more "basic" for their survival and the fact that foreclosures, because of costs and legal regulations, often take many months to be completed. Credit cards accounts are frequently cancelled after a small number of missed payments.[6]

An average U.S. household with at least one credit card carries close to $11,000 in credit card debt.[7] Millions of families have sought bankruptcy protection in recent years. In almost all bankruptcy cases, the credit card companies receive next to nothing and have to write off the outstanding balance as uncollectible debt. When credit card issuers write off bad debt, the losses are spread out across a vast ocean of shareholders. When a major bank has a new million dollars in credit card defaults, no particular person feels a dramatic impact—the losses are widely diluted.

When homes are foreclosed upon, communities feel significant effects. Property values drop for everyone in areas with a high concentration of foreclosures. The properties themselves tend to be neglected and are sometimes abandoned, which can lead to an increase in crime. Decreasing property values impact a community's tax base and hurt its ability to provide basic services and maintain schools. Losses are more concentrated when mortgage loans go into default.

Because of the likelihood of significant losses described earlier, lenders often face difficult decisions about when to press forward with foreclosures. The right to foreclose often arises after a second missed payment, but many lenders do not exercise it immediately. Similarly, many Americans must decide if and when to make mortgage payments if they do not have enough money to pay all their bills.[8]

## CHECKPOINT **9–2**

**1.** Define the following terms in your own words:

mortgage

foreclosure

[6]Luke Mullins, "Forget the Mortgage, I'm Paying My Credit Card Bill," *U.S. News and World Report*, Feb. 8, 2010, http://money.usnews.com/money/personal-finance/articles/2010/02/08/forget-the-mortgage-im-paying-my-credit-card-bill.html.

[7]"Top Things to Know," Money 101, Lesson 9: Controlling Debt, CNNMoney.com, http://money.cnn.com/magazines/moneymag/money101/lesson9.

[8]From Bredeson. *Applied Business Ethics*, 1e. © 2012 South-Western, a part of Cengage Learning, Inc. Reproduced by permission. www.cengage.com/permissions.

deficiency judgment

negative equity

strategic default

2. Are strategic defaults ethical actions by borrowers? Why or why not?

3. Should banks and other lenders foreclose less frequently, or should they step in and protect their interests whenever a borrower fails to make timely payments? Is seeking a deficiency judgment acceptable?

## ■ Applying Ethical Principles to Financial Issues

As you have learned, legal standards and ethical standards are not always the same. The ethical standard is based on universal ethical principles—the kind you read about in Chapter 2. This section will take a fresh look at those principles to see how they apply to ethical issues in finance.

### The Egoism Principle

The *egoism principle* is the idea that the right thing for a person to do in any situation is the action that best serves that person's long-term interests. At first glance, this principle might seem to justify some unethical actions on the part of financial professionals. Remember, though, the key is *long-term*. What are the long-term consequences of payday loans? of high interest rates on credit cards? of foreclosures?

Smart business leaders and policy makers think long-term. Banks that consistently lure customers into excessive and unmanageable debt may eventually face an angry backlash from the public. Another result may be new laws that protect consumers from exploitive lenders.

### The Utility Principle

The *utility principle* is the idea that the morally right action is the one that produces the greatest possible good for the greatest number of people. Since there are more customers and consumers than businesses that serve them,

> Capital as such is not evil; it is its wrong use that is evil. Capital in some form or other will always be needed.
>
> —MAHATMA GANDHI

this would seem, on the surface, to mean that whatever is best for consumers must be right. Perhaps banks should not charge interest for loans, but, instead, should offer high interest rates for savings accounts. What a wonderful world it could be!

The reason those ideas won't work may sound familiar—because of the long-term implications. What would happen in the long term if banks and investment companies gave out more money than they took in? They would go out of business. Consumers would then be worse off without those important services. What is actually the greatest good for the greatest number is to allow financial companies to earn sustainable profits, but to diligently protect consumers from exploitation.

## The Principle of Rights

According to the *principle of rights*, an action is considered moral when it respects the rights of others and is considered immoral when it violates another's rights. On the surface, the application of this principle seems simple. Financial service companies should respect the rights of their customers. However, this is one of those situations in which *legal* and *ethical* are not quite the same.

Laws allow people to forfeit or sign away their basic rights. If Erica takes Manny's money by force, Manny's rights are violated. However, what if Manny voluntarily signs a contract stating that Erica may take his money? That fact changes everything.

You can compare that situation to the argument made by credit card companies and other lenders: "If people have other borrowing options and still choose to borrow money from us, and if our terms are clearly stated in the contract, then how can we be exploiting people?" However, individuals with poor credit histories may not have other borrowing options. Since they represent higher risks for lenders, many banks and credit card companies will not loan money to them. The ones that do offer loans are likely to charge higher interest rates.

## The Principle of Duties

The *principle of duties* maintains that you should do what is ethically right purely because you have a moral obligation to do what is ethically right. Do the right thing, not because good consequences will result, but because it's the right thing to do. The important point is that the duty is not to one's company, one's customers, or even one's community. The duty is simply to do the right thing.

### Ethics & Law

The general purpose of laws is to reinforce social ethical standards. Societies that value honesty and fairness have laws designed to impose those standards on businesses. However, people eventually stop conforming to laws that are not enforced. Therefore, federal, state, and local governments are charged with the responsibility of ensuring that people in businesses and professions obey the laws.

At the federal level, the Federal Trade Commission (FTC) regulates general business practices. The Securities and Exchange Commission (SEC) regulates investment-related trade, such as the stock market. The Federal Communications Commission (FCC) regulates issues related to broadcasting and telecommunications.

**Go online and find an example of a government agency in your state that regulates businesses. What is one thing that the agency is currently focused upon?**

How can people know their moral duties—the right things to do? Philosopher Immanuel Kant maintained that people's duties boil down to two basic concepts—universality and respect for persons. *Universality* is the idea that you should act as you would want others to act in the same situation. *Respect for persons* is the idea that it is always wrong to take unfair advantage of others for personal gain.

Applying those concepts to ethical issues in finance is not difficult, at least in principle. No rational person would want deception to be a universal moral standard because that would mean allowing oneself to be deceived. The same is true for actions that can harm people financially. Since a person can't logically want others to harm him or her, it can't be right for that person to harm others. In addition, the concept of respect for persons prohibits tactics that exploit others for personal gain, such as manipulating people into borrowing more money than they can afford to repay.

However, the concepts are more difficult to live by in the real world. Pressure from stockholders to increase profits and dividends, combined with pressure from employees for increased wages and benefits, can lead company policy makers to seek profit-raising shortcuts. The short-term pressures make it more difficult for executives to keep their eyes on the long-term picture.

## The Principle of Virtues

The *principle of virtues* is the idea that ethics is based on being a good person, that is, on incorporating ideal character traits, or virtues, into one's life. Proponents of this virtue tend to sum up the goal of ethics as *being good*. That viewpoint is currently very popular in business. Corporate leaders identify key virtues they want their company to exhibit, such as integrity, fairness, truthfulness, respect, and generosity. Then the leaders work with employees and other stakeholder groups to determine the most effective ways to incorporate the virtues into company policies and practices. A common theme in current business ethics discussions is that good ethics is good business.

A strength of this approach is that people generally agree on the worthiness of the virtues. Not many people will argue that fairness and honesty are bad character traits. A potential weakness is the difficulty of translating the ideal traits into specific actions. For example, the interest rate on a loan doubles in six months. That fact is spelled out in small print on the credit application in the middle of several paragraphs of legal text. Is that arrangement sufficient for the company to praise itself for being honest and fair?

An important point to remember is that ethics is about being a good person, a good employee, a good citizen, and a good company. However, ethics is also about doing the right thing and making the right decision when the pressure to do the wrong thing is strong. Wise business leaders who think in the long term and want their companies to earn reputations for integrity and fairness try to incorporate as many universal ethical principles as possible into their decision-making processes.

# CHECKPOINT **9–3**

1. Return to the opening passage. Would the company change its credit card practices or expand into payday loans if it followed the . . .

   egoism principle?          Yes // No

   utility principle?          Yes // No

   principle of rights?          Yes // No

   principle of duties?          Yes // No

   principle of virtues?          Yes // No

2. Which of the ethical principles discussed do you find yourself relying on most often when you are making ethical decisions? Which do you rely on the least? Why do you suppose that is?

3. Which of the ethical principles discussed do you think *businesses* rely on most often when making ethical decisions? Which do they rely on the least? Why do you suppose that is?

This chapter has presented ideas related to ethical lending practices. The following scenario is your chance to apply the concepts to a business situation. Which ideas make the most sense to you? Why? Answer the questions that follow the scenario, and be prepared to respectfully argue for your point of view in class.

## Main Issues and Options

**Issues:** Should the bank foreclose on any or all of the four homes? Should the residents of 123 Elm Street practice a strategic default?

**Options:** The bank is legally free to foreclose or to give the customers more time to make mortgage payments. The homeowners are free to make a strategic default if they are willing to risk a foreclosure.

## Strategic Defaults

### Greentown Bank

"OK," Ann frowned and grimaced. "Let's move on to this month's foreclosures. How many this time?"

"Four possibles," Reggie reported.

"Let's hear it."

"First up—the house at 123 Oak Street is three months behind on payments. We've been in contact with them, and he's lost his job. She's still employed as a teacher."

"What kind of job did the husband lose?"

"Sales."

"OK, go on."

"He says he's looking and I believe him. They hadn't missed any payments for the six years we've held their mortgage until the last three."

"What would the house fetch at auction?"

"Maybe $30,000 less than what they owe us."

"They have any assets?"

"Nothing major as far as I can tell. We could try to garnish her wages, and his when he has another job. A default judgment might cut our losses over the long term."

Ann made some notes. "OK," she said, "moving on."

"House number two is 123 Pine Street. Single guy, laid-off autoworker."

"Ouch."

"Yep, those jobs aren't coming back, at least not here."

"How far behind is he?"

"Just two months. He's had some money from a severance package, but that appears to be just about dried up. No other assets to speak of."

"How much will we lose if we foreclose?"

"About $50,000."

"All right. Next."

"Next is 123 Birch Street. Way behind, ah . . . six months. The wife was in a one-car accident last year and has had a lot of problems—medical expenses, had to cut back on hours at work, that kind of thing."

"Any record of what happened with the accident?"

"No police record or anything—she wasn't ticketed. All I can verify is it happened at ten o'clock at night and an ambulance took her to the hospital."

"OK. Any signs of improvement?"

"The husband talks to me regularly, but he seems to make promises that don't end up happening."

"Yeah. Any assets?"

"Not really. We'll lose about $40,000 overall in the short term."

"OK," Ann said as she made more notes. "You have one more?"

"Yep. Last one is 123 Elm Street. This one is kind of scary."

Ann smiled for the first time in a while. "A 'Nightmare on Elm Street,' Reggie?"

Reggie smiled, too. "You might say that."

"Scary as in how?"

"Scary as in these people are both employed, and they have the money to pay their mortgage, and they're just not doing it."

"How far behind are they?"

"Two months."

"Are they aware of it?"

"I talked to them yesterday. 'We've had some problems, but we'll catch up real soon,' they told me."

"Hmm . . ."

"It's almost as if they're daring us to foreclose."

"How much do you think we'd lose?"

"That loan is way underwater—maybe $70,000."

"Do you really think they're playing chicken with us?"

"I don't know, but if everybody who's underwater starts doing this . . ."

"I know. We can't afford to foreclose on everybody at once."

"Scary," said Reggie.

"Scary," agreed Ann.

## 123 Elm Street

Tom and Ellen Smith sat at their kitchen table. A large number of bills and bank statements lay spread out before them. Tom rubbed a hand through his hair. "Look," he said, "if we declare bankruptcy, we'll lose the house for sure. If we do it this way, we might not lose the house."

"We're already two payments behind," Ellen answered. "If we miss another payment, they'll foreclose on us anyway."

"Maybe not!" Tom replied, a bit too loudly. "I'm sorry," he said, lowering his voice. "Look, we know people who have

gotten a lot longer from the bank. Ed and Mary were eight months behind before they lost the house. They'll call and send letters and make threats, but everybody's in trouble and they can't foreclose on the whole town at once."

"What'll we tell the kids if we have to go?"

"We won't have to tell the kids anything. I'm trying to save the house, and I think we will save the house. Look here," he said, pointing to a legal pad. "Last month, we had $400 in checking at the end of the month and $12,000 on the credit cards. This month, we have $800 in checking and $11,800 on the cards. We came out $600 better this month by cutting back on everything."

"And by skipping the $1,000 mortgage payment again."

"Yes, but we're closer to being able to make it. If we can save that $600 every month, and if I can get just a little more overtime, we can make it work."

"But you said you wouldn't be able to get more overtime for another couple of months."

"Right, so we just have to hang on to everything until then."

"I'd still feel better if we made the mortgage payment."

"So would I, but that will make us $400 short on something else. We've cut our spending as much as we can—we don't even have cable anymore. Which $400 worth of other bills should we not pay?"

"I don't know, Tom."

"Look, we have to pay the utilities. We can't do without electricity and water. The only other thing is the $400 minimum payments on the credit cards."

"We can't skip those?"

"Come on, Elly, you know those guys are ruthless. They'll close the accounts after two months, tops."

"But they can't take our house, and we can just pay cash for everything."

"But they can take our cushion. What happens if the cards get cancelled and one of the kids gets sick? What about last month when my car broke down? We didn't have two grand in the bank. It would still be parked on the mechanic's back lot if I hadn't been able to put the repairs on a credit card."

"I don't know, Tom."

"Look, it'll get better. I'll get the overtime eventually. They owe me. And you'll get a raise in May."

"Maybe."

"Look, we just have to keep everything going for now. And banks just take longer to act than credit card companies. If it were the other way around, I'd say we should pay the mortgage this month."

"I guess so."

"This is the best way to keep everything together."

## What Do You Think?

1. If you were Ann, which of the four houses would you foreclose on, and which customers would get more time? Why?

   123 Oak Street

   123 Pine Street

   123 Birch Street

   123 Elm Street

2. Would your answer to Question 1 change if the economy were significantly better than it is currently? What if it were significantly worse?

3. If you were in Tom and Ellen's position, would you give priority to making the mortgage payment or the credit card payments? Why?

4. Debt trade-offs aside, could you get along without credit cards if necessary? What would be the biggest problems you would have if you no longer had credit cards?

5. During the recession, some lenders have "frozen" foreclosures for a time, which means they have suspended all foreclosures for weeks or months. Some state governments have at least considered requiring statewide freezes. Are such policies reasonable during an economic downturn? Would they be better or worse if they were required by the government?

# Summary

Unethical lending practices can have serious economic consequences for customers. Particular care must be given when issuing credit cards and when making payday loans.

Defaults on millions of mortgages and the ensuing wave of foreclosures helped to create the current recession. Some consumers have even been led to the practice of strategic defaults.

The universal ethical principles of egoism, utility, rights, duties, and virtues can be applied to lending issues to help professionals make wise decisions. As with other business ethics issues, combining principles like these with long-term thinking can help prevent unethical actions.

# Key Terms and Concepts

Match each definition with a key term or concept.

_____ 1. The practice of charging excessively high interest rates

_____ 2. The process of repossessing a home from a homeowner

_____ 3. A short-term loan made at a high rate of interest

_____ 4. The consumer practice of paying credit card bills before making mortgage payments

_____ 5. An action that a lender may take when a foreclosure does not generate enough money to pay off a mortgage loan

_____ 6. A loan balance that is larger than the value of the asset for which the loan was made

_____ 7. A loan made for the purpose of buying a home

_____ 8. A law that sets maximum acceptable rates of interest

a. deficiency judgment

b. foreclosure

c. mortgage

d. negative equity

e. payday loan

f. strategic default

g. usury

h. usury law

# Review

1. Name two ethically questionable behaviors of banks and credit card companies.

2. Payday loans tend to carry a rate of interest of

   a. less than 25 percent.

   b. about 25 percent.

   c. about 50 percent.

   d. about 100 percent.

   e. more than 100 percent.

3. Give two reasons why foreclosures are bad for borrowers and two reasons why they are bad for lenders.

4. Which of the following is a practice that *borrowers* choose to engage in?

   a. foreclosures

   b. deficiency judgments

   c. strategic defaults

   d. all of the above

5. True or false: Charging high interest rates is an ethically sound practice according to the egoism principle.

6. Name one advantage and one drawback for corporate leaders of using the principle of virtues as a guide in making ethical decisions (*good ethics is good business*).

# Critical Thinking

7. Farah is a freshman at State University. One aspect of college life that has surprised her is the many credit card applications she receives. When she checks her mailbox, she often finds three or four new credit card ads. During orientation, credit card companies set up tables all around campus, offering T-shirts, dorm supplies, and other gifts to students who submitted applications. One credit card rep told Farah, "You're an adult now and legally responsible for your financial decisions."

   Her older sister cautioned her. "Many students don't have much spending money and often don't understand how credit cards work. They think it's free money. By the time they figure out the truth, they may be thousands of dollars in debt, and their credit is ruined for years.

In fact, some people I know graduated owing more on their credit cards than on their student loans!"

Farah is tempted by the offers. Many of the advertisements offer 0 percent interest. Besides, she's sure she will find a great job when she graduates. She can pay off the credit cards then.

What pitfalls might Farah face if she forms bad borrowing habits?

# Applications

8. Apply each of the universal ethical principles reviewed in this chapter to the ethical issue of foreclosing on mortgages and seeking deficiency judgments. Would each principle imply that the practices are right or wrong? Why?

   a. egoism principle

   b. utility principle

   c. principle of rights

   d. principle of duties

   e. principle of virtues

9. A credit card company advertises an initial interest rate of 0 percent. In small print on the back of the ad are the facts that the rate jumps to 13.99 percent after six months and to 24.99 percent if the consumer ever makes a late payment. The company reserves the right to change the terms at any time. Is this practice ethically sound? Why or why not?

# Digging Deeper

10. Visit the Web site that is home to the federal government's Making Home Affordable Program at http://makinghomeaffordable.gov/. Learn about government assistance available for homeowners who find themselves underwater. Cite three specific provisions of the program, and assess whether you think each will be very helpful, somewhat helpful, or unhelpful to a typical struggling homeowner.

# The Bottom Line

11. Evaluate your feelings toward the following:

### Mortgage Foreclosures and Deficiency Judgments

← COMPLETELY UNACCEPTABLE                    COMPLETELY ACCEPTABLE →

1        2        3        4        5        6        7

### Payday Loans

← COMPLETELY UNACCEPTABLE                    COMPLETELY ACCEPTABLE →

1        2        3        4        5        6        7

# Two Global Issues: The Environment and Sweatshops

## CHAPTER 10

This chapter will examine two issues, each of which has a broad scope. What steps should a company take to protect the environment? What steps should a company take to protect overseas contract workers?

## Objectives

- Discuss the circumstances under which businesses should adopt sustainability initiatives and green building practices.
- Identify issues related to the use of sweatshop labor outside the United States.

## Key Terms and Concepts

environmental law, p. 154

Environmental Protection Agency, p. 154

sustainability, p. 155

green building, p. 155

sweatshop labor, p. 156

labor union, p. 157

Occupational Safety and Health Act, p. 157

race to the bottom, p. 157

Ron greets his vice president, Jack, and gestures to the chair in front of his desk. He opens the folder with his notes on the consultants' presentation. He's asked Jack to review their recommendations and advise him. Ron is leaving for Singapore in two days. He wants to decide which proposals to adopt so the company can start taking bids while he is away.

"All right," Jack begins. "I thought we might go through what I think are the best ideas the consultants presented. Water usage is the biggest problem. I think our clients will appreciate water conservation efforts."

"Any data on that? Any evidence of our competitors winning clients because of those kinds of efforts?"

"Not directly, no, but people are aware of the issue. It can't hurt."

"It probably can't. I'm just wondering if it can help. Go ahead."

"First, install a rainwater collection system on the roof. It adds only $50,000 to a $15,000,000 building, and it can save a great deal of water, which we'd have to pay for otherwise."

"I had notes on that being a sensible idea as well. Let's add it."

"The next water saver is the landscaping idea. I agree with the consultants that we should have limited grass on the grounds and use native plants and native rock wherever possible. The artist's rendition looked really good, and we can water 50 percent less."

"People like lawns, though," Ron says. "All companies have lush green lawns around their space. I don't want our building landscaped like a desert."

"I'm not saying we shouldn't have any grass—just limit the amount. Maybe a nice lawn surrounding the clients' parking lot and native landscaping in other places. It would cost about $100,000 for the initial landscaping, but less to maintain—less mowing, lower watering costs."

"OK. What else?"

"We use packed gravel and not concrete for the employees' parking lot. That lets rainwater return to the aquifer more efficiently—it doesn't puddle and evaporate as much as with concrete. The cost is about the same."

"Yeah, but do people want to walk on gravel? Scuff up their shoes?"

"They'll get used to it."

"You ever try to walk on gravel in high heels, Jack?"

"Ah, no, but it's packed gravel, not the old-style loose gravel."

"Maybe. Moving on . . ."

"The next few ideas are related to energy usage. I know you don't like solar panels."

"Ugly," Ron says.

"I'd argue no one will see them on top of a five-story building with a flat roof, so what does it matter what they look like?"

"Expensive," the CEO counters.

"Up front, yes, $200,000. If we generate our own power, though, we'll make money off them eventually."

"How much can we generate? With a roof full of solar panels?"

"Fifteen, maybe twenty percent of what we need. If you want all the power from solar cells, we also have that option."

"Yeah, but if we buy our energy from the, what, the solar energy farm, we pay 30 percent more than if we buy it from the city."

"If energy prices don't go up. The solar farm is offering us a 15-year deal. Its prices might start to look pretty good if regular energy prices double."

"That's true. I'll think about that one."

"The next energy idea is to use local building materials. If we bring in less from far away, the builders use less energy to get everything to the site."

"What's the price?"

"$300,000."

"OK." Ron makes some notes.

"The last two energy ideas I like are efficient windows and upgraded insulation. They're expensive—$400,000 and $200,000—but our heating and cooling costs will fall dramatically. We'll recapture our full costs in six years or less."

"Yeah, I noted those as well during the presentation."

"That's almost everything. Just two things with the restrooms."

"Oh, no," the CEO says.

"Now I know you're probably . . ."

"You're not going to bring up those. Nobody wants those."

"In a company our size, bidets would save a tremendous amount of toilet paper per year."

"No one wants to use a bidet."

"That's because they're uncommon. They're standard in many countries—"

"We're not in those countries, Jack," Ron interrupts.

"You'd save $50,000 a year on toilet paper, and the sewers would have . . ."

"Fifty thousand isn't worth the grief I'd get."

"So make them an option—people can use another stall if they want toilet paper. One bidet per restroom. One hundred thousand added to the building costs."

Ron grunts, but doesn't say anything. Eventually, Jack continues.

"The other restroom idea I like is the hand driers. We can save $100,000 per year on paper towels and send a lot less to the landfill. The new models are very energy-efficient, and it's more sanitary."

"Yeah, people are used to hand dryers, but they're expensive, right?"

"One hundred fifty thousand for the building. They'll pay for themselves in a year and a half."

"OK. So your proposals total," the CEO checks his notes, "a million and a half?"

"That's right. Don't think of it in terms of construction costs, though. A lot of these ideas will make money eventually."

"That's true, but I pitched $15,000,000 to the board last quarter. I need good reasons to OK a higher figure."

"I think all these ideas are in our shareholders' best interests."

"I know you do. I have to decide whether I agree."

## {**WHAT** Do You Think?}

1. **Rank the ideas presented from best (1) to worst (10).**

   _____ rainwater collection system ($50,000)

   _____ native landscaping ($100,000)

   _____ packed gravel parking lot ($0)

   _____ solar panels ($200,000)

   _____ contract to buy solar-generated energy ($0 up front; future cost depends on energy prices)

   _____ local building materials ($300,000)

   _____ efficient windows ($400,000)

   _____ upgraded insulation ($200,000)

   _____ bidets ($100,000)

   _____ hand dryers ($150,000)

2. **Focus on your top two and bottom two choices. Why did you rank them as you did?**

# ■ Environmental Ethics

Few issues generate more passion and debate than those surrounding the environment. People like green spaces; we are hard-wired to like nature. However, many products and processes that generate pollution are essential to our society. We need computers. We need roads and vehicles to get us from place to place. We need affordable energy. Other products and processes are not essential, but people desire them. Often, there is no easy answer to environmental questions.

A majority of companies face difficult environmental decisions. Frequently, leaders must balance laws, profits, the expectations of their customers, and their own desire to do what is right.

## Environmental Laws

There are a great many **environmental laws**, but many of them are fairly new. Until 1970, there was essentially no environmental regulation from the federal government. Before then, companies generally operated in the cheapest way possible, even if it meant creating massive and obvious pollution. Factories were located near rivers specifically so any waste materials created in manufacturing could be dumped into the river and washed away. Cars had no emission control systems. Absolutely everything, toxic or not, was sent to the same dump or landfill. Many companies have had to change their ways substantially within the careers of the people who now lead them.

In recent decades, Congress has created the **Environmental Protection Agency** (EPA) and has charged it with enforcing environmental regulations. The EPA has taken action countless times to stop practices that were perfectly legal for most of our nation's history, but that violate new laws.

## Ethics & Law

The Environmental Protection Agency is the federal agency in charge of enforcing environmental laws. One law that has been a "hot topic" in recent years is the Clean Air Act.

In 2010, the EPA celebrated the Clean Air Act's fortieth birthday. The agency noted that, in its first 20 years, the law prevented more than 200,000 premature deaths and almost 700,000 cases of chronic bronchitis by requiring improvements in air quality.

Go to http://www.epa.gov. Describe the EPA's current efforts to improve the following:

1. ozone protection

2. car and truck emissions

3. fuel standards for cars and trucks

Source: "40th Anniversary of the Clean Air Act," Sept. 14, 2010, U.S. Environmental Protection Agency, http://www.epa.gov/oar/caa/40th.html.

## The Environment and Business

Profits and meeting the expectations of customers often go hand in hand. In recent years, many consumers have started to pay close attention to the environment and to demand that the companies they do business with respect it. Often, sales increase dramatically if a company gains a reputation for being green. As a result, many firms strive to operate more cleanly and efficiently and to support environmental causes with corporate donations.

Pro-environment decisions are easy in win-win cases. If a company can both care for the planet and make more money doing so, there is no ethical dilemma. The real choices come when profits and the environment seem to be at odds. For example, what should a CEO do if an environmental project does not seem likely to generate increased sales? Should he or she pass on the project and not spend the shareholders' money? A great many business leaders say, often off the record, that they will observe environmental practices only if the law requires them. They contend that if they make changes their competitors aren't required to make, and they don't generate revenue by making them, they place their company at a competitive disadvantage. If the environment needs protecting in a new way, these leaders argue, the law needs to change so everyone plays by the same rules.

Some decisions are even harder. What if the likely costs and benefits of an environmental action are not uncertain? What if the green option will definitely lose large amounts of money? If a company does not break the law, and if its customers don't seem to mind, can losing money on green projects be justified? Can the environment be a stakeholder (Chapter 4) that takes priority over shareholders and others?

## Sustainability

**Sustainability** has become a tremendously powerful idea in recent years. It is the idea that our limited natural resources should be used in such a way that they will not be diminished over time. For example, oil will not "run out" in our lifetime, but it will run out eventually, and our ability to increase annual supply may well end in the near term. Therefore, sensible energy conservation efforts are entirely reasonable. Water for household use and irrigation is already in short supply in many parts of the world, and problems are starting to occur in the United States. "Rare earth" minerals that are essential in the manufacturing of hybrid cars are in short supply, as are many other commodities.

Governments, citizens, interest groups, and corporations have taken a keen interest in making wise long-term use of resources. Many sustainability efforts are simple and cheap and have been widely adopted. Recycling, for example, is becoming universal. Recycling bins for plastic bottles, aluminum cans, and newspapers are everywhere, and most garbage companies offer curbside pickup for home recyclables. Other ideas are useful in conserving resources, but come with a higher price tag.

## Green Building

Many options exist for building facilities, and some have a more limited environmental impact than others. **Green building** is the use of construction practices that seek to minimize environmental impact. Leaders who evaluate new construction choices must make decisions about energy, wastewater, materials, and a range of other items, which were discussed in the Hard Choices scenario. The basic trade-off usually involves costs. A state-of-the-art green building tends to cost about 10 percent more than a "regular" building to construct. A building designed to send less waste to sewers and landfills costs more money. A building designed to make use of renewable energy also costs more up front.

Many company leaders have been persuaded to look at long-term costs. Green buildings cost more to build but, depending on features, can cost less to operate. Some environmental upgrades can pay for themselves over time. Cost issues aside, many leaders have decided to "go green" because they have concluded that it is the right thing to do.[1]

## CHECKPOINT 10-1

1. In your opinion, is a company under a moral obligation to follow green practices if they are not legally required? Why or why not?

2. Return to the opening scenario and your rankings. If you were Ron (the CEO), where would you draw the line? Which of the ten ideas would you OK? Why?

3. For this last question, knock two zeros off every figure in the opening scenario. Imagine you are signing a contract to build a home for your family with a "base price" of $150,000. The upgrades cost 1/100 of the office building prices. So, a basic rainwater collection system would cost $500, native landscaping would add $1,000, efficient windows are $4,000 extra, and so on. Which upgrades would you approve? Did you make different choices than in Question 3? If so, why?

## ■ International Ethics: Sweatshop Labor

Another business issue with a worldwide reach has to do with American companies using overseas workers to produce goods for the U.S. market. A huge proportion of consumer goods are manufactured abroad. It can be difficult to find clothes, toys, or household goods made in the United States.

I am working on a laptop that was made in China at a table that was manufactured in Indonesia. I am wearing a shirt from India and a baseball cap that was stitched together in Bangladesh. The pen I am using to take notes bears a "Mexico" stamp on the bottom. My cat/research assistant was made in the United States, but her collar and food dish are from China.

Some foreign employees are treated well, but some work exhausting schedules for poor wages in harsh living and working environments. In June 2010, the media reported on ten suicides at a Foxconn factory in China. The story reignited debate on the use of **sweatshop labor**—workers who labor for low pay in poor conditions, often for long hours—in developing nations.

[1]From Bredeson. *Applied Business Ethics*, 1e. © 2012 South-Western, a part of Cengage Learning, Inc. Reproduced by permission. www.cengage.com/permissions.

## Factory Workers in the United States

Factory workers have made substantial gains in the United States over the past century. They have, in most industries, won the right to form **labor unions** and bargain collectively with their employers. They have secured a minimum wage that, at the time of this writing, stands at $7.25 per hour. This is not a large sum, but it generates about $15,000 per year in income for a full-time worker, which is enough to live above the poverty line in the wealthiest country in the world. Most assembly-line workers must be paid 1.5 times their regular wages if they work more than 40 hours per week. The **Occupational Safety and Health Act** and similar laws have established numerous workplace safety requirements for companies.

## Factory Workers Outside the United States and the "Race to the Bottom"

Few, if any, of these protections exist in many nations that have become manufacturing hot spots. Free-trade policies are beneficial in that they make the global economy work more efficiently. They have the effect, however, of creating a "**race to the bottom**." Manufacturers constantly seek the lowest labor costs in the world. Nations with millions of workers in desperate circumstances tend to win the battle.

U.S. workers can compete with anyone in the world if the issue is making things well. They are often completely uncompetitive when it comes to the wages for which they are willing to work. The $7.25 an American worker expects per hour will buy 20 hours of labor somewhere else.

## Foxconn Technology Group

You likely own more than one gadget that was assembled at a Foxconn factory in China. Intel®, HP, and Dell all contract work to Foxconn. The Apple iPhone® and iPad® mobile digital devices are made by Foxconn, as are Amazon's Kindle, Motorola cell phones, Sony's PlayStation 3, Nintendo's Wii, and Microsoft's Xbox 360®.

Foxconn may represent the natural endgame of free trade. The company wins big contracts with many of the world's largest technology companies because it offers, in its own words, "the lowest 'total cost' solution." * Foxconn generally complies with Chinese law, but it works its employees hard. A typical employee works 10- to 12-hour shifts six days a week and, at the time of the unwanted publicity in 2010, was paid about $130 per month. Discipline is strict, and mistakes seldom pass without criticism. The company defends itself by pointing to practices such as maintaining a swimming pool for employees and holding chess tournaments for them. Critics dismiss such perks as trivial, however, and point to the at least ten employees who, in 2010, decided life was no longer worth living.

---

*"About Foxconn," http://www.foxconn.com/CompanyIntro.html.

Foxconn is certainly not the worst employer in China, and it will improve. For example, following the 2010 suicides, the company announced a number of changes, including substantially higher wages. Its partners have too much to lose, because bad publicity costs large companies millions of dollars.

## Do the RIGHT THING

When Nike was a target of bad publicity in the 1980s, it established closer oversight of its overseas contractors and minimized its problem. Today's companies will follow the Nike blueprint. Apple will lead the way, will demand that workers be treated better, and will get results. Wages will continue to increase, and Foxconn workers will be treated less harshly. Nintendo, Dell, and other U.S. clients will do their part as well.

The interesting ethics question is whether more CEOs will choose to act *before* a crisis. Information control is tight in some nations, and few stories leak out. For every employee who works at an operation that makes headlines, hundreds labor at similar jobs in obscurity.

Have you ever refused to buy a product because of a company's mistreatment of its workers? If so, what was the product?

Large U.S. companies have clout with their partners regardless of whether the media are paying any attention. They can demand better working conditions for workers or seek partners that treat workers reasonably in the first place. The Ethics @ Work scenario investigates whether they should act.[2]

## CHECKPOINT 10–2

**1.** Define the following terms in your own words:

a. sweatshop labor

b. labor union

c. race to the bottom

**2.** Evaluate the Foxconn Technology Group practices described in this section. Do they seem acceptable to you? Why or why not?

[2]Ibid.

# ETHICS@WORK

This chapter has presented ethical dilemmas that sometimes arise when using an international labor force to manufacture products. The following scenario is your chance to apply the concepts to a business situation. What should the CEO do? Why? Answer the questions that follow the scenario, and be prepared to respectfully argue for your point of view in class.

## Main Issue and Options

**Issue:** Should the CEO renew the contract with Quality Dragon, Limited, or should he seek other options?

**Options:** Randolph is free to continue the relationship with Quality Dragon or not, after the current contract expires.

## Sweatshop Labor

### President's Office

"We need to cut ties with Quality Dragon, Limited," the vice president said, summing up her argument. "The contract is up in six months, Randolph. I'd love to end it now, but I'm resigned that the best-case scenario is just that we go with somebody else in six months."

"I don't think that's necessary," the president replied.

"They abuse their employees," the vice president replied with quiet insistence. "It's wrong to continue our relationship with them."

"Their workers are not prisoners!" the president said sharply. Calming down somewhat, he continued. "They are free to end their employment at any time. They are not beaten. In all the reports about them, there are no documented cases of physical abuse. They are paid on time. They work there because they want to work there. It is better than the alternatives. Just because you would not want to take those jobs doesn't mean that no one else does."

The vice president set her jaw. "You're wrong."

"Excuse me?"

"I said you're wrong, Randolph. Even if it costs me my job, you're wrong." She paused for a moment. "You are . . .

brilliant . . . when it comes to controlling costs, and that's almost always a good thing. It's why we're growing. We were nearly bankrupt when you came aboard. But it's not a good thing this time."

"Go on."

"We are morally required to use our negotiating power to insist upon humane treatment of the people who make our products," the vice president insisted. "Even if our labor costs increase, and I don't think they'll increase by much. I'm not talking about paying them a fortune, just . . ." she trailed off. "Look, you're going over there next month. Just talk to one of them. You'll see."

"Hmmph. Maybe I will—just so I can tell you that *you're* wrong." Randolph smiled slightly.

### A Month Later—China—Hotel Suite

"We have a worker downstairs in the conference room, boss," said the executive assistant.

"Excellent!" Randolph replied. "No problems?"

"Not on Sunday. They're not on a fixed schedule, and surveillance is light. I found the guy wandering around the edge of the property by himself. I had the interpreter explain who I was and asked if he could leave the property.

He said yes, that it was allowed. So we offered him $10 for his trouble and arranged to pick him up a mile down the road. Piece of cake."

"How does he seem?"

"Quiet. Thin. What can I say?"

"OK. I'm headed downstairs."

## Hotel Conference Room

"Explain to him that I am the president of his employer's largest client," Randolph said to the interpreter. "That . . . I can make demands . . . if I am unhappy with how his factory is run."

The interpreter spoke at some length. The Quality Dragon worker nodded once when the interpreter had finished and uttered a single syllable. He did not look up from the table. "He understands," the interpreter said.

"Good, good," Randolph responded. "Ask him his name."

The interpreter relayed the question. "Ping," the worker said softly.

"Hello, Ping. I'm Randolph." Ping nodded once.

Randolph: "Ping, will you help me to understand how Quality Dragon treats its workers?"

Ping (*through the interpreter*): "Yes, sir."

Randolph: "I will not let them fire you, whatever you say. Do you believe me?"

Ping: "Yes, I would like to believe you, sir."

Randolph: "OK, then, the truth, please. Will you tell me what a workday is like for you?"

Ping did not answer, and a long silence stretched out.

Randolph: "Ping? I want to help. I need to understand."

Ping (*after another lengthy pause*): "My mother lives alone. She is very poor."

Randolph: "Ah." (*smiling*) "Very noble of you. Very. All right, then. My company sponsors a school where American students learn Mandarin. It's about 100 miles from here. I will guarantee to find your mother a job there, doing anything she is able to do. Fair enough?"

The translator conveyed the message, and Ping absorbed it.

Ping: "That would be most kind, sir. She will work happily and well for your school. Thank you."

Randolph: "Consider it done. Now. Back to my question. What is a workday like for you?"

Ping collected his thoughts for a moment. He began to speak, slowly at first, and then with increasing pace and volume. Randolph listened to the interpreter, but kept his eyes on Ping.

Ping: "We are awakened at 5 a.m. They shout at us and order us to hurry. We are fed a poor meal and are at our stations by 5:30, although work does not begin until 6. We work from 6 until 1 p.m. We have one restroom break at 9 a.m. for 10 minutes. I have time to smoke one cigarette. We are not permitted to talk to other workers. If we do, even quietly, we lose pay and the supervisors scream at us. If we make an assembly error, we lose pay and the supervisors scream at us. If we yawn, we lose pay and the supervisors scream at us. If we fail to meet an hourly quota, we lose pay and the supervisors scream at us.

"I drill holes into the outer casing of your phones. It is the place where a charger can be plugged in. I must process 120 per hour. And the holes must be perfectly located and perfectly straight. Every 30 seconds a new one. It is difficult to keep focus. I try to make fewer than 10 errors per day. One day I made only 4 errors. Another day I made 18. On that day, my supervisor slapped me and docked me my entire day's pay.

"We have 30 minutes for lunch. The company provides a poor meal. We can pay for better food at the cafeteria, but it is very expensive. I only buy the good meal once a month. One time, I bought a Pepsi. (*smiling*) It was wonderful.

"We may speak quietly at lunch. I have a friend, but we are often too tired to speak.

"At 1:30, we go back to work until 8:30. We have another 10-minute break at 4:30. Work is more difficult in the afternoon. The sun warms the factory, especially in the summer. Water is not allowed on the assembly floor. Sometimes, water is available at the restroom break. The supervisors are angrier and less patient. They call us names that no one should be called, but I am numb to them. Most days.

"If we miss our quota, or if we have a heavy order from a client, we work late. This happens several times a month.

"Eventually, we are fed, and we are returned to our dorm. We have 12 men to a room, and we sleep in bunk beds that are three bunks high. The room smells bad, and there are ants. We usually fall asleep quickly.

"We work six days per week. On Sundays like today, we do not work. I spend much of the day sleeping. There are televisions in the recreation building, and there are chess sets. I like to play chess with my friend on Sunday. Sometimes, we share a pack of cigarettes and play all afternoon. It is pleasant to do something slowly and to have time to think.

"I am supposed to be paid $150 per month. But the supervisors always look for reasons to dock your pay. No one gets his full pay. I usually get about $110 at the end of the month. I keep $50 for myself and send $60 to my mother. There are things you must buy here. They require you to shave, but do not give you razor blades. You have to buy soap. They provide you a jumpsuit once a year, but you have to buy socks and underwear. And I have to buy cigarettes. What else do I have?

"That is what it is like for me, sir."

The translator trailed off. Randolph shook his head slightly, as if to emerge from a trance. Ping returned his gaze to the table in front of him and fell silent.

## What Do You Think?

1. To what degree do you agree with the vice president's statement: "We are morally required to use our negotiating power to insist upon humane treatment of the people who make our products"?

| COMPLETELY DISAGREE | | | | | | COMPLETELY AGREE |
|---|---|---|---|---|---|---|
| 1 | 2 | 3 | 4 | 5 | 6 | 7 |

2. If you were Randolph, would you renew the contract with Quality Dragon, Limited, if no changes were made to its operations?

3. What parts of Ping's story indicate to you that he is being treated wrongfully, or is he treated reasonably in your opinion?

4. Assume again that you are Randolph and that you are considering the following changes. Each will result in a 1 percent cost increase for your company. Check the items you would choose.

_____ Reducing employees' workdays to a maximum of 12 hours

_____ Improving the quality of food served to employees

_____ Eliminating reduced pay for employees who exceed their quota for errors

_____ Building additional dorms so workers sleep no more than four to a room

_____ Prohibiting unpaid overtime

5. As a consumer, are you keenly aware of how much goods and services cost? Would you notice if food prices rose by 5 percent? What about smartphones, computers, and TVs—would a 5 percent increase in price for these items be noticeable? What if the increase was 2 percent?

# Summary

Consumers and regulators are keenly interested in the environment and preserving scarce natural resources. Business leaders must be aware of large numbers of regulations and must be sensitive to consumers and their preference for companies that operate with sustainable and green practices in evidence.

International ethics often involve ensuring that overseas contract workers are well treated and fairly compensated. Too often, the "race to the bottom" creates pressures that can be damaging to large numbers of people who manufacture items for sale in the U.S. market.

# Key Terms and Concepts

**Match each definition with a key term or concept.**

a. environmental law

b. Environmental Protection Agency

c. green building

d. labor union

e. Occupational Safety and Health Act

f. race to the bottom

g. sustainability

h. sweatshop labor

_____ 1. The use of construction practices that seek to minimize environmental impact

_____ 2. An organization that allows workers to bargain with their employers collectively

_____ 3. Workers who labor in difficult and perhaps unsafe conditions, often for long hours, while receiving unreasonably low wages

_____ 4. The practice of seeking the lowest possible labor costs worldwide

_____ 5. The part of the U.S. government in charge of enforcing environmental regulations

_____ 6. A law that prohibits some actions that harm the environment

_____ 7. The concept of making wise long-term use of scarce natural resources

_____ 8. A U.S. law that requires companies to provide employees with a working environment free from unnecessary dangers

# Review

1. The Environmental Protection Agency is a

    a. part of the U.S. government.

    b. consumer watchdog group.

    c. for-profit corporation that encourages the adoption of sustainability initiatives.

2. Name a reason why a company would not pursue a pro-environment decision unless it was legally required.

3. List three ideas for green building.

4. The main U.S. law that seeks to ensure workplace safety for workers is the

    a. Fair Labor Standards Act.

    b. Securities Act of 1933.

    c. Occupational Safety and Health Act.

    d. Norris-LaGuardia Act.

5. Why are many of the consumer goods purchased by Americans manufactured outside the United States?

6. List three examples of the difficult working conditions experienced by sweatshop labor.

# Critical Thinking

7. To what degree should a corporation seek to care for the environment? To what degree do you think a typical corporation does protect the environment? To what degree would you seek to protect the environment if you owned your own business? If you gave different answers to the three questions, explain the reasons for the differences on a separate piece of paper.

# Applications

8. Assume you own a company that makes outdoor furniture. Your manufacturing plant is in the United States. Draft a model set of environmentally friendly rules containing at least five specific ideas your company will follow.

9. Assume you own a company that makes watches. You hire a firm in China to manufacture the watches for you, and you sell them in the United States. Draft a model set of rules containing at least five specific ideas that will seek to guarantee the workers in China are treated reasonably.

# Digging Deeper

10. Spend some time online researching low wages around the world. Find examples of countries with very low average wages. Should anything be done about these wages? If so, what and by whom?

# The Bottom Line

11. Evaluate your feelings toward the two models presented in this chapter.

## Sustainability Initiatives

UNIMPORTANT            HIGHLY IMPORTANT

| 1 | 2 | 3 | 4 | 5 | 6 | 7 |

## Green Building Practices

UNIMPORTANT            HIGHLY IMPORTANT

| 1 | 2 | 3 | 4 | 5 | 6 | 7 |

## Reducing the Use of Sweatshop Labor

UNIMPORTANT            HIGHLY IMPORTANT

| 1 | 2 | 3 | 4 | 5 | 6 | 7 |

# Critical Thinking in Ethics

**Critical thinking** is the process of logical problem solving. People use critical thinking skills in math to resolve mathematics problems, in science to resolve scientific problems, and in ethics to resolve ethical and moral problems. The goal in ethics is for a person to use sound critical thinking skills so that his or her opinions about ethical issues are logical and well-founded.

## Objectives

- Identify common ethical fallacies.
- Apply several ideas from the text to a new ethical dilemma.

## Key Terms and Concepts

critical thinking, p. 165
logical fallacy, p. 168
post hoc, p. 168
inconsistency, p. 169
two wrongs make a right, p. 169
either/or, p. 169
is/ought, p. 169

red herring, p. 169
hasty generalization, p. 170
slippery slope, p. 170
provincialism, p. 170
false appeal to authority, p. 171
false appeal to popularity, p. 171

Ricardo's department is in the process of filling some new positions. Last week, Ricardo was instructed by his manager, Mary, to review the resumes of 40 recent job applicants and to verify that the information they contained was accurate. In most of the resumes, 32 in fact, he found no inaccuracies. The remaining 8 had a questionable item or at least something he thought he should bring up. He spoke with Mary, and they arranged a meeting for this afternoon to discuss the results.

Ricardo looks through one of the neat blue folders in front of him as he sips from a cup of steaming coffee. After a few minutes, Mary enters the conference room and slides into a seat across the table from him. "I'm sorry, Ricardo. The budget meeting always seems to run late when I have another meeting scheduled after it."

"That's fine, Ms. Walker," Ricardo replies, smiling.

"So what have you got for me?"

Ricardo picks up the second blue folder and hands it across the table to her. She removes a slim document from it. Ricardo takes a second copy from his own folder and places it on the table in front of him.

"The first four resumes," he begins, "are from college applicants, and the other resumes are from people with industry experience. On most of the college ones, the issues have to do with grades.

"Anderson," says Ricardo, picking up the document, "rounded her GPA up. Her resume lists a 3.7; her actual GPA is a 3.65." He moves on, glancing at his report from time to time to check a figure or quote as he speaks.

"Benson's resume says that his 'Major GPA' is 3.9, which is true, but his overall GPA is 3.2, and his resume doesn't say anything about that. Cisneros just flat-out lied about her GPA. She listed it as a 3.5, and it's really a 2.8.

"Davis was, ah, his deal was different. One of his references was his boss during an internship. He listed the manager as 'James Cox' and gave a phone number. I called it and talked to "James

Cox,' and he gave Davis a really terrific reference, but he didn't seem to know a lot about our industry.

"After I hung up, I looked up the phone number, and it belonged to someone named Avery Sanderson, who is also listed as a senior at Davis's college. I called the number again from my cell phone so that, you know, the company's name wouldn't come up on the guy's caller ID. He answered and said, 'S'up?' Same voice as 'James Cox.' I said, 'Avery? Hey, man, it's John.' He said, 'John who? Miller? S'up, dog?'"

Mary smiles. "Very creative. This is why I like you."

"Thanks."

"What did you say then?"

"I, ah, I just hung up on him. I couldn't really think of anything else. Anyway, then I found the number for the real James Cox and talked to him. He said that Davis did intern for him over the summer and that he was not a standout but not terrible. He didn't really recommend or not recommend him."

"You did well. That's all the college applicants?"

"Yes. Then there were four others. Edwards listed his current position as '2006–present,' but he was laid off three months ago.

"Franklin is currently employed, but she stretched her dates of employment twice in the work history section of her resume. Reading through it, it looks as if she's always had a job, but she wasn't working for one stretch of six months in 2006 and another stretch of ten months in 2008. So she would claim she worked for a company from January 2006 to January

2008, when she really worked only 18 of those 24 months—that kind of thing.

"Green exaggerated his job duties. His resume claims he supervised 20 people at his last job and managed a budget of $3 million. His former employer disputes that. She told me he might have supervised a total of 20 different people over the three years he worked there, but never more than seven at a time. She also said he never had a personal say in more than about $750,000 of the budget.

"The last was Henderson. She listed 'to start my own business' as her reason for leaving her last employer. She did start a business, but her former employer told me that she didn't leave voluntarily. In fact, she was fired for cursing out a supervisor after he confronted her about being late repeatedly."

Ricardo sets the document down and looks at Mary. "Ah, that's all of them," he says. " These people are all finalists for positions. What do you want me to tell HR?"

# {WHAT Do You Think?}

1. Rate the resume discrepancies of the four applicants who are soon-to-be college graduates.

UNACCEPTABLE                        NOT A PROBLEM

Anderson    1       2       3       4       5       6       7

UNACCEPTABLE                        NOT A PROBLEM

Benson      1       2       3       4       5       6       7

UNACCEPTABLE                        NOT A PROBLEM

Cisneros    1       2       3       4       5       6       7

UNACCEPTABLE                        NOT A PROBLEM

Davis       1       2       3       4       5       6       7

2. Now rate the resume discrepancies of the four applicants who are workers with industry experience.

UNACCEPTABLE                        NOT A PROBLEM

Edwards     1       2       3       4       5       6       7

UNACCEPTABLE                        NOT A PROBLEM

Franklin    1       2       3       4       5       6       7

UNACCEPTABLE                        NOT A PROBLEM

Green       1       2       3       4       5       6       7

UNACCEPTABLE                        NOT A PROBLEM

Henderson   1       2       3       4       5       6       7

3. If you were Mary, which of the eight would you tell HR to no longer consider for employment? Why?

# ■ Logical Fallacies and Ethical Reasoning

The desire to have others agree with one's opinions seems to be a part of human nature. So a discussion with a friend over a difference of opinion usually involves each person sharing and arguing his or her own point of view. However, your main goal as a critical thinker is not so much to win arguments as it is to seek truth—that is, to find the best answers to life's questions and problems. To achieve that, you need to acknowledge strengths in the arguments of others and admit any weaknesses in your own. If someone's arguments are stronger than your own, you haven't lost a contest; you've learned something new.

When people seek to justify bad behavior, they often cheat. They stop looking for the best possible answers and start trying to win arguments at all costs. In doing so, they may resort to the use of fallacies.

**Logical fallacies** are illogical or deceptive arguments. Ideally, an argument should appeal to other people's intellects. Fallacies, however, are frequently aimed at people's emotions. They are often based on ignorance and are sometimes used to manipulate or trick others into agreeing with unethical propositions. Critical thinking in ethics includes trying to avoid the use of fallacies in arguments and noticing fallacies in arguments made by others. Many common fallacies (Figure 11-1) are identified in the following paragraphs.

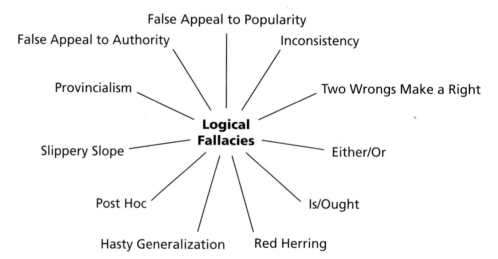

**FIGURE 11-1**
Logical fallacies

## Post Hoc

**Post hoc** is the fallacy of assuming that because two events happened within a short period of time, the first action must have caused the second action. People's minds interpret events this way so they can make sense of what they see around them. This assumption is not always accurate, however. Many superstitions and myths are a result of post hoc fallacies. For example, "A black cat crossed my path on Tuesday; then on Wednesday, my car was hit by a bus. That proves black cats are bad luck!" Wouldn't you like to know what happened to the person who started the superstition that walking under a ladder causes bad luck? Sometimes one event or action does cause another, but not always. Many times, what looks like a cause is really a coincidence.

## Inconsistency

**Inconsistency** is the fallacy of contradicting oneself in words or actions without being able to logically defend the contradictions. It is the error of saying one thing while doing the opposite or of saying two things that contradict each other. For example, a manager lectures a worker about the importance of honesty, but acts dishonestly herself.

## Two Wrongs Make a Right

**Two wrongs make a right** is the fallacy of defending a wrongful action by pointing out that someone else did it, too. An employee who is disciplined for spending too much time online protests, "Everyone does the same thing!" Similarly, what do people often say (or at least think) when a police officer pulls them over for driving too fast? "Yes, officer, I was going over the speed limit, but you should have seen the car that just passed me! It was really flying!" A person's wrongful actions do not become acceptable just because other people have done them, too.

## Either/Or

**Either/or** is the fallacy of making it appear that there are only two possible sides to an issue, one good and one bad. This fallacy is an attempt to make other people think that they are in some kind of logical trap, when in fact, the trap does not exist. A coach may tell an athlete that unless the athlete takes illegal steroids or continues to play while injured, she has no commitment to the team. Real-life situations usually involve more than two choices.

## Is/Ought

**Is/ought** is the fallacy of stating that because things are a certain way now, they should remain that way. In other words, whatever *is* now *ought* to be that way always, so nothing should change. This fallacy is often used by people who fear change. A famous example of the is/ought fallacy was used to warn against the invention of the airplane. Skeptics said that if people were meant to fly, they'd have wings. In other words, people are earthbound now, so that is how they should remain. Today similar arguments are used against adopting new forms of technology—from experimenting in genetics to expanding the role of computers in society. Some people see change as frightening and find security in keeping things the way they are.

## Red Herring

**Red herring** is the fallacy of using an unrelated idea in an argument to distract your opponent. It is said that the name came from a once-common practice in English fox hunting. To get the hounds to stop chasing the fox, the hunters would drag a smoked fish across the fox's trail. The dogs, charging down the path, would be diverted by the stronger, more interesting scent. The red herring fallacy accomplishes the same goal by using interesting but irrelevant arguments. For example, an office manager complains that an employee is consistently late for work. The worker responds that the company's compensation policies are unfair.

Some politicians seem particularly fond of this tactic. In a recent one-hour television debate, this author's scorecard had nine red herring answers from one candidate and seven from the other. (I voted for the guy who had only seven red herring answers.)

## Hasty Generalization

**Hasty generalization** is the fallacy of assuming that most members of a group share a common characteristic, when this assumption is actually based on only a few observations. For example, because two older employees spoke harshly to Mitsu, she assumes that all older people are irritable. Many of the unfair stereotypes and prejudices that a person has about other groups of people are based on hasty generalizations.

## Slippery Slope

The **slippery slope** fallacy is an attempt to frighten others into rejecting an idea by trying to show that accepting it would start a chain reaction of terrible events. This chain reaction often involves a series of steps that keep getting worse. At the end of the chain reaction is a terrifying consequence that no rational person would want.

A school recently expelled a third grader for having a small orange squirt gun in his backpack. There was no water in the reservoir, so the squirt gun wasn't even "loaded." In defending the school's "zero tolerance" policy, the principal argued that no exception, no matter how small, could be made without endangering children. Her slippery slope argument implied that if an exception is made for squirt guns, then another must be made for BB guns, and then another for real guns, bazookas, and so on. It would have been more sensible to give a lighter punishment to the kid with the squirt gun.

### Ethics & Law

As stated earlier, your main goal as an ethical thinker is to discover the truth—or at least the best answers you can find to your problems. However, that isn't always the case. The goal of an attorney arguing a case is to win the argument, not necessarily to learn the truth. Thus, attorneys are sometimes put in the position of arguing points that they don't personally believe. There are some limits, though. For example, lawyers are not allowed to lie or to put someone on the stand who they know will lie. Nevertheless, that still leaves ethical dilemmas, such as the professional mandate to zealously argue for a criminal defendant that the attorney strongly suspects is guilty.

**Would you be able to justify such actions to yourself if you were an attorney?**

## Provincialism

**Provincialism** is the fallacy of looking at an issue or a question strictly from your point of view or from the point of view of people like you. It is a fallacy of narrow-mindedness, of not trying to see the viewpoints of others. This fallacy is an easy trap to fall into because the first tool that many people have in interpreting the world around them is their own point of view. However, most people also use *empathy,* the skill of understanding the feelings and perspectives of others. A person applying the provincialism fallacy does not have the ability to use empathy or simply chooses not to empathize.

## False Appeal to Authority

**False appeal to authority** is the fallacy of incorrectly relying on authority figures or experts to support your argument. It is not always a fallacy to rely on authority figures to back up your point of view. After all, that is one purpose of research. However, the authorities referred to should be *real* experts and should have some special insight into the issue being discussed. The fallacy occurs when your expert is not an authority in the area you are talking about or when other experts seem to agree that your expert is wrong. For example, if you want to convince a friend that using animals in medical experiments is not always morally wrong, it would not be appropriate for you to quote a famous movie star who happens to agree with your opinion. All by itself, having a famous name does not make anyone an authority. A more appropriate expert on using animals for experiments would be a doctor or a scientist.

## False Appeal to Popularity

**False appeal to popularity** is the fallacy of assuming that an idea is right because many people believe it is right. People using this fallacy believe that if an idea is popular, it must be true. Do you know people who often base their opinions on what others think? At different times in history, a majority of humans have believed that the earth was flat; that it was the center of the universe; and that the stars were small holes in the night sky, letting in light from the other side. No idea becomes true just because it is popular.

---

## CHECKPOINT **11–1**

Identify the logical fallacies in the following statements:

1.  Adults are all alike! They are never satisfied with anything you do!

2.  Either you join the protest against the death penalty, or you don't respect human life.

3.  Most elementary school math teachers agree that physical education classes are important to a child's growth and development; therefore, it must be true.

4.  I'll never go on another cruise. My family went on a cruise when I was ten. A month later my parents decided to get a divorce. Cruises are bad news!

5.  Yes, I cheated on the exam, but you shouldn't fail me because Clara turned in a paper she bought off the Internet!

# ■ Ethical Dilemmas and Reasoning

Countless ethical dilemmas, both large and small, confront workers on a daily basis. It is often easy to determine the appropriate course of action, but some calls are quite difficult to make. This last section of the book presents a model for reasoning through difficult decisions based on ideas presented in earlier chapters.

When faced with a difficult decision, start with the big picture, taking in all the details and complexities of the situation. Then begin analyzing the information, gradually narrowing the scope until you identify the central ethical decision you must make and the options available to you. In comparing the options, it is often useful to consider stakeholders and ethical principles.

## Stakeholders

Remember stakeholder ethics from Chapter 4? Stakeholders are the individuals, groups, or entities that might be affected by a specific decision. It is important to include as many stakeholders as possible when faced with a difficult decision. They might include (among others):

- A worker
- A group of workers
- A company
- A community
- Customers
- Society
- The environment

The consequences of ethical and unethical actions are like ripples on a pond. They may affect only a few people at first, but they frequently spread wider to include many more people than originally anticipated. The more stakeholders you consider, the more balanced and fair your final decision will be.

## Ethical Principles

Once the stakeholders have been identified, it is often useful to try to apply one or more of the ethical principles presented in Chapter 2. A quick review of those principles follows:

- **Egoism principle:** The right thing for a person to do in any situation is the action that best serves that person's own long-term interests.

- **Utility principle:** The morally right action is the one that produces the best consequences for everyone involved, not just for one individual.

- **Principle of rights:** An action is considered moral when it respects the rights of others and is considered immoral when it violates another's rights.

- **Principle of duties:** People should do what is ethically right purely because they have a moral obligation to do so. People should do the right thing because it's the right thing to do.

- **Principle of virtues:** Ethics is based on being a good person, that is, on incorporating ideal character traits into your life.

So how do you go about applying those principles to the central ethical decision to be made? You simply look at the situation from each principle's perspective. What would each principle suggest is the most ethical course of action?

Consider, for example, an employee who repeatedly witnesses a coworker stealing from the store where they both work. Based on each principle, what should the witnessing employee do? Figure 11-2 addresses that question.

| EMPLOYEE THEFTS | |
|---|---|
| **Principle** | **Application** |
| **Egoism** | The witnessing employee should do whatever is in his or her long-term best interests. Reporting the thefts would impress company managers and might lead to a reward. On the other hand, not reporting the thefts might be easier period. |
| **Utility** | What action would produce the most overall happiness for the most people? The answer to that question depends largely on the situation. If the thefts are significant, they are affecting many people. Other employees may be under suspicion, and money that could have gone toward increases in employee pay may be spent on security instead. Customers may be paying higher prices to make up for the lost profits. Reporting the thefts would likely be the best choice. |
| **Rights** | The thief is clearly violating the rights of others and, therefore, forfeiting any rights he or she might have in expecting loyalty from coworkers. Reporting the thefts does not violate anyone's rights. Not reporting them would violate the rights of the store owners, honest employees, and perhaps the customers. |
| **Duties** | This is the duty to do the right thing, no matter what. So what's the right thing to do? Somehow you already know, don't you? If someone was stealing from the witnessing employee, the employee would want others to report what they knew and put an end to the stealing. Therefore, that is what the employee should do now. |
| **Virtues** | What ethical virtues apply to situations like this? Honesty, integrity, trustworthiness, courage, and fairness, among others. All of those virtues seem to suggest that the witnessing employee should report the thefts. |

**FIGURE 11-2**
Applying the five ethical principles

Remember that principles may apply better to some ethical questions and situations than others. Different principles also sometimes conflict with one another. So the process is not as simple as completing a yes/no checklist. When most of the principles end up suggesting the same course of action, as in the preceding example, the decision maker can have some measure of confidence that a particular option is a good moral choice.

## CHECKPOINT **11–2**

Return to the opening scenario about the resume misrepresentations and answer the following questions:

 **1.** Identify the stakeholders involved.

 **2.** Apply the ethical principles discussed to the scenario. What does each suggest?

 **3.** Now which of the applicants do you think should no longer be considered by the company?

# ETHICS @ WORK

This chapter has defined many common logical fallacies and has presented a method for making tough ethical decisions. The following scenario is your chance to apply the method to a business situation. What should be done? Why? Answer the questions that follow the scenario, and be prepared to respectfully argue for your point of view in class.

## Main Issue and Options

**Issue:** In light of Terry's special situation, should he be laid off?

**Options:** The sales director is free to adopt any policy she wishes.

## Unusual Needs and Layoffs

### Sales Director's Office

"I don't like layoffs any more than you do, but . . ." Carl said.

"We have to do it," the sales director finished. She took off her glasses, leaned back in her chair, and sighed.

"Yeah."

"Yeah. How many?"

"I'd recommend five. No, six. If we lay off six, we probably won't have to do this again, at least not this year. So, ah, do you want to go by seniority?" Carl asked.

The sales director thought about it for a minute. "No," she said, "let's stick with the numbers. Rank everybody from top to bottom, first place to . . . how many do we have?"

"Forty-one."

"First to forty-first. Let's average the last three years if they've been around that long, just this year if not. The bottom six will go."

Carl made some notes on his laptop. "I'll get right on it."

### Two Days Later

"Here's the report," Carl said. "Benjamin is tops, of course. Over $350,000 a year."

"He's a machine," the sales director said.

"He is. The, ah, bottom six are highlighted. Below the line."

The sales director looked over the spreadsheet. The bottom portion read as follows:

| 34. | Roger | $143,000 |
| 35. | Susan | $140,000 |
| --- | --- | --- |
| 36. | Javier | $126,000 |
| 37. | Ellen | $120,000 |
| 38. | Terry | $110,000 |
| 39. | Fred | $92,000 |
| 40. | Irene | $90,000 |
| 41. | Stan | $52,000 |

"I didn't know Stan was this bad," she said. "I mean, this is just dreadful."

"He hasn't been pulling his weight for some time."

"We should have cut him loose a long time ago."

"I can't argue with you there."

"OK. Ellen's been with us a long time.

"That she has."

The sales director looked over the numbers for a while longer. Then she opened a drawer and slid the spreadsheet into it. "All right. The decision's been made, so let's get this done."

"Agreed."

"Stop by human resources and tell Jane what's going on."

"Will do," Carl nodded. He picked up his laptop and left the office.

## Later That Day

"Hi, Jane," the sales director said as she looked up from her screen. "What's up?"

"Do you have a few minutes?"

"Yes."

"Can I shut the door?"

"Sure."

Jane shut the door softly. The sales director closed the document she had been working on and nodded to a chair. Jane sat down.

"Carl told me about the layoffs."

"Yeah. I hate to do it, but we're sunk if we don't get our costs under control."

"Yes, I know, and I don't want to argue against all of them. Just one of them."

The sales director took off her glasses and laid them on the desk. "Which one?"

"Terry."

"Terry's a great guy, and I'd keep him on if the company was in better shape, but his numbers just aren't there."

"True," Jane responded, tapping the arm of her chair, "but I know something about him that I don't think you do."

"Which is . . ."

"Terry's a hemophiliac."

"OK." The sales director thought for a moment. "That's . . . a bleeding disorder, right?"

"Right. He's had the condition since birth."

"OK, but . . . that's never been an issue here. He's got low numbers; that's it."

"The issue is that Terry's condition is one of the most expensive health problems there is," Jane replied. "He has to receive regular injections to help his blood clot, and each

round of treatment costs thousands of dollars. His medical bills," she continued, "are over $150,000 per year. Without health insurance, he can't possibly cover that amount."

"And he has our insurance."

"Of course."

"Well . . ." the sales director paused. "He'll get another job. And he can get COBRA coverage in the meantime, right?"

"For a while, yes, but COBRA doesn't last forever."

"But it lasts for what, 18 months?" the sales director asked.

"Yes, that's right."

"He can find another job with health coverage in 18 months," the sales director said.

"A mediocre salesman in this economy? Perhaps, but it's hardly a sure thing."

"Aren't there . . . special programs for problems like his, though? " asked the sales director. "Won't the government pick up the bill?"

"Maybe so; maybe not. It's hard to say whether someone can enroll in something like that or what level of coverage the person will receive."

"But nobody gets turned away from the ER," the sales director pointed out, "even if they don't have any insurance at all."

"Yes," Jane replied, "but Terry might not make it to the ER. If he doesn't get his regular injections, even a small cut can be life-threatening. He can literally bleed to death in minutes because without the injections, he can't stop bleeding."

The sales director's phone buzzed.

"Yes?"

"Your three o'clock appointment is here," her assistant's voice said over the speaker.

"That's all I wanted to tell you about this anyway," Jane said. She stood and moved toward the door. "It's your call, of course. I just thought that this was something you should know."

"Yeah, you're right," the sales director replied. "I'll think it over, Jane."

1. If you were the sales director, would you lay off Terry?

2. If Terry is not laid off, how should the other "below-the-line" workers on the partial spreadsheet be treated? Is it fair to terminate Javier and Ellen when they had higher numbers than Terry? Should Susan be terminated, since she is in the bottom six among the "not-Terry" employees?

3. If Terry's job is spared, should the company create a policy for layoffs and workers with unusual medical needs, or should it continue to make exceptions on a case-by-case basis?

4. If Terry's job is spared, what should be done if his performance slips even further? Say, for example, that next year he bills only the $52,000 that last-place Stan billed in this scenario. Should he be terminated at that point?

5. Assume that Terry is not a hemophiliac. Rather than a genetic condition that he has had since birth, suppose that instead he has huge medical bills because of a problem created by his behavior. Assume that Terry was driving drunk and ran his SUV into a concrete pillar. He has ongoing substantial bills related to physical therapy and a series of reconstructive surgeries that are not yet complete. Would you give less consideration to his potential problems if he loses his health insurance? Specifically, why or why not?

# Summary

Logical fallacies are inappropriate or deceptive arguments. They are often used from ignorance, but are sometimes utilized to manipulate or trick others into agreeing.

A good approach to a difficult ethical decision is to consider the situation broadly with all its details and intricacies and then to analyze the information and narrow the scope until the main decision and available options are clear. In weighing options, it is useful to identify the stakeholders who will be affected and to apply ethical principles. Decisions may not always be easy to execute, but the proper course of action usually becomes apparent.

# Key Terms and Concepts

**Match each definition with a key term or concept.**

a. critical thinking

b. either/or

c. false appeal to authority

d. false appeal to popularity

e. hasty generalization

f. inconsistency

g. is/ought

h. logical fallacy

i. post hoc

j. provincialism

k. red herring

l. slippery slope

m. two wrongs make a right

_____ 1. An attempt to frighten others into rejecting an idea by trying to show that accepting it would start a chain reaction of terrible events

_____ 2. An illogical or deceptive argument

_____ 3. The fallacy of assuming that an idea is right because many people believe it is right

_____ 4. The fallacy of assuming that because two events happened in a short period of time, the first action must have caused the second action

_____ 5. The fallacy of assuming that most members of a group share a common characteristic, when this assumption is actually based on only a few observations

6. The fallacy of contradicting oneself in words or actions without being able to logically defend the contradictions

_____ 7. The fallacy of defending a wrongful action by pointing out that someone else did it, too

_____ 8. The fallacy of incorrectly relying on authority figures or experts to support an argument

_____ 9. The fallacy of a person's looking at an issue or a question strictly from his or her point of view or from the point of view of people like him or her

_____ 10. The fallacy of making it appear that there are only two possible sides to an issue, one good and one bad

_____ 11. The fallacy of stating that because things are a certain way now, they should remain that way

_____ 12. The fallacy of using an unrelated idea in an argument to distract an opponent

_____ 13. The process of logical problem solving

# Review

1. On Monday, Sofia notices that her coworker Marcia is sneezing a lot. On Tuesday, Sofia comes down with a cold. "I caught a cold from Marcia," Sofia concludes. The logical fallacy Sofia has committed is

   a. a hasty generalization.

   b. post hoc.

   c. red herring.

   d. either/or.

2. True or false: When making a difficult ethical decision, you should narrow the stakeholders involved to those that will be most affected by the action.

3. Which are commonly identified as stakeholders?

   a. communities

   b. employees

   c. customers

   d. all of the above

4. According to the _____, the morally right action is the one that produces the best consequences for everyone involved, not just for one individual.

   a. utility principle

   b. principle of rights

   c. principle of duties

   d. principle of virtues

5. True or false: In applying ethical principles to a decision, if most of the principles support a particular course of action, it is probably a good choice.

# Critical Thinking

6. Create an original example of each fallacy.

   a. post hoc:


   b. inconsistency:


   c. two wrongs make a right:

d. either/or:

e. is/ought:

f. red herring:

g. hasty generalization:

h. slippery slope:

i. provincialism:

j. false appeal to authority:

k. false appeal to popularity:

7. Consider Robin Hood. As the legend goes, he stole from the rich and gave to the poor. Evaluate his actions in terms of the five ethical principles reviewed in the chapter. Was Robin's operation ethical? Why or why not?

## Applications

8. On the blank after each statement, write the name of the fallacy that best describes it.

a. I think you are wrong about the danger of the sun's ultraviolet rays. After all, look how well our company has been performing lately!

_____

b. I can't support your idea about reserving the closest parking places for seniors. I don't care about the great things they've done for this school. I'm a sophomore, and on rainy days, I sometimes have to park half a mile away.

_____

c. Either you participate in the event this weekend, or you don't really care about our firm!

_____

d. If we don't let Luisa be the yearbook editor, she might tell her mother, who happens to be the principal. Then she might accuse us of breaking a rule and suspend us. Then we might get behind in school and not graduate on time. Then we might not get accepted into college or technical school. We might never get a job! Let's just let Luisa be the editor.

_____

e. It is absolutely wrong to use drugs. People should protect their minds and bodies. Relying on drugs is no way to deal with problems. It's just wrong! Now, let's go downtown and have a few drinks.

_____

f. I know for a fact that the square root of 16 is 8. I heard it directly from the sportscaster on Channel 8.

_____

g. A tradition at this company is that managers always get an all-expenses-paid vacation in June. That's just the way it is, so that's how it should stay.

_____

h. Gina and Marie both have brown eyes, and they're two of the smartest people I know. Therefore, all brown-eyed people are intelligent.

_____

i. Yes, I took $50 from the petty cash drawer. But Al took $300—he's the one who should be punished!

_____

j. This morning I had leftover pizza for breakfast. Then I wrecked my car. Evidently, pizza causes car accidents.

_____

k. In a school survey, 90 percent of students said they would learn more if they did not have reading assignments. Therefore, it must be true that we need fewer reading assignments.

_____

9. Refer back the previous question. Which three statements do you find to be most deceptive? Why?

## Digging Deeper

10. Try to find examples of people using some of the fallacies discussed in this chapter. Good resources may include newspapers, television and radio talk shows, articles about controversial issues, television news programs, and political debates.

## The Bottom Line

11. The logical fallacy that I myself fall for most often, and that I should be more on guard against, is . . .

# Glossary

## A

**affirmative action** the practice of taking active measures to ensure equal opportunity in hiring and advancement decisions (p. 104)

**authority** a source of ethical beliefs holding that an action is right or wrong because someone important said so (p. 4)

## B

**bait and switch** the practice of advertising a product at a low price while intentionally stocking only a limited number in hopes of luring shoppers to buy more expensive items (p. 71)

**boycott** a group agreement not to buy products or conduct business with a certain company to protest a perceived injustice (p. 105)

## C

**Civil Rights Act of 1964** the most important federal law that addresses discrimination (p. 103)

**code of ethics** a written set of principles and rules intended to serve as a guideline for ethical behavior for individuals under an organization's authority (p. 71)

**commission** a method of compensation in which salespeople are rewarded with a percentage of the money from the sales they make, in addition to a salary or hourly wage (p. 76)

**consequences** the effects or results of what people do (p. 17)

**critical thinking** the process of logical problem solving (p. 165)

**culture** a source of ethical beliefs holding that the morality of an action depends on the beliefs of one's culture or nation (p. 4)

## D

**deficiency judgment** an action that a lender may take when a foreclosure does not generate enough money to pay off a mortgage loan (p. 136)

**discrimination** illegal treatment of a person or group based on prejudice (p. 103)

**distributor** a business that sells to retailers a product manufactured by others (p. 56)

**diversity** the inclusion in a company workforce of people who differ in culture, background, personality, and other ways (p. 103)

**drug and alcohol abuse** a major concern of employers, according to a recent survey (p. 92)

**duty** an ethical obligation that one individual has to others (p. 20)

## E

**egoism principle** the idea that the right thing for a person to do in any situation is the action that best serves that person's long-term interests (p. 17)

**either/or** the fallacy of making it appear that there are only two possible sides to an issue, one good and one bad (p. 169)

**Employee Polygraph Protection Act** a law that sets ground rules for companies and workers when companies ask workers to take a certain kind of exam (p. 94)

**environmental law** a law that prohibits some actions that harm the environment (p. 154)

**Environmental Protection Agency** the part of the U.S. government in charge of enforcing environmental regulations (p. 154)

**ethical character** a group of qualities such as courage and self-discipline belonging to a person (p. 41)

**ethical judgment** the ability to determine the morally right or best course of action (p. 39)

**ethical motivation** the inner desire to do the right thing (p. 40)

**ethical principles** ideas that act as guides for behaving ethically (p. 3)

# F

**false advertising** the practice of making statements about products that the advertiser knows are not true (p. 69)

**false appeal to authority** the fallacy of incorrectly relying on authority figures or experts to support an argument (p. 171)

**false appeal to popularity** the fallacy of assuming that an idea is right because many people believe it is right (p. 171)

**false prizes** a sales technique that seeks to trick potential customers into thinking they have won valuable items such as cash, cars, and cruises (p. 76)

**fear of change** the internal force that holds people back from ethical growth (p. 42)

**foreclosure** the process of repossessing a home from a homeowner (p. 136)

# G

**golden mean** the method of defining virtues as perfect balances between opposite and undesirable extremes (p. 22)

**green building** the use of construction practices that seek to minimize environmental impact (p. 155)

# H

**hasty generalization** the fallacy of assuming that most members of a group share a common characteristic, when this assumption is actually based on only a few observations (p. 170)

**honesty** the character trait of consistently telling the truth, the whole truth, and nothing but the truth (p. 120)

**hostile work environment** a type of harassment in which supervisors or coworkers use embarrassment, humiliation, or fear to create a negative climate that interferes with the ability of others to perform their jobs (p. 106)

# I

**inconsistency** the fallacy of contradicting oneself in words or actions without being able to logically defend the contradictions (p. 169)

**industriousness** the character trait of consistently demonstrating perseverance and hard work (p. 122)

**inner conflict** the internal force that motivates people to move up toward higher levels of ethical thinking (p. 41)

**integrity** the character trait of maintaining adherence to a strict personal ethical code (p. 122)

**intuition** a source of ethical beliefs holding that principles of right and wrong have been built into a person's conscience (p. 4)

**is/ought** the fallacy of stating that because things are a certain way now, they should remain that way (p. 169)

# J

**judicial activism** the liberal approach to interpreting laws that calls for considering their purpose (p. 90)

**judicial restraint** the conservative approach to interpreting laws that calls for applying laws literally (p. 90)

**justice** impartial fairness, or equity (p. 33)

# L

**labor union** an organization that allows workers to bargain with their employers collectively (p. 157)

**legalism** the belief that because there are laws and policies to cover issues of right and wrong, ethics is irrelevant (p. 3)

**logical fallacy** an illogical or deceptive argument (p. 168)

**loyalty** the character trait of maintaining allegiance to a person, an organization, a cause, or an idea (p. 122)

## M

**moral development** the process by which people develop an understanding of right and wrong (p. 33)

**moral sensitivity** the ability to recognize ethical issues, questions, and temptations and how your actions could affect the people involved (p. 39)

**morality** the part of human conduct that can be evaluated in terms of right and wrong (p. 4)

**mortgage** a loan made for the purpose of buying a home (p. 136)

## N

**negative equity** a loan balance that is larger than the value of the asset for which the loan was made (p. 137)

## O

**Occupational Safety and Health Act** a U.S. law that requires companies to provide employees with a working environment free from unnecessary dangers (p. 157)

## P

**payday loan** a short-term loan made at a high rate of interest (p. 135)

**philanthropy** efforts to improve the well-being of others through charitable donations (p. 57)

**post hoc** the fallacy of assuming that because two events happened in a short period of time, the first action must have caused the second action (p. 168)

**post-offer drug testing** drug testing of applicants who are offered jobs (p. 93)

**pre-employment drug testing** drug testing of job applicants (p. 93)

**price gouging** the practice of pricing a product far above the normal market value on the assumption that consumers have no other way to buy the product (p. 76)

**principle of duties** the idea that people should do what is ethically right purely because they have a moral obligation to do so (p. 21)

**principle of rights** the idea that an action is considered moral when it respects the rights of others and immoral when it violates another's rights (p. 20)

**principle of virtues** the idea that ethics is based on being a good person, on incorporating ideal character traits into one's life (p. 22)

**profit maximization** a business practice that favors increasing shareholder wealth over all other objectives (p. 53)

**provincialism** the fallacy of a person's looking at an issue or a question strictly from his or her point of view or from the point of view of people like him or her (p. 170)

**puffery** a term used to describe statements that are not outright lies, but merely exaggerations (p. 70)

## Q

**quid pro quo** a type of harassment in which sexual demands are directly tied to a person's keeping his or her job or receiving a promotion or another job benefit (p. 106)

## R

**race to the bottom** the practice of seeking the lowest possible labor costs worldwide (p. 157)

**random drug testing** drug testing that may be administered to any employee with little or no advance notice (p. 93)

**reason** a source of ethical beliefs holding that consistent, logical thinking should be the primary tool used in making ethical decisions (p. 4)

**red herring** the fallacy of using an unrelated idea in an argument to distract an opponent (p. 169)

**relativism** the belief that because ethical values vary widely, there can be no universal ethical principles that apply to everyone (p. 3)

**respect** the character trait of showing consideration and appreciation for others (p. 121)

**respect for persons** the idea that it is wrong to use other people in ways that harm them for one's own benefit (p. 21)

**reverse discrimination** the alleged practice of giving jobs and promotions to minority applicants at the expense of better-qualified members of majority groups (p. 104)

**right** a term used to describe how an individual is entitled to be treated by others (p. 19)

**right to privacy** a constitutional liberty first recognized in the cases *Griswold v. Connecticut* and *Roe v. Wade* (p. 90)

## S

**sexual harassment** unwelcome physical or verbal behavior directed at employees because of their sex (p. 106)

**shareholder model** the theory that a company's only obligation is to try to make as much money as possible for its investors and owners (p. 54)

**shareholders** the owners of a corporation (p. 53)

**slippery slope** an attempt to frighten others into rejecting an idea by trying to show that accepting it would start a chain reaction of terrible events (p. 170)

**social contract** the deepest values and beliefs of a society (p. 36)

**stakeholder model** the theory that a company has ethical responsibilities to many people affected by the decisions and actions of the business (p. 55)

**standard of ethics** refers to social expectations of people's moral behavior (p. 7)

**standard of etiquette** refers to social expectations concerning manners or social graces (p. 6)

**standard of law** refers to rules of behavior imposed on people by governments (p. 7)

**statute** a law passed by Congress (p. 91)

**stock** a financial instrument the sale of which is used to raise capital for a corporation (p. 53)

**straight commission** a method of compensation in which income is based entirely on what a person sells (p. 76)

**strategic default** the consumer practice of paying credit card bills before making mortgage payments (p. 138)

**substantiation** the validation of advertising claims with objective data from independent research (p. 73)

**supplier** a business that provides a particular service or commodity that other businesses require (p. 56)

**sustainability** the concept of making wise long-term use of scarce natural resources (p. 155)

**sweatshop labor** workers who labor in difficult and perhaps unsafe conditions, often for long hours, while receiving unreasonably low wages (p. 156)

## T

**telemarketing** the practice of selling directly to individuals through unsolicited phone calls, e-mails, or faxes (p. 71)

**testimonial** an endorsement of a product by someone claiming to have benefited from its use (p. 74)

**turnover** the number of employees a business is required to hire in order to replace workers who have left the company (p. 55)

**two wrongs make a right** the fallacy of defending a wrongful action by pointing out that someone else did it, too (p. 169)

## U

**universality** the idea that people should act as they would want others to act in the same situation (p. 21)

**usury** the practice of charging excessively high interest rates (p. 134)

**usury law** a law that sets maximum acceptable rates of interest (p. 134)

**utility principle** the idea that the morally right action is the one that produces the best consequences for everyone involved, not just for one individual (p. 18)

## V

**value system** a way of viewing ethical right and wrong, often unique to an individual, a culture, or a subculture (p. 17)

**virtue** an ideal character trait that people should try to incorporate into their lives (p. 21)

## W

**warranty** a written promise to repair or replace a product if it breaks or becomes defective within a specified period of time (p. 74)

**whistle-blowing** the act of reporting unethical or illegal actions by one's superiors or peers to authorities or the media (p. 123)

# Index

## A

AAF, 72, 75
Abortion, 90
Abstract stakeholders, 57–58
Adult Web sites, at work, 118–119
Advertising, ethics in, 69–75
  code of ethics limitations, 75
  ethical problems
    bait and switch, 70–71
    children, advertising to, 71
    false advertising, 69–70
    puffery, 70
    telemarketing and spam, 71
  ethical standards
    comparisons, 72, 73
    guarantees and
      warranties, 72, 73–74
    price claims, 72, 74
    substantiation, 72, 73
    taste and decency, 72, 74
    testimonials, 72, 74
    truth, 72–73
Advertising Ethics and Principles
    (AAF), 72
Affirmative action, 104
Age-related discrimination, 103
Alcohol abuse, employee, 92–93
American Advertising Federation
    (AAF), 72, 75
American Honda Motor
    Company, 104
Aristotle, 22, 23, 123
Authority, 4

## B

Bait and switch, 70–71
Banking, ethical issues in,
    133–134
Behavior, standards of, 6–8
Body Shop, The, 58

Boston Community Capital
    (BCC), 138
Boycotts, 105
Business, the environment and,
    154–155
Business partners, as direct
    stakeholders, 56

## C

Children
  advertising to, 71
  moral development of. *See*
    Kohlberg's Justice Model
    of Moral Development
Civil Rights Act of 1964,
    103
Clean Air Act 154
Code of ethics, 71
Commission, 76–77
Communities, as direct
    stakeholders, 56–57
Comparisons, in advertising,
    72, 73
Computers, misuse by employees,
    118–119
Concordance, 34
Confidential information,
    disclosure of by
    employees, 119
Consequences, 17
Consequential ethics
  basing morality
    on, 17–18
  long-term, 77–78
  strengths and weaknesses
    of, 18–19
Constitution, United States,
    19, 69, 90
Constitutional rights, 69
Corporate speech, 69

Corporation, purpose of, history,
    53–54
Courage, 22
Court cases
  *Griswold v. Connecticut*, 90
  *Roe v. Wade*, 90
Cowardice, 22
*Crazy People* (movie), 69
Credit cards, ethical issues with,
    134–135, 139
Culture, 4
Customers
  as direct stakeholders,
    55–56
  ethical selling to, 77–78

## D

Decency in advertising, 72, 74
Deception, intentional, 8–11
Declaration of
    Independence, 19
Defaults on loans, strategic,
    138–139
Deficiency judgment, 136–137
Direct stakeholders, 55–57
Disabilities, discrimination
    and, 103
Discrimination
  Civil Rights Act of
    1964, 103
  diversity programs,
    103–104
  equal opportunity, 104–105
  laws and, 103
Dishonesty, in employees, 120
Distributors, as direct
    stakeholders, 56
Diversity, 103
Diversity programs, 103–104
Dodge brothers, 53

Do the Right Thing (feature)
   affirmative action policies, 104
   ethical lending, 138
   ethical treatment of overseas
      contractors, 158
   ethics at work, 22
   Johnson & Johnson
      *Credo,* 5
   most honest professions, 77
   stakeholder ethics, 58
   treat workers with respect,
      121
   whistle-blowing, 123
Drug abuse, employee, 92–93
Drug testing, employee, 92–94
   pre-employment, 93
   post-offer, 93
   random, 93–94
Duty, 20


**E**

Egoism principle, 17–18,
   140, 172
Eighth Amendment, to U.S.
   Constitution, 90
Either/or (logical
   fallacy), 169
Elevate the goal, 78
Eminent domain, 20
Employee Polygraph Protection
   Act (EPPA), 94
Employee(s)
   as direct stakeholders, 55
   character traits of
      excellent
         honesty, 120–121
         industriousness, 122
         integrity, 122
         loyalty, 122–123
         respect, 121
   drug testing of, 93–94
   ethical violations by
      confidential information,
         disclosure of, 119
      technology, misuse of,
         118–119
      theft, 117, 173

polygraph examinations
   of, 94–95
wasted time, 117–118
Environment, as indirect
   stakeholder, 57–58, 155
Environmental ethics
   business and, 154–155
   green building, 155–156
   laws and, 154
   sustainability, 155
Environmental laws, 154
Environmental Protection Agency
   (EPA), 154
Equal Employment Opportunity
   Commission (EEOC),
   105, 106
Equal opportunity, 104–105
Erikson, Erik 41
Ethical beliefs, sources of, 4
Ethical character, 41
Ethical development, personal
   Kohlberg's Justice Model of
      Moral Development, 32–38
   opposing forces, 41–42
   Rest's Four Components of
      Moral Behavior, 39–41
Ethical dilemmas, reasoning and,
   172–174
   ethical principles, 172–174
   stakeholders, 172
Ethical judgment, 39–40
Ethical motivation, 40
Ethical principles
   defined, 3
   dilemmas, reasoning and,
      172–174
   egoism principle, 17–18, 140,
      172, 173
   principle of duties, 20–21,
      141–142, 173
   principle of rights, 19–20,
      141, 172, 173
   principle of virtues, 21–23,
      142, 173
   respect for persons, 141
   universality, 141
   utility principle, 18, 140–141,
      172, 173

Ethical reasoning, logical
   fallacies and, 168–171.
   *See also* Logical fallacies
Ethics
   beliefs, sources of, 4
   principles of, 17–30
   right and wrong, 3–4
   standards of behavior, 6–8
Ethics & Law (feature)
   Environmental Protection
      Agency, 154
   ethical dilemmas for attorneys,
      170
   government regulation of
      advertising, 70
   government regulation of
      business, 141
   individual versus public
      rights, 20
   judges as "literalist" or
      "not literalist," 90
Ethics @ Work (feature)
   deception, intentional, 8–11
   "don't be a hero" policies,
      125–127
   drug and polygraph testing,
      96–98
   employee dating bans,
      108–110
   employee layoffs, 175–177
   ethics in advertising, 79–81
   misleading the customer
      44–46
   shareholders and stakeholders,
      60–63
   strategic defaults, 144–146
   sweatshop labor, 159–161
   unsafe products, 24–26
Etiquette, standards of, 6–7


**F**

Factory workers
   labor unions and, 157
   race to the bottom, 157
   sweatshop conditions for,
      156–158
False advertising, 69–70

False appeal to authority (logical fallacy), 171
False appeal to popularity (logical fallacy), 171
False prizes, 76
Fear of change, 42
Federal Communications Commission, 141
Federal Trade Commission (FTC), 70, 141
Fifth Amendment, to U.S. Constitution, 90
Figure(s)
    AAF code of ethics, 72
    consequences, 17
    direct and indirect stakeholders, 56
    egoism, 18
    employee theft, ethical principles and, 173
    individual rights, 20
    Kohlberg's justice model, 33–38
    logical fallacies, 168
    moral duties, 21
    opposing forces, 42
    Rest's components of moral behavior, 39–41
    utility, 18
    virtues, 23
    workplace substance abuse, 93
First Amendment, to U.S. Constitution, 69, 90
Ford, Henry, 53
Foreclosures, ethical issues in lending and, 136–137
Foxconn Technology Group, 157–158
Free speech, 69
Free trade, 157
Friedman, Milton, 54

**G**

Gandhi, Mahatma, 38
Generosity, 22
Goals, in selling, 78
Golden mean, 22

Government regulation
    of business, 141
    privacy and, 90
*Griswold v. Connecticut,* 90
Green building, 155–156
Guarantees, in advertising, 72, 73–74

**H**

Hard Choices (feature)
    ethical advertising, 68
    ethical lending, 132–133
    ethical principles, 16
    ethics, 2
    green building, 152–153
    lying in resumes, 166–167
    personal ethical development, 32
    shareholders and stakeholders, 52–53
    social networking sites and privacy, 88–89
    unethical work environment, 116
    weight-based discrimination, 102
Hasty generalization (logical fallacy), 170
Honesty, employee character trait, 120–121
Hostile work environment sexual harassment, 106

**I**

Inconsistency (logical fallacy), 169
Individual rights, 19–20
Indirect stakeholders, 57–58
Industriousness, as employee character trait, 122
Inner conflict, 41
Instrument and relativity, in Kohlberg's Justice Model, 34
Integrity, as employee character trait, 122

International ethics
    factory workers, in the U.S., 157
    Foxconn Technology Group, 157–158
    race to the bottom, 157
    sweatshop labor, 156–158
Internet, misuse at work, 118
Interpersonal concordance, in Kohlberg's Justice Model, 34–35
Intuition, 4
Is/ought (logical fallacy), 169

**J**

Johnson & Johnson *Credo,* 5
Judicial activism, 90
Judicial restraint, 90
Justice, 33

**K**

Kant, Immanuel, 21, 78, 142
King, Martin Luther, Jr., 38
Kohlberg, Lawrence, 33
Kohlberg's Justice Model of Moral Development, 33–38
    instrument and relativity, 34
    interpersonal concordance, 34–35
    law and order, 35–36
    punishment and obedience, 33–34
    social contract, 36–37
    universal ethical principles, 37–38

**L**

Labor unions, 157
Law(s)
    discrimination and, 103
    environmental, 154
    ethics and (feature). *See* Ethics & Law
    privacy, 90–94. *See also* Privacy law

Law and order, in Kohlberg's Justice Model, 35–36
Legalism, 3
Lending, ethical issues in
  banking, 133–134
  credit cards, 134–135
  foreclosures, 136–137
  negative equity, 137
  payday loans, 135
  strategic defaults, 138–139
Learn to listen, 78
Literalist versus non-literalist judges, 90
Loan defaults, strategic, 138–139
Logical fallacies
  defined, 168
  either/or, 169
  false appeal to authority, 171
  false appeal to popularity, 171
  hasty generalization, 170
  inconsistency, 169
  is/ought, 169
  post hoc, 168
  provincialism, 170–171
  red herring, 169–170
  slippery slope, 170
  two wrongs make a right, 169
Long-term consequences, 77–78, 142
Love contracts, 107
Loyalty, as employee character trait, 122–123
Lying, 120

**M**

Moral development, 33
Morality
  as source of ethical beliefs, 4
  based on consequences, 17–19
  based on rights, duties, and virtues, 19–23
  defined, 4
Moral sensitivity, 39
Mortgage
  defined, 136
  ethical issues with, 139

**N**

Negative equity, 137
Nike 158

**O**

Occupational Safety and Health Act, 157
Online gambling, 118
Opposing forces, 41–42

**P**

Payday loans, ethical issues and, 135
Peer pressure, 34–35
Philanthropy, 57
Plato, 23
Polygraph examinations, of employees, 94–95
Post hoc (logical fallacy), 168
Post-offer drug testing, 93
Pre-employment drug testing, 93
Price claims, in advertising, 72, 74
Price gouging, 76
Principle of duties, 20–21, 141–142, 173
Principle of rights, 19–20, 141, 172, 173
Principle of virtues, 21–23, 142, 173
Principles of ethics, morality and
  basing on consequences, 17–19
  basing on rights, duties, and virtues, 19–23
Privacy law
  drug and alcohol abuse at work, 92–93
  drug-testing employees, 93–94
  origins of, 90–91
  privacy at work, 91
Professions, perceptions of honesty, 77
Profit maximization, 53
Provincialism (logical fallacy), 170–171
Puffery, 70
Punishment and obedience, Kohlberg's Justice Model, 33–34

**Q**

Quid pro quo sexual harassment, 106

**R**

Race, civil rights and, 103
Race to the bottom, 157
Rain checks, 71
Random drug testing, 93–94
Reason
  as source of ethical beliefs, 4
  defined, 4
  ethical, logical fallacies and. See Logical fallacies
  ethical dilemmas and. See Ethical dilemmas, reasoning and
Red herring (logical fallacy), 169–170
Relativism, 3
Respect
  employee character trait, 121
  for persons, 21, 142
Rest's Four Components of Moral Behavior, 39–41
  ethical character, 41
  ethical judgment, 39–40
  ethical motivation, 40–41
  moral sensitivity, 39
Rest, James, 59
Reverse discrimination, 104
Right, 19
Right and wrong, 3
Right to life, 19
Right to privacy, 90–91
Right to property, 19
Roddick, Anita, 58
Roe v. Wade, 90

**S**

Securities and Exchange Commission (SEC), 141
Self-discipline, 41
Selling, ethics in, 75–78
  ethical problems
    commissions vs. straight commissions, 76–77

false prizes, 76
price gouging, 76
principles of ethical selling
elevate the goal, 78
learn to listen, 78
think long-term, 77–78
Seriousness, in standards of
behavior, 7
Sexual harassment
combating in the workplace,
107
hostile work environment, 106
love contracts, 107
quid pro quo, 106
Sexual orientation, discrimination
and, 103
Shareholder ethics
defined, 53
justification, 54
purpose of a corporation,
53–54
Shareholder model, 54
Shareholders, 53
Slippery slope (logical fallacy),
170
Social contract
defined, 36
in Kohlberg's justice
model, 36–37
Social networking sites
misuse of at work, 118
use to check job applicants'
information, 88–89
Society/"all mankind," as indirect
stakeholder, 58
Spam, 71
Stakeholder ethics
direct stakeholders
communities, 56–57
customers, 55–56
employees, 55
stockholders, 57
suppliers and distributors, 56

ethical dilemmas, 172
indirect/abstract stakeholders
environment, 57–58, 155
society/"all mankind", 58
Stakeholder model, 55
Stakeholders, 55–58, 172
direct, 55–57
indirect, 57–58
Standard of ethics, 6–7
Standard of etiquette, 6
Standard of law, 7
Standards of behavior, 6–8
ethics, 7
etiquette, 6–7
law, 7
Statutes, 91
Stewart, Potter (Justice), 90
Stock, 53
Stockholders, as direct
stakeholders, 57
Straight commission, 76–77
Strategic defaults, 138–139
Substance abuse, at work,
92–93
Substantiation, in advertising,
72, 73
Suppliers, as direct stakeholders,
56
Supreme Court, U.S., 90, 95
Sustainability, 155
Sweatshop labor
defined, 156
international ethics and,
156–158

T

Taste in advertising, 72, 74
Technology, misuse of by
employees, 118–119
Telemarketing, 71
Testimonials, in advertising,
72, 74

Theft, employee, 117, 173
Think long-term, 77–78
Time, wasted by employees,
117–118
Trade groups, 75
Truth
in advertising, 72–73
from employees, 120–121
Two wrongs make a right (logical
fallacy), 169

U

Universal ethical principles, in
Kohlberg's Justice Model,
37–38
Universality, 21, 142
Usury, 134
Usury laws, 134
Utility principle, 18, 140–141,
172

V

Value system, 17
Virtue, 21

W

Walmart, 121
Walton, Sam, 121
Warranties, in advertising, 72,
73–74
Warranty, 74
Whistle-blowing, 123
World War II, 54